JOHN NEWTON'S OLNEY HYMNS.

ILLUSTRATION DRAWN BY M. I. DICKSEE.

John Newton's
Olney Hymns

—————*Cantabitis, Arcades, inquit,*
Montibus hæc vestris: soli cantare periti
Arcades. O mihi tum quàm molliter ossa quiescant,
Vestra meos olim si fistula dicat amores!—Virgil, Eclogues 10:31.

And they sang as it were a new song before the throne;—and no man could learn that song, but the redeemed from the earth.—Revelation 14:3.

As sorrowful—yet always rejoicing.—2 Corinthians 6:10.

Compiled by
Charles J. Doe

Minneapolis
2011

Published by Curiosmith.
P. O. Box 390293, Minneapolis, Minnesota, 55439.
Internet: curiosmith.com.
E-mail: shopkeeper@curiosmith.com.

Scripture quotations are from *The Holy Bible*, King James Version.
The full verse text has been added to this edition.

The cover portrait was taken from the *Olney Hymns* first edition, published by W. Oliver in 1779.
The frontispiece illustration was taken from *Quiver Magazine*, 1887.

ISBN 9781935626343

Publisher's notes:
The text of this edition is uniform with the wording, punctuation, contractions and stanza formatting of the first edition *Olney Hymns* published by W. Oliver in 1779. The 1779 errata has been incorporated. Additional corrections incorporated in this edition:
Book I. Hymn 42 - Nehemiah 8:10 was substituted for Nehemiah 9:10.
Book I. Hymn 60 - Matthew 16:18 was substituted for Matthew 16:16.
Book I. Hymn 70 - Ezekiel 16:64 does not exist. Ezekiel 16:6 and 16:63 have been substituted.
Book I. Hymn 102 - "Worldling" was substituted for "Wordling" in the title.
Book II. Hymn 26 - "Travailing" was substituted for "Travelling" in the title.
Book II. Hymn 64 - 2 Samuel 24:16 was substituted for 1 Samuel 24:16.
Book III. Hymn 27 - Deleted one of a double "hear."

CONTENTS.

PREFACE.

Copies of a few of these Hymns have already appeared in periodical publications, and in some recent collections. I have observed one or two of them attributed to persons who certainly had no concern in them, but as transcribers. All that have been at different times parted with in manuscript are included in the present volume; and (if the information were of any great importance) the public may be assured, that the whole number were composed by two persons only. The original design would not admit of any other association. A desire of promoting the faith and comfort of sincere christians, though the principal, was not the only motive to this undertaking. It was likewise intended as a monument, to perpetuate the remembrance of an intimate and endeared friendship. With this pleasing view I entered upon my part, which would have been smaller than it is, and the book would have appeared much sooner, and in a very different form, if the wise, though mysterious providence of God, had not seen fit to cross my wishes. We had not proceeded far upon our proposed plan, before my dear friend was prevented, by a long and affecting indisposition, from affording me any farther assistance. My grief and disappointment were great; I hung my harp upon the willows, and for some time thought myself determined to proceed no farther without him. Yet my mind was afterwards led to resume the service. My progress in it, amidst a variety of other engagements, has been slow, yet in a course of years the hymns amounted to a considerable number. And my deference to the judgment and desires of others, has at length overcome the reluctance I long felt to see them in print, while I had so few of my friend's hymns to insert in the collection. Though it is possible a good judge of composition might be able to distinguish those which are his, I have thought it proper to preclude a misapplication, by prefixing the letter C to each of them. For the rest, I must be responsible.

There is a stile and manner suited to the composition of hymns, which may be more successfully, or at least more easily attained by a versifier, than by a poet. They should be *Hymns*, not *Odes*, if designed for public worship, and for the use of plain people. Perspicuity, simplicity and ease, should be chiefly attended to; and the imagery and coloring of poetry, if admitted at all, should be indulged very sparingly and with great judgment. The late Dr. *Watts*, many of whose hymns are admirable patterns in this species of writing, might, as a poet, have a right to say, That it cost him some labor to restrain his fire, and to accommodate himself to the capacities of common readers. But it would not become me to make such a declaration. It behoved me to do my best. But though I would not offend readers of taste by a wilful coarseness, and negligence, I do not write professedly for them. If the Lord whom I serve, has been pleased to favor me with that mediocrity of talent, which may qualify me for usefulness to the weak and the poor of his flock, without quite disgusting persons of superior discernment, I have reason to be satisfied.

As the workings of the heart of man, and of the Spirit of God, are in general the same, in all who are the subjects of grace, I hope most of these hymns, being the fruit and expression of my own experience, will coincide with the views of real christians of all denominations. But I cannot expect that every sentiment I have advanced will be universally approved. However, I am not conscious of having written a single line with an intention, either to flatter, or to offend any party or person upon earth. I have simply declared my own views and feelings, as I might have done if I had composed hymns in some of the newly discovered islands in the South-Sea, where no person had any knowledge of the name of JESUS, but myself. I am a friend of peace, and being deeply convinced that no one can profitably understand the great truths and doctrines of the gospel, any farther than he is taught of GOD, I have not a wish to obtrude my own tenets upon others, in a way of controversy: yet I do not think myself bound to conceal them. Many gracious persons (for many such I am persuaded there are) who differ from me, more or less, in those points which are called Calvinistic, appear desirous that the Calvinists should, for their sakes, studiously avoid every expression which they cannot approve. Yet few of them, I believe, impose a like restraint upon themselves, but think the importance of what they deem to be truth, justifies them in speaking their sentiments plainly, and strongly. May I not plead for an equal liberty? The views I have received of the doctrines of grace are essential to my peace, I could not live comfortably a day or an hour without them. I likewise believe, yea, so far as my poor attainments warrant me to speak, I know them to be friendly to holiness, and to have a direct influence in producing and maintaining a gospel conversation, and therefore I must not be ashamed of them.

The Hymns are distributed into three Books. In the first I have classed those which are formed upon select passages of Scripture, and placed them in the order of the books of the Old and New Testament. The second contains occasional Hymns, suited to particular seasons, or suggested by particular events or objects. The third Book is miscellaneous, comprising a variety of subjects relative to a life of faith in the Son of GOD, which have no express reference either to a single text of Scripture, or to any determinate season or incident. These are farther subdivided into distinct heads. This arrangement is not so accurate but that several of the hymns might have been differently disposed. Some attention to method may be found convenient, though a logical exactness was hardly practicable. As some subjects in the several books are nearly co-incident, I have, under the divisions in the third book, pointed out those which are similar in the two former. And I have likewise here and there in the first and second, made a reference to hymns of a like import in the third.

This publication, which, with my humble prayer to the LORD for his blessing upon it, I offer to the service and acceptance of all who love the LORD JESUS CHRIST in sincerity, of every name and in every place, into whose hands it may come; I more particularly dedicate to my dear friends in the parish and neighborhood of *Olney*, for whose use the hymns were originally composed; as a testimony of the sincere love I bear them, and as a token of my gratitude to the LORD, and to them, for the comfort and satisfaction with which the discharge of my ministry among them has been attended.

The hour is approaching, and at my time of life cannot be very distant, when my heart, my pen, and my tongue, will no longer be able to move in their service. But I trust, while my heart continues to beat, it will feel a warm desire for the prosperity of their souls; and while my hand can write, and my tongue speak, it will be the business and the pleasure of my life, to aim at promoting their growth and establishment in the grace of our GOD and SAVIOUR. To this precious grace I commend them, and earnestly entreat them, and all who love his name, to strive mightily with their prayers to GOD for me, that I may be preserved faithful to the end, and enabled at last to finish my course with joy.

Olney, Bucks,
Feb. 15, 1779.

JOHN NEWTON.

JOHN NEWTON'S
OLNEY HYMNS.

ADAM.

And the LORD God called unto Adam, and said unto him, Where art thou?—GENESIS 3:9.

ON man, in his own image made,
 How much did GOD bestow?
The whole creation homage paid,
 And own'd him, LORD, below!

He dwelt in Eden's garden, stor'd
 With sweets for ev'ry sense;
And there with his descending LORD
 He walk'd in confidence.

But oh! by sin how quickly chang'd!
 His honor forfeited,
His heart, from GOD and truth, estrang'd,
 His conscience fill'd with dread!

Now from his Maker's voice he flees,
 Which was before his joy:
And thinks to hide, amidst the trees,
 From an All-seeing eye.

Compell'd to answer to his name;
 With stubbornness and pride
He cast, on GOD himself, the blame,
 Nor once for mercy cry'd.

But grace, unask'd, his heart subdu'd
 And all his guilt forgave;
By faith, the promis'd seed he view'd,
 And felt his pow'r to save.

Thus we ourselves would justify,
 Tho' we the Law transgress;
Like him, unable to deny,
 Unwilling to confess.

But when by faith the sinner sees
 A pardon bought with blood;
Then he forsakes his foolish pleas,
 And gladly turns to GOD.

CAIN AND ABEL.

And in process of time it came to pass, that Cain brought of the fruit of the ground an offering unto the LORD. And Abel, he also brought of the firstlings of his flock and of the fat thereof. And the LORD had respect unto Abel and to his offering: But unto Cain and to his offering he had not respect. And Cain was very wroth, and his countenance fell. And the LORD said unto Cain, Why art thou wroth? and why is thy countenance fallen? If thou doest well, shalt thou not be accepted? and if thou doest not well, sin lieth at the door. And unto thee shall be his desire, and thou shalt rule over him. And Cain talked with Abel his brother: and it came to pass, when they were in the field, that Cain rose up against Abel his brother, and slew him.—GENESIS 4:3–8.

WHEN Adam fell he quickly lost
GOD's image, which he once possest:
See *All* our nature since could boast
In Cain, his first-born son, express'd!

The sacrifice the LORD ordain'd
In type of the Redeemer's blood,
Self-righteous reas'ning Cain disdain'd,
And thought his own first-fruits as good.

Yet rage and envy fill'd his mind,
When, with a sullen, downcast look,
He saw his brother favor find,
Who GOD's appointed method took.

By Cain's own hand, good Abel dy'd,
Because the LORD approv'd his faith;
And, when his blood for vengeance cry'd,
He vainly thought to hide his death.

Such was the wicked murd'rer Cain,
And such by nature still are we,
Until by grace we're born again,
Malicious, blind and proud, as he.

Like him the way of grace we slight,
And in our own devices trust;
Call evil good, and darkness light,
And hate and persecute the just.

(Continued on the next page.)

The saints, in ev'ry age and place,
Have found this history fulfill'd;
The numbers all our thoughts surpass
Of Abels, whom the Cains have kill'd![1]

Thus JESUS fell—but oh! his blood
Far better things than Abel's cries;[2]
Obtains his murd'rers peace with GOD,
And gains them mansions in the skies.

WALKING WITH GOD.

And Enoch walked with God: and he was not; for God took him.—GENESIS 5:4.

By faith in CHRIST I walk with GOD,
With heav'n, my journeys'-end, in view;
Supported by his staff and rod,[3]
My road is safe and pleasant too.

I travel thro' a desart wide,
Where many round me blindly stray;[4]
But He vouchsafes to be my guide,
And will not let me miss my way.

Tho' snares and dangers throng my path,
And earth and hell my course withstand;
I triumph over all by faith,[5]
Guarded by his Almighty hand.

The wilderness affords no food,
But GOD for my support prepares;
Provides me ev'ry needful good,
And frees my soul from wants and cares.

With him sweet converse I maintain,
Great as he is I dare be free;
I tell him all my grief and pain,
And he reveals his love to me.

Some cordial from his word he brings,
Whene'er my feeble spirit faints;
At once my soul revives and sings,
And yields no more to sad complaints.

I pity all that worldlings talk
Of pleasures that will quickly end;
Be this my choice, O LORD, to walk
With thee, my Guide, my Guard, my Friend.

---

1 Romans 8:36—As it is written, For thy sake we are killed all the day long; we are accounted as sheep for the slaughter.
2 Hebrews 12:24—And to Jesus the mediator of the new covenant, and to the blood of sprinkling, that speaketh better things than that of Abel.

3 Psalm 23:4—Yea, though I walk through the valley of the shadow of death, I will fear no evil: for thou art with me; thy rod and thy staff they comfort me.
4 Psalm 107:7—And he led them forth by the right way, that they might go to a city of habitation.
5 Psalm 27:1–2—The LORD is my light and my salvation; whom shall I fear? the LORD is the strength of my life; of whom shall I be afraid? When the wicked, even mine enemies and my foes, came upon me to eat up my flesh, they stumbled and fell.

LOT IN SODOM.

And Lot lifted up his eyes, and beheld all the plain of Jordan, that it was well watered every where, before the LORD destroyed Sodom and Gomorrah, even as the garden of the LORD, like the land of Egypt, as thou comest unto Zoar.—GENESIS 13:10.

How hurtful was the choice of Lot,
  Who took up his abode
(Because it was a fruitful spot)
  With them who fear'd not GOD!

A pris'ner he was quickly made,
  Bereav'd of all his store;
And, but for Abraham's timely aid,
  He had return'd no more.

Yet still he seem'd resolv'd to stay
  As if it were his rest;
Altho' their sins from day to day[1]
  His righteous soul distress'd.

Awhile he stay'd with anxious mind,
  Expos'd to scorn and strife;
At last he left his all behind,
  And fled to save his life.

In vain his sons-in-law he warn'd,
  They thought he told his dreams;
His daughters too, of them had learn'd,
  And perish'd in the flames.

His wife escap'd a little way,
  But dy'd for looking back:
Does not her case to pilgrims say,
  "Beware of growing slack?"

Yea, Lot himself could ling'ring stand,
  Tho' vengeance was in view;
'Twas mercy pluck'd him by the hand,
  Or he had perish'd too.

The doom of Sodom will be ours
  If to the earth we cleave;
LORD quicken all our drowsy pow'rs,
  To flee to thee and live.

---

[1] 2 Peter 2:8—For that righteous man dwelling among them, in seeing and hearing, vexed his righteous soul from day to day with their unlawful deeds.

THE LORD WILL PROVIDE.

THO' troubles assail
And dangers affright,
Tho' friends should all fail
And foes all unite;
Yet one thing secures us,
Whatever betide,
The scripture assures us,
The LORD will provide.

The birds without barn
Or storehouse are fed,
From them let us learn
To trust for our bread:
His saints, what is fitting,
Shall ne'er be deny'd,
So long as 'tis written,
The LORD will provide.

We may, like the ships,
By tempests be tost
On perilous deeps,
But cannot be lost:
Tho' Satan enrages
The wind and the tide,
The promise engages,
The LORD will provide.

His call we obey
Like Abra'm of old,
Not knowing our way,
But faith makes us bold;
For tho' we are strangers
We have a good Guide,
And trust in all dangers,
The LORD will provide.

When Satan appears
To stop up our path,
And fill us with fears,
We triumph by faith;
He cannot take from us,
Tho' oft he has try'd,
This heart-cheering promise,
The LORD will provide.

(Continued on the next page.)

He tells us we're weak,
Our hope is in vain,
The good that we seek
We ne'er shall obtain;
But when such suggestions
Our spirits have ply'd,
This answers all questions,
The LORD will provide.

No strength of our own,
Or goodness we claim,
Yet since we have known
The Saviour's great name;
In this our strong tower
For safety we hide,
The LORD is our power,
The LORD will provide.

When life sinks apace
And death is in view,
This word of his grace
Shall comfort us thro':
No fearing or doubting
With CHRIST on our side,
We hope to die shouting,
The LORD will provide.

ESAU.

Then Jacob gave Esau bread and pottage of lentiles; and he did eat and drink, and rose up, and went his way: thus Esau despised his birthright.
—GENESIS 25:34.

Lest there be any fornicator, or profane person, as Esau, who for one morsel of meat sold his birthright.—HEBREWS 12:16.

POOR Esau repented too late
That once he his birth-right despis'd;
And sold, for a morsel of meat,
What could not too highly be priz'd:
How great was his anguish when told,
The *blessing* he sought to obtain,
Was gone with the *birth-right* he sold,
And none could recall it again!

He stands as a warning to all,
Wherever the gospel shall come;
O hasten and yield to the call,
While yet for repentance there's room!
Your season will quickly be past,
Then hear and obey it to-day;
Lest when you seek mercy at last,
The Saviour should frown you away.

What is it the world can propose?
A morsel of meat at the best!
For this are you willing to lose
A share in the joys of the bless'd?
Its pleasures will speedily end,
Its favor and praise are but breath;
And what can its profits befriend
Your soul in the moment of death?

If JESUS for these you despise,
And sin to the Saviour prefer;
In vain your entreaties and cries,
When summon'd to stand at his bar:
How will you his presence abide?
What anguish will torture your heart?
The saints all enthron'd by his side,
And you be compell'd to depart.

(Continued on the next page.)

Too often, dear Saviour, have I
Preferr'd some poor trifle to thee;
How is it thou dost not deny
The blessing and birth-right to me?
No better than Esau I am,
Tho' pardon and heav'n be mine;
To me belongs nothing but shame,
The praise and the glory be thine.

JACOB'S LADDER.

And he dreamed, and behold a ladder set up on the earth, and the top of it reached to heaven: and behold the angels of God ascending and descending on it.—GENESIS 28:12.

IF the LORD our leader be,
We may follow without fear;
East or West, by land or sea,
Home, with him, is ev'ry where:
When from Esau Jacob fled,
Tho' his pillow was a stone,
And the ground his humble bed,
Yet he was not left alone.

Kings are often waking kept,
Rack'd with cares on beds of state;
Never king like Jacob slept,
For he lay at heaven's gate:
Lo! he saw a ladder rear'd,
Reaching to the heav'nly throne;
At the top the LORD appear'd,
Spake and claim'd him for his own.

"Fear not, Jacob, thou art mine,
And my presence with thee goes;
On thy heart my love shall shine,
And my arm subdue thy foes:
From my promise comfort take,
For my help in trouble call;
Never will I thee forsake,
'Till I have accomplish'd all."

Well does Jacob's ladder suit
To the gospel throne of grace;
We are at the ladder's foot,
Ev'ry hour, in ev'ry place:
By assuming flesh and blood,
JESUS heav'n and earth unites;
We by faith ascend to GOD,[1]
GOD to dwell with us delights.

(Continued on the next page.)

---

1 2 Corinthians 6:16—And what agreement hath the temple of God with idols? for ye are the temple of the living God; as God hath said, I will dwell in them, and walk in them; and I will be their God, and they shall be my people.

They who know the Saviour's name,
Are for all events prepar'd;
What can changes do to them,
Who have such a Guide and Guard?
Should they traverse earth around,
To the ladder still they come;
Ev'ry spot is holy ground,
GOD is there—and he's their home.

MY NAME IS JACOB.

And he said unto him, What is thy name? And he said, Jacob.—GENESIS 32:27.

NAY, I cannot let Thee go,
Till a blessing thou bestow;
Do not turn away thy face,
Mine's an urgent pressing case.

Dost thou ask me, who I am?
Ah, my LORD, thou know'st my name!
Yet the question gives a plea,
To support my suit with thee.

Thou didst once a wretch behold,
In rebellion blindly bold;
Scorn thy grace, thy pow'r defy,
That poor rebel, LORD, was I.

Once a sinner near despair,
Sought thy mercy-seat by pray'r;
Mercy heard and set him free,
LORD, that mercy came to me,

Many years have pass'd since then,
Many changes I have seen;
Yet have been upheld till now,
Who could hold me up but thou?

Thou hast help'd in ev'ry need,
This emboldens me to plead;
After so much mercy past,
Canst thou let me sink at last?

No—I must maintain my hold,
'Tis thy goodness makes me bold;
I can no denial take,
When I plead for JESU's sake.

PLENTY IN A TIME OF DEARTH.

And the famine was over all the face of the earth: and Joseph opened all the storehouses, and sold unto the Egyptians; and the famine waxed sore in the land of Egypt.—GENESIS 41:56.

My soul once had its plenteous years,
And throve, with peace and comfort fill'd,
Like the fat kine and ripen'd ears,
Which Pharaoh in his dream beheld.

With pleasing frames and grace receiv'd,
With means and ordinances fed;
How happy for a while I liv'd,
And little fear'd the want of bread.

But famine came and left no sign,
Of all the plenty I had seen;
Like the dry ears and half-starv'd kine,
I then look'd wither'd, faint and lean.

To Joseph the Egyptians went,
To JESUS I made known my case;
He, when my little stock was spent,
Open'd *his* magazine of grace.

For he the time of dearth foresaw,
And made provision long before;
That famish'd souls, like me, might draw
Supplies from his unbounded store.

Now on his bounty I depend,
And live from fear of dearth secure;
Maintain'd by such a mighty friend,
I cannot want till he is poor.

O sinners hear his gracious call!
His mercy's door stands open wide;
He has enough to feed you all,
And none who come shall be deny'd.

JOSEPH MADE KNOWN TO HIS BRETHREN.

And Joseph said unto his brethren, I am Joseph; doth my father yet live? And his brethren could not answer him; for they were troubled at his presence. And Joseph said unto his brethren, Come near to me, I pray you. And they came near. And he said, I am Joseph your brother, whom ye sold into Egypt.—GENESIS 45:3–4.

When Joseph his brethren beheld,
Afflicted and trembling with fear;
His heart with compassion was fill'd,
From weeping he could not forbear.
Awhile his behaviour was rough,
To bring their past sin to their mind;
But when they were humbled enough,
He hasted to shew himself kind.

How little they thought it was he,
Whom they had ill treated and sold!
How great their confusion must be,
As soon as his name he had told!
"I am Joseph, your brother, he said,
And still to my heart you are dear,
You sold me, and thought I was dead,
But GOD, for your sakes, sent me here."

Tho' greatly distressed before,
When charg'd with purloining the cup;
They now were confounded much more,
Not one of them durst to look up.
"Can Joseph, whom we would have slain,
Forgive us the evil we did?
And will he our households maintain?
O this is a brother indeed!"

Thus dragg'd by my conscience, I came,
And laden with guilt, to the LORD;
Surrounded with terror and shame,
Unable to utter a word.
At first he look'd stern and severe,
What anguish then pierced my heart!
Expecting each moment to hear
The sentence, "Thou cursed, depart!"

(Continued on the next page.)

But oh! what surprize when he spoke,
While tenderness beam'd in his face;
My heart then to pieces was broke,
O'erwhelm'd and confounded by grace:
"Poor sinner, I know thee full well,
By thee I was sold and was slain;
But I dy'd to redeem thee from hell,
And raise thee in glory to reign.

I am JESUS, whom thou hast blasphem'd,
And crucify'd often afresh;
But let me henceforth be esteem'd,
Thy brother, thy bone, and thy flesh:
My pardon I freely bestow,
Thy wants I will fully supply;
I'll guide thee and guard thee below,
And soon will remove thee on high.

Go, publish to sinners around,
That they may be willing to come,
The mercy which now you have found,
And tell them that yet there is room."
Oh, sinners, the message obey!
No more vain excuses pretend;
But come, without farther delay,
To JESUS our brother and friend.

THE BITTER WATERS.

And when they came to Marah, they could not drink of the waters of Marah, for they were bitter: therefore the name of it was called Marah. And the people murmured against Moses, saying, What shall we drink? And he cried unto the LORD; and the LORD shewed him a tree, which when he had cast into the waters, the waters were made sweet: there he made for them a statute and an ordinance, and there he proved them.—EXODUS 15:23–25.

BITTER, indeed, the waters are
    Which in this desart flow;
Though to the eye they promise fair,
    They taste of sin and woe.

Of pleasing draughts I once could dream,
    But now, awake, I find,
That sin has poison'd ev'ry stream,
    And left a curse behind.

But there's a wonder-working wood,
    I've heard believers say,
Can make these bitter waters good,
    And take the curse away.

The virtues of this healing tree
    Are known and priz'd by few;
Reveal this secret, LORD, to me,
    That I may prize it too.

The cross on which the Saviour dy'd,
    And conquer'd for his saints;
This is the tree, by faith apply'd,
    Which sweetens all complaints.

Thousands have found the bless'd effect,
    Nor longer mourn their lot;
While on his sorrows they reflect,
    Their own are all forgot.

When they, by faith, behold the cross,
    Tho' many griefs they meet;
They draw again from ev'ry loss,
    And find the bitter sweet.

MANNA.

And when they did mete it with an omer, he that gathered much had nothing over, and he that gathered little had no lack; they gathered every man according to his eating.—EXODUS 16:18.

MANNA to Israel well supply'd
 The want of other bread;
While GOD is able to provide,
 His people shall be fed.

(Thus tho' the corn and wine should fail,
 And creature-streams be dry;
The pray'r of faith will still prevail,
 For blessings from on high.)

Of his kind care how sweet a proof!
 It suited ev'ry taste;
Who gather'd most, had just enough,
 Enough, who gather'd least.

'Tis thus our gracious LORD provides
 Our comforts and our cares;
His own unerring hand provides,
 And gives us each our shares.

He knows how much the weak can bear,
 And helps them when they cry;
The strongest have no strength to spare,
 For such he'll strongly try.

Daily they saw the Manna come,
 And cover all the ground;
But what they try'd to keep at home,
 Corrupted soon was found.

Vain their attempt to store it up,
 This was to tempt the LORD;
Israel must live by faith and hope,
 And not upon a hoard.

MANNA HOARDED.

Notwithstanding they hearkened not unto Moses; but some of them left of it until the morning, and it bred worms, and stank: and Moses was wroth with them.—EXODUS 16:20.

THE manna favor'd Israel's meat,
 Was gather'd day by day;
When all the host was serv'd, the heat
 Melted the rest away.

In vain to hoard it up they try'd,
 Against to-morrow came;
It then bred worms and putrefy'd,
 And prov'd their sin and shame.

'Twas daily bread and would not keep,
 But must be still renew'd;
Faith should not want a hoard or heap,
 But trust the LORD for food.

The truths by which the soul is fed,
 Must thus be had afresh;
For notions resting in the head,
 Will only feed the flesh.

However true, they have no life,
 Or unction to impart;
They breed the worms of pride and strife,
 But cannot cheer the heart.

Nor can the best experience past,
 The life of faith maintain;
The brightest hope will faint at last,
 Unless supply'd again.

Dear LORD, while we in pray'r are found,
 Do thou the Manna give;
Oh! let it fall on all around,
 That we may eat and live.

THE GOLDEN CALF.

And he received them at their hand, and fashioned it with a graving tool, after he had made it a molten calf: and they said, These be thy gods, O Israel, which brought thee up out of the land of Egypt.
—EXODUS 32:4.

And Moses returned unto the LORD, and said, Oh, this people have sinned a great sin, and have made them gods of gold.—EXODUS 32:31.

WHEN Israel heard the fiery law,
    From Sinai's top proclaim'd;
Their hearts seem'd full of holy awe,
    Their stubborn spirits tam'd.

Yet, as forgetting all they knew,
    Ere forty days were past;
With blazing Sinai still in view,
    A molten calf they cast.

Yea, Aaron, GOD's anointed priest,
    Who on the mount had been;
He durst prepare the idol-beast,
    And lead them on to sin.

LORD, what is man! and what are we,
    To recompense thee thus!
In their offence our own we see,
    Their story points at us.

From Sinai we have heard thee speak,
    And from mount Calv'ry too;
And yet to idols oft we seek,
    While thou art in our view.

Some golden calf, or golden dream,
    Some fancy'd creature-good,
Presumes to share the heart with him,
    Who bought the whole with blood.

LORD, save us from our golden calves,
    Our sin with grief we own;
We would no more be thine by halves,
    But live to thee alone.

THE TRUE AARON.

And he put upon him the coat, and girded him with the girdle, and clothed him with the robe, and put the ephod upon him, and he girded him with the curious girdle of the ephod, and bound it unto him therewith. And he put the breastplate upon him: also he put in the breastplate the Urim and the Thummim. And he put the mitre upon his head; also upon the mitre, even upon his forefront, did he put the golden plate, the holy crown; as the LORD commanded Moses.—LEVITICUS 8:7–9.

SEE Aaron, GOD's anointed priest,
    Within the vail appear;
In robes of mystic meaning drest,
    Presenting Israel's pray'r.

The plate of gold which crowns his brows,
    His holiness describes;
His breast displays, in shining rows,
    The names of all the tribes.

With the atoning blood he stands,
    Before the mercy-seat;
And clouds of incense from his hands,
    Arise with odour sweet.

Urim and Thummim near his heart,
    In rich engravings worn;
The sacred light of truth impart,
    To teach and to adorn.

Thro' him the eye of faith descries,
    A greater Priest than he;
Thus JESUS pleads above the skies,
    For you, my friends, and me.

He bears the names of all his saints,
    Deep on his heart engrav'd;
Attentive to the state and wants
    Of all his love has sav'd.

In him a holiness complete,
    Light and perfections shine;
And wisdom, grace, and glory meet;
    A Saviour all divine.

(Continued on the next page.)

The blood, which as a Priest he bears
    For sinners, is his own;
The incense of his pray'rs and tears
    Perfume the holy throne.

In him my weary soul has rest,
    Tho' I am weak and vile;
I read my name upon his breast,
    And see the Father smile.

BALAAM'S WISH.[1]

*Who can count the dust of Jacob, and the number
of the fourth part of Israel? Let me die the death
of the righteous, and let my last end be like his!*
          —NUMBERS 23:10.

How blest the righteous are
    When they resign their breath!
No wonder Balaam wish'd to share
    In such a happy death.

"Oh! let me die, said he,
    The death the righteous do;
When life is ended let me be
    Found with the faithful few."

The force of truth how great!
    When enemies confess,
None but the righteous whom they hate,
    A solid hope possess.

But Balaam's wish was vain,
    His heart was insincere;
He thirsted for unrighteous gain,
    And sought a portion here.

He seem'd the LORD to know,
    And to offend him loth;
But Mammon prov'd his overthrow,
    For none can serve them both.

May you, my friends, and I,
    Warning from hence receive;
If like the righteous we would die,
    To choose the life they live.

---

1 Book III. Hymn 71.

GIBEON.

And the men of Gibeon sent unto Joshua to the camp to Gilgal, saying, Slack not thy hand from thy servants; come up to us quickly, and save us, and help us: for all the kings of the Amorites that dwell in the mountains are gathered together against us.—JOSHUA 10:6.

WHEN Joshua, by GOD's command,
Invaded Canaan's guilty land;
Gibeon, unlike the nations round,
Submission made and mercy found.

Their stubborn neighbours who enrag'd,
United war against them wag'd,
By Joshua soon were overthrown,
For Gibeon's cause was now his own.

He from whose arm they ruin fear'd,
Their leader and ally appear'd;
An emblem of the Saviour's grace,
To those who humbly seek his face.

The men of Gibeon wore disguise,
And gain'd their peace by framing lies;
For Joshua had no pow'r to spare,
If he had known from whence they were.

But JESUS invitations sends,
Treating with rebels as his friends;
And holds the promise forth in view,
To all who for his mercy sue.

Too long his goodness I disdain'd,
Yet went at last and peace obtain'd;
But soon the noise of war I heard,
And former friends in arms appear'd.

Weak in myself, for help I cry'd,
"LORD, I am press'd on ev'ry side;
The cause is thine, they fight with me,
But ev'ry blow is aim'd at thee."

With speed to my relief he came,
And put my enemies to shame;
Thus sav'd by grace I live to sing
The love and triumphs of my King.

GIDEON'S FLEECE.

Behold, I will put a fleece of wool in the floor; and if the dew be on the fleece only, and it be dry upon all the earth beside, then shall I know that thou wilt save Israel by mine hand, as thou hast said. And it was so: for he rose up early on the morrow, and thrust the fleece together, and wringed the dew out of the fleece, a bowl full of water. And Gideon said unto God, Let not thine anger be hot against me, and I will speak but this once: let me prove, I pray thee, but this once with the fleece; let it now be dry only upon the fleece, and upon all the ground let there be dew. And God did so that night: for it was dry upon the fleece only, and there was dew on all the ground.—JUDGES 6:37–40.

THE signs which GOD to Gideon gave,
His holy Sov'reignty made known;
That He alone has pow'r to save,
And claims the glory as his own.

The dew which first the fleece had fill'd,
When all the earth was dry around;
Was from it afterwards withheld,
And only fell upon the ground.

To Israel thus the heavenly dew
Of saving truth was long restrain'd;
Of which the Gentiles nothing knew,
But dry and desolate remain'd.

But now the Gentiles have receiv'd
The balmy dew of gospel peace;
And Israel, who his spirit griev'd,
Is left a dry and empty fleece.

This dew still falls at his command,
To keep his chosen plants alive;
They shall, tho' in a thirsty land,
Like willows by the waters thrive.[1]

But chiefly when his people meet,
To hear his word and seek his face;
The gentle dew, with influence sweet,
Descends and nourishes their grace.

(Continued on the next page.)

---

1 Isaiah 44:4—And they shall spring up as among the grass, as willows by the water courses.

But ah! what numbers still are dead,
Tho' under means of grace they lie!
The dew still falling round their head,
And yet their heart untouch'd and dry.

Dear Saviour, hear us when we call,
To wrestling pray'r an answer give;
Pour down thy dew upon us all,
That all may feel, and all may live.

SAMPSON'S LION.

And after a time he returned to take her, and he turned aside to see the carcase of the lion: and, behold, there was a swarm of bees and honey in the carcase of the lion.—JUDGES 14:8.

THE lion that on Sampson roar'd,
    And thirsted for his blood;
With honey afterwards was stor'd,
    And furnish'd him with food.

Believers, as they pass along,
    With many lions meet;
But gather sweetness from the strong,
    And from the eater, meat.

The lions rage and roar in vain,
    For JESUS is their shield;
Their losses prove a certain gain,
    Their troubles comfort yield.

The world and Satan join their strength,
    To fill their souls with fears;
But crops of joy they reap at length,
    From what they sow in tears.

Afflictions make them love the word,
    Stir up their hearts to pray'r;
And many precious proofs afford,
    Of their Redeemer's care.

The lions roar but cannot kill,
    Then fear them not, my friends,
They bring us, tho' against their will,
    The honey JESUS sends.

HANNAH; OR THE THRONE OF GRACE.

And she said, Let thine handmaid find grace in thy sight. So the woman went her way, and did eat, and her countenance was no more sad.
—1 SAMUEL 1:18.

WHEN Hannah press'd with grief,
 Pour'd forth her soul in pray'r;
She quickly found relief,
 And left her burden there:
Like her, in ev'ry trying case,
Let us approach the throne of grace.

When she began to pray,
 Her heart was pain'd and sad;
But ere she went away,
 Was comforted and glad:
In trouble, what a resting place,
Have they who know the throne of grace!

Tho' men and devils rage,
 And threaten to devour;
The saints, from age to age,
 Are safe from all their pow'r:
Fresh strength they gain to run their race,
By waiting at the throne of grace.

Eli her case mistook,
 How was her spirit mov'd
By his unkind rebuke?
 But GOD her cause approv'd.
We need not fear a creature's face,
While welcome at a throne of grace.

She was not fill'd with wine,
 As Eli rashly thought;
But with a faith divine,
 And found the help she sought:
Tho' men despise and call us base,
Still let us ply the throne of grace.

Men have not pow'r or skill,
 With troubled souls to bear;
Tho' they express good-will,
 Poor comforters they are:
But swelling sorrows sink apace,
When we approach the throne of grace.

(Continued in the next column.)

Numbers before have try'd,
 And found the promise true;
Nor one been yet deny'd,
 Then why should I or you?
Let us by faith their footsteps trace,
And hasten to the throne of grace.

As fogs obscure the light,
 And taint the morning air;
But soon are put to flight,
 If the bright sun appear;
Thus JESUS will our troubles chase,
By shining from the throne of grace.[1]

---

1 Book II. Hymn 61.

DAGON BEFORE THE ARK.

And when they arose early on the morrow morning, behold, Dagon was fallen upon his face to the ground before the ark of the LORD; and the head of Dagon and both the palms of his hands were cut off upon the threshold; only the stump of Dagon was left to him. Therefore neither the priests of Dagon, nor any that come into Dagon's house, tread on the threshold of Dagon in Ashdod unto this day.
—1 SAMUEL 5:4–5.

WHEN first to make my heart his own,
The LORD reveal'd his mighty grace;
Self reign'd, like Dagon, on the throne,
But could not long maintain its place.

It fell, and own'd the pow'r divine,
(Grace can with ease the vict'ry gain)
But soon this wretched heart of mine,
Contriv'd to set it up again.

Again the LORD his name proclaim'd,
And brought the hateful idol low;
Then self, like Dagon, broken, maim'd,
Seem'd to receive a mortal blow.

Yet self is not of life bereft,
Nor ceases to oppose his will;
Tho' but a maimed stump be left,
'Tis Dagon, 'tis an idol still.

LORD! must I always guilty prove,
And idols in my heart have room?[1]
Oh! let the fire of heavenly love,
The very stump of self consume.

---

1 Hosea 14:8—Ephraim shall say, What have I to do any more with idols? I have heard him, and observed him: I am like a green fir tree. From me is thy fruit found.

THE MILCH KINE DRAWING THE ARK: FAITH'S SURRENDER OF ALL.

And the kine took the straight way to the way of Bethshemesh, and went along the highway, lowing as they went, and turned not aside to the right hand or to the left; and the lords of the Philistines went after them unto the border of Bethshemesh.
—1 SAMUEL 6:12.

THE kine unguided went
By the directest road;
When the Philistines homeward sent
The ark of Israel's GOD.

Lowing they pass'd along,
And left their calves shut up;
They felt an instinct for their young,
But would not turn or stop.

Shall brutes, devoid of thought,
Their Maker's will obey;
And we, who by his grace are taught,
More stubborn prove than they?

He shed his precious blood
To make us his alone;
If wash'd in that atoning flood
We are no more our own.

If he his will reveal,
Let us obey his call;
And think whate'er the flesh may feel,
His love deserves our all.

We should maintain in view
His glory, as our end;
Too much we cannot bear, or do,
For such a matchless friend.

His saints should stand prepar'd
In duty's path to run;
Nor count their greatest trials hard,
So that his will be done.

With JESUS for our guide,
The path is safe though rough;
The promise says, "I will provide,"
And faith replies, "Enough!"

SAUL'S ARMOR.

And Saul armed David with his armour, and he put an helmet of brass upon his head; also he armed him with a coat of mail. And David gird-ed his sword upon his armour, and he assayed to go; for he had not proved it. And David said unto Saul, I cannot go with these; for I have not proved them. And David put them off him. And he took his staff in his hand, and chose him five smooth stones out of the brook, and put them in a shepherd's bag which he had, even in a scrip; and his sling was in his hand: and he drew near to the Philistine.
—1 Samuel 17:38–40.

WHEN first my soul enlisted
    My Saviour's foes to fight;
Mistaken friends insisted
    I was not arm'd aright:
So Saul advised David
    He certainly would fail;
Nor could his life be saved
    Without a coat of mail.

But David, tho' he yielded
    To put the armor on,
Soon found he could not wield it,
    And ventur'd forth with none.
With only sling and pebble
    He fought the fight of faith;
The weapons seem'd but feeble,
    Yet prov'd Goliath's death.

Had I by him been guided,
    And quickly thrown away
The armor men provided,
    I might have gain'd the day;
But arm'd as they advis'd me,
    My expectations fail'd;
My enemy surpriz'd me,
    And had almost prevail'd.

Furnish'd with books and notions,
    And arguments and pride;
I practis'd all my motions,
    And Satan's pow'r defy'd:

(Continued in the next column.)

But soon perceiv'd with trouble,
    That these would do no good;
Iron to him is stubble,[1]
    And brass like rotten wood.

I triumph'd at a distance
    While he was out of sight;
But faint was my resistance
    When forc'd to join in fight:
He broke my sword in shivers,
    And pierc'd my boasted shield;
Laugh'd at my vain endeavors,
    And drove me from the field.

Satan will not be braved
    By such a worm as I;
Then let me learn with David,
    To trust in the Most High;
To plead the name of JESUS,
    And use the sling of pray'r;
Thus arm'd, when Satan sees us
    He'll tremble and despair.

---

1 Job 41:27—He esteemeth iron as straw, and brass as rotten wood.

DAVID'S FALL.

And when the mourning was past, David sent and fetched her to his house, and she became his wife, and bare him a son. But the thing that David had done displeased the LORD.—2 SAMUEL 11:27.

How David, when by sin deceiv'd,
   From bad to worse went on!
For when the Holy Spirit's griev'd,
   Our strength and guard are gone.

His eye on Bathsheba once fix'd,
   With poison fill'd his soul;
He ventur'd on adult'ry next,
   And murder crown'd the whole.

So from a spark of fire at first,
   That has not been descry'd;
A dreadful flame has often burst,
   And ravag'd far and wide.

When sin deceives it hardens too,
   For tho' he vainly sought
To hide his crimes from public view,
   Of GOD he little thought.

He neither would, or could repent,
   No true compunction felt;
'Till GOD in mercy Nathan sent,
   His stubborn heart to melt.

The parable held forth a fact,
   Design'd his case to shew;
But tho' the picture was exact,
   Himself he did not know.

"Thou art the man," the prophet said,
   That word his slumber broke;
And when he own'd his sin, and pray'd,
   The LORD forgiveness spoke.

Let those who think they stand beware,
   For David stood before;
Nor let the fallen soul despair,
   For mercy can restore.

IS THIS THY KINDNESS TO THY FRIEND.

And Absalom said to Hushai, Is this thy kindness to thy friend? why wentest thou not with thy friend?—2 Samuel 16:17.

POOR, weak, and worthless tho' I am,
I have a rich almighty friend;
JESUS, the Saviour, is his name,
He freely loves, and without end.

He ransom'd me from hell with blood,
And by his pow'r my foes controll'd;
He found me, wand'ring far from GOD,
And brought me to his chosen fold.

He cheers my heart, my wants supplies,
And says that I shall shortly be
Enthron'd with him above the skies,
Oh! what a friend is CHRIST to me.

But ah! I my inmost spirit mourns,
And well my eyes with tears may swim,
To think of my perverse returns;
I've been a faithless friend to him.

Often my gracious Friend I grieve,
Neglect, distrust, and disobey,
And often Satan's lies believe,
Sooner than all my Friend can say.

He bids me always freely come,
And promises whate'er I ask:
But I am straitned, cold and dumb,
And count my privilege a task.

Before the world that hates his cause,
My treach'rous heart has throbb'd with shame;
Loth to forego the world's applause,
I hardly dare avow his name.

Sure were not I most vile and base,
I could not thus my friend requite!
And were not he the GOD of grace,
He'd frown and spurn me from his sight.

ASK WHAT I SHALL GIVE THEE.

In Gibeon the Lord appeared to Solomon in a dream by night: and God said, Ask what I shall give thee.—1 KINGS 3:5.

COME, my soul, thy suit prepare,
JESUS loves to answer pray'r;
He himself has bid thee pray,
Therefore will not say thee nay.

Thou art coming to a King,[1]
Large petitions with thee bring;
For his grace and pow'r are such,
None can ever ask too much.

With my burden I begin,
LORD, remove this load of sin!
Let thy blood, for sinners spilt,
Set my conscience free from guilt.

LORD! I come to thee for rest,
Take possession of my breast;
There thy blood-bought right maintain,
And without a rival reign.

As the image in the glass
Answers the beholder's face;
Thus unto my heart appear,
Print thine own resemblance there.

While I am a pilgrim here,
Let thy love my spirit cheer;
As my Guide, my Guard, my Friend,
Lead me to my journey's end.

Shew me what I have to do,
Ev'ry hour my strength renew;
Let me live a life of faith,
Let me die thy peoples death.

ASK WHAT I SHALL GIVE THEE.

IF Solomon for wisdom pray'd,
The LORD before had made him wise;
Else he another choice had made,
And ask'd for what the worldlings prize.

Thus he invites his people still,
He first instructs them how to choose;
Then bids them ask whate'er they will,
Assur'd that He will not refuse.

Our wishes would our ruin prove,
Could we our wretched choice obtain;
Before we feel the Saviour's love,
Kindle our love to him again.

But when our hearts perceive his worth,
Desires, till then unknown, take place;
Our spirits cleave no more to earth,
But pant for holiness and grace.

And dost thou say, "Ask what thou wilt?"
LORD, I would seize the golden hour;
I pray to be releas'd from guilt,
And freed from sin and Satan's pow'r.

More of thy presence, LORD, impart,
More of thine image let me bear;
Erect thy throne within my heart,
And reign without a rival there.

Give me to read my pardon seal'd,
And from thy joy to draw my strength;
To have thy boundless love reveal'd
In all its height, and breadth, and length.

Grant these requests, I ask no more,
But to thy care the rest resign;
Sick or in health, or rich, or poor,
All shall be well if thou art mine.

---

1 Psalm 81:10—I am the LORD thy God, which brought thee out of the land of Egypt: open thy mouth wide, and I will fill it.

ASK WHAT I SHALL GIVE THEE.

BEHOLD the throne of grace!
The promise calls me near;
There JESUS shews a smiling face,
And waits to answer pray'r.

That rich atoning blood,
Which sprinkled round I see;
Provides for those who come to GOD,
An all-prevailing plea.

My soul ask what thou wilt,
Thou canst not be too bold;
Since his own blood for thee he spilt,
What else can he withhold.

Beyond thy utmost wants
His love and pow'r can bless;
To praying souls he always grants,
More than they can express.

Since 'tis the LORD's command,
My mouth I open wide;
LORD open thou thy bounteous hand,
That I may be supply'd.

Thine image, LORD, bestow,
Thy presence and thy love;
I ask to serve thee here below,
And reign with thee above.

Teach me to live by faith,
Conform my will to thine;
Let me victorious be in death,
And then in glory shine.

If Thou these blessings give,
And wilt my portion be;
Cheerful the world's poor toys I leave,
To them who know not thee.

QUEEN OF SHEBA.

And when the queen of Sheba heard of the fame of Solomon concerning the name of the LORD, she came to prove him with hard questions. And she came to Jerusalem with a very great train, with camels that bare spices, and very much gold, and precious stones: and when she was come to Solomon, she communed with him of all that was in her heart. And Solomon told her all her questions: there was not any thing hid from the king, which he told her not. And when the queen of Sheba had seen all Solomon's wisdom, and the house that he had built, And the meat of his table, and the sitting of his servants, and the attendance of his ministers, and their apparel, and his cupbearers, and his ascent by which he went up unto the house of the LORD; there was no more spirit in her. And she said to the king, It was a true report that I heard in mine own land of thy acts and of thy wisdom. Howbeit I believed not the words, until I came, and mine eyes had seen it: and, behold, the half was not told me: thy wisdom and prosperity exceedeth the fame which I heard. Happy are thy men, happy are these thy servants, which stand continually before thee, and that hear thy wisdom. Blessed be the LORD thy God, which delighted in thee, to set thee on the throne of Israel: because the LORD loved Israel for ever, therefore made he thee king, to do judgment and justice.—1 KINGS 10:1–9.

FROM Sheba a distant report
Of Solomon's glory and fame,
Invited the queen to his court,
But all was outdone when she came;
She cry'd, with a pleasing surprize,
When first she before him appear'd,
"How much, what I see with my eyes,
"Surpasses the rumor I heard!"

When once to Jerusalem come,
The treasure and train she had brought;
The wealth she possessed at home,
No longer had place in her thought:
His house, *his* attendants, *his* throne,
All struck her with wonder and awe;
The glory of Solomon shone,
In every object she saw.

(Continued on the next page.)

But Solomon most she admir'd,
Whose spirit conducted the whole;
His wisdom, which GOD had inspir'd,
His bounty and greatness of soul;
Of all the hard questions she put,
A ready solution he shew'd;
Exceeded her wish and her suit,
And more than she ask'd him bestow'd.

Thus I when the gospel proclaim'd
The Saviour's great name in my ears,
The wisdom for which he is fam'd,
The love which to sinners he bears;
I long'd, and I was not deny'd,
That I in his presence might bow;
I saw, and transported I cry'd,
"A greater than Solomon Thou!"

My conscience no comfort could find,
By doubt and hard questions oppos'd;
But He restor'd peace to my mind,
And answer'd each doubt I propos'd:
Beholding me poor and distress'd,
His bounty supply'd all my wants;
My pray'r could have never express'd
So much as this Solomon grants.

I heard, and was slow to believe,
But now with my eyes I behold,
Much more than my heart could conceive,
Or language could ever have told:
How happy thy servants must be,
Who always before thee appear!
Vouchsafe, LORD, this blessing to me,
I find it is good to be here.

ELIJAH FED BY RAVENS.[1]

And the ravens brought him bread and flesh in the morning, and bread and flesh in the evening; and he drank of the brook.—1 KINGS 17:6.

ELIJAH'S example declares,
Whatever distress may betide;
The saints may commit all their cares
To him who will surely provide:
When rain long withheld from the earth
Occasion'd a famine of bread;
The prophet, secure from the dearth,
By ravens was constantly fed.

More likely to rob than to feed,
Were ravens who live upon prey;
But when the LORD's people have need,
His goodness will find out a way:
This instance to those may seem strange,
Who know not how faith can prevail;
But sooner all nature shall change,
Than one of GOD's promises fail.

Nor is it a singular case,
The wonder is often renew'd;
And many can say, to his praise,
He sends them by ravens their food:
Thus worldlings, tho' ravens indeed,
Tho' greedy and selfish their mind,
If GOD has a servant to feed,
Against their own wills can be kind.

Thus Satan, that raven unclean,
Who croaks in the ears of the saints;
Compell'd by a power unseen,
Administers oft to their wants:
GOD teaches them how to find food
From all the temptations they feel;
This raven, who thirsts for my blood,
Has help'd me to many a meal.

How safe and how happy are they
Who on the good Shepherd rely!
He gives them out strength for their day,
Their wants he will surely supply:
He ravens and lions can tame,
All creatures obey his command;
Then let me rejoice in his name,
And leave all my cares in his hand.

1 Book III. Hymn 57.

THE MEAL AND CRUISE OF OIL.

And the barrel of meal wasted not, neither did the cruse of oil fail, according to the word of the Lord, which he spake by Elijah.—1 KINGS 17:16.

By the poor widow's oil and meal
   Elijah was sustain'd;
Tho' small the stock it lasted well,
   For GOD the store maintain'd.

It seem'd as if from day to day,
   They were to eat and die;
But still, tho' in a secret way,
   He sent a fresh supply.

Thus to his poor he still will give
   Just for the present hour;
But for to-morrow they must live
   Upon his word and pow'r.

No barn or storehouse they possess
   On which they can depend;
Yet have no cause to fear distress,
   For JESUS is their friend.

Then let not doubts your mind assail,
   Remember, GOD has said,
"The cruise and barrel shall not fail,
   "My people shall be fed."

And thus tho' faint it often seems,
   He keeps their grace alive;
Supply'd by his refreshing streams,
   Their dying hopes revive.

Tho' in ourselves we have no stock,
   The LORD is nigh to save;
His door flies open when we knock,
   And 'tis but ask and have.

JERICHO; OR, THE WATERS HEALED.

And the men of the city said unto Elisha, Behold, I pray thee, the situation of this city is pleasant, as my lord seeth: but the water is naught, and the ground barren. And he said, Bring me a new cruse, and put salt therein. And they brought it to him. And he went forth unto the spring of the waters, and cast the salt in there, and said, Thus saith the Lord, I have healed these waters; there shall not be from thence any more death or barren land. So the waters were healed unto this day, according to the saying of Elisha which he spake.—2 KINGS 2:19–22.

Tho' Jericho pleasantly stood,
And look'd like a promising soil;
The harvest produc'd little food,
To answer the husbandman's toil.
The water some property had,
Which poisonous prov'd to the ground;
The springs were corrupted and bad,
The streams spread a barreness round.

But soon by the cruise and the salt,
Prepar'd by Elisha's command;
The water was cur'd of its fault,
And plenty enriched the land:
An emblem sure this of the grace
On fruitless dead sinners bestow'd;
For man is in Jericho's case,
Till cur'd by the mercy of GOD.

How noble a creature he seems!
What knowledge, invention and skill!
How large and extensive his schemes!
How much can he do if he will!
His zeal to be learned and wise,
Will yield to no limits or bars;
He measures the earth and the skies,
And numbers and marshals the stars.

Yet still he is barren of good;
In vain are his talents and art;
For sin has infected his blood,
And poison'd the streams of his heart:

(Continued on the next page.)

Tho' cockatrice eggs he can hatch,[1]
Or, spider like, cobwebs can weave;
'Tis madness to labour and watch
For what will destroy or deceive.

But grace, like the salt in the cruise,
When cast in the spring of the soul;
A wonderful change will produce,
Diffusing new life thro' the whole:
The wilderness blooms like a rose,
The heart which was vile and abhorr'd;
Now fruitful and beautiful grows,
The garden and joy of the LORD.

NAAMAN.

Then went he down, and dipped himself seven times in Jordan, according to the saying of the man of God: and his flesh came again like unto the flesh of a little child, and he was clean.—2 KINGS 5:14.

BEFORE Elisha's gate
    The Syrian leper stood;
But could not brook to wait,
    He deem'd himself too good:
He thought the prophet would attend,
And not *to him* a message send.

Have I this journey come,
    And will he not be seen?
I were as well at home,
    Would washing make me clean:
Why must I wash in Jordan's flood?
Damascus' rivers are as good.

Thus by his foolish pride
    He almost miss'd a cure;
Howe'er at length he try'd,
    And found the method sure:
Soon as his pride was brought to yield,
The leprosy was quickly heal'd.

Leprous and proud as he,
    To JESUS thus I came;
From sin to set me free,
    When first I heard his fame:
Surely, thought I, my pompous train
Of vows and tears will notice gain.

My heart devis'd the way
    Which I suppos'd he'd take;
And when I found delay,
    Was ready to go back:
Had he some painful task enjoin'd,
I to performance seem'd inclin'd.

When by his word he spake,
    "That fountain open'd see;
'Twas open'd for thy sake,
    Go wash, and thou art free:"
Oh! how did my proud heart gainsay,
I fear'd to trust this simple way.

---

1 Isaiah 59:5—They hatch cockatrice' eggs, and weave the spider's web: he that eateth of their eggs dieth, and that which is crushed breaketh out into a viper.

(Continued on the next page.)

At length I trial made,
    When I had much endur'd;
The message I obey'd,
    I wash'd, and I was cur'd:
Sinners this healing fountain try,
Which cleans'd a wretch so vile as I.

THE BORROWED AXE.

But as one was felling a beam, the axe head fell into the water: and he cried, and said, Alas, master! for it was borrowed. And the man of God said, Where fell it? And he shewed him the place. And he cut down a stick, and cast it in thither; and the iron did swim.—2 KINGS 6:5–6.

THE prophets sons, in time of old,
    Tho' to appearance poor;
Were rich without possessing gold,
    And honor'd, tho' obscure.

In peace their daily bread they eat,
    By honest labour earn'd;
While daily at Elisha's feet,
    They grace and wisdom learn'd.

The prophet's presence cheer'd their toil,
    They watch'd the words he spoke;
Whether they turn'd the furrow'd soil,
    Or fell'd the spreading oak.

Once as they listen'd to his theme,
    Their conference was stopp'd;
For one beneath the yielding stream,
    A borrow'd axe had dropp'd.

"Alass! it was not mine, he said,
    How shall I make it good?"
Elisha heard, and when he pray'd,
    The iron swam like wood.

If GOD, in such a small affair,
    A miracle performs;
It shews his condescending care
    Of poor unworthy worms.

Tho' kings and nations in his view
    Are but as motes and dust;
His eye and ear are fix'd on you,
    Who in his mercy trust.

Not one concern of ours is small,
    If we belong to him;
To teach us this, the LORD of all,
    Once made the iron swim.

MORE WITH US THAN WITH THEM.

And he answered, Fear not: for they that be with us are more than they that be with them.
        —2 KINGS 6:16.

ALAS! Elisha's servant cry'd,
When he the Syrian army spy'd;
But he was soon releas'd from care,
In answer to the prophet's pray'r.

Straitway he saw, with other eyes,
A greater army from the skies;
A fiery guard around the hill,
Thus are the saints preserved still.

When Satan and his host appear,
Like him of old, I faint and fear;
Like him, by faith, with joy I see,
A greater host engag'd for me.

The saints espouse my cause by pray'r,
The angels make my soul their care;
Mine is the promise seal'd with blood,
And JESUS lives to make it good.

FAITH'S REVIEW AND EXPECTATION.

And David the king came and sat before the LORD, and said, Who am I, O LORD God, and what is mine house, that thou hast brought me hitherto? And yet this was a small thing in thine eyes, O God; for thou hast also spoken of thy servant's house for a great while to come, and hast regarded me according to the estate of a man of high degree, O LORD God.—1 CHRONICLES 17:16–17.

AMAZING grace! (how sweet the sound)
    That sav'd a wretch like me!
I once was lost, but now am found,
    Was blind, but now I see.

'Twas grace that taught my heart to fear,
    And grace my fears reliev'd;
How precious did that grace appear,
    The hour I first believ'd!

Thro' many dangers, toils and snares,
    I have already come;
'Tis grace has brought me safe thus far,
    And grace will lead me home.

The LORD has promis'd good to me,
    His word my hope secures;
He will my shield and portion be,
    As long as life endures.

Yes, when this flesh and heart shall fail,
    And mortal life shall cease;
I shall possess, within the vail,
    A life of joy and peace.

The earth shall soon dissolve like snow,
    The sun forbear to shine;
But GOD, who call'd me here below,
    Will be for ever mine.

THE JOY OF THE LORD IS YOUR STRENGTH.

Then he said unto them, Go your way, eat the fat, and drink the sweet, and send portions unto them for whom nothing is prepared: for this day is holy unto our LORD: neither be ye sorry; for the joy of the LORD is your strength.—NEHEMIAH 8:10.

JOY is a fruit that will not grow
    In nature's barren soil;
All we can boast, till CHRIST we know,
    Is vanity and toil.

But where the LORD has planted grace,
    And made his glories known;
There fruits of heavenly joy and peace
    Are found, and there alone.

A bleeding Saviour seen by faith,
    A sense of pard'ning love;
A hope that triumphs over death,
    Give joys like those above.

To take a glimpse within the vail,
    To know that GOD is mine;
Are springs of joy that never fail,
    Unspeakably divine!

These are the joys which satisfy,
    And sanctify the mind;
Which make the spirit mount on high,
    And leave the world behind.

No more, believers, mourn your lot,
    But if you are the LORD's;
Resign to them that know him not,
    Such joys as earth affords.

OH THAT I WERE AS IN MONTHS PAST!

Oh that I were as in months past, as in the days when God preserved me.—JOB 29:2.

SWEET was the time when first I felt
    The Saviour's pard'ning blood
Apply'd, to cleanse my soul from guilt,
    And bring me home to GOD.

Soon as the morn the light reveal'd,
    His praises tun'd my tongue;
And when the ev'ning shades prevail'd,
    His love was all my song.

In vain the tempter spread his wiles,
    The world no more could charm;
I liv'd upon my Saviour's smiles,
    And lean'd upon his arm.

In pray'r my soul drew near the LORD,
    And saw his glory shine;
And when I read his holy word,
    I call'd each promise mine.

Then to his saints I often spoke,
    Of what his love had done;
But now my heart is almost broke,
    For all my joys are gone.

Now when the evening shade prevails,
    My soul in darkness mourns;
And when the morn the light reveals,
    No light to me returns.

My prayers are now a chatt'ring noise,
    For JESUS hides his face;
I read, the promise meets my eyes,
    But will not reach my case.

Now Satan threatens to prevail,
    And make my soul his prey;
Yet, LORD, thy mercies cannot fail,
    O come without delay.

THE CHANGE.[1]

SAVIOUR shine and cheer my soul,
Bid my dying hopes revive;
Make my wounded spirit whole,
Far away the tempter drive:
Speak the word and set me free,
Let me live alone to thee.

Shall I sigh and pray in vain,
Wilt thou still refuse to hear;
Wilt thou not return again,
Must I yield to black despair?
Thou hast taught my heart to pray,
Canst thou turn thy face away?

Once I thought my mountain strong,
Firmly fix'd no more to move;
Then thy grace was all my song,
Then my soul was fill'd with love:
Those were happy golden days,
Sweetly spent in pray'r and praise.

When my friends have said, "Beware,
Soon or late you'll find a change;"
I could see no cause for fear,
Vain their caution seem'd and strange:
Not a cloud obscur'd my sky,
Could I think a tempest nigh?

Little, then, myself I knew,
Little thought of Satan's pow'r;
Now I find their words were true,
Now I feel the stormy hour!
Sin has put my joys to flight,
Sin has chang'd my day to night.

Satan asks, and mocks my woe,
"Boaster, where is now your GOD?"
Silence, LORD, this cruel foe,
Let him know I'm bought with blood:
Tell him, since I know thy name,
Tho' I change thou art the same.

PLEADING FOR MERCY.

Have mercy upon me, O LORD; for I am weak: O LORD, heal me; for my bones are vexed.—PSALM 6:2.
(The entire chapter of Psalm 6 was referenced.)

IN mercy, not in wrath, rebuke
    Thy feeble worm, my GOD!
My spirit dreads thine angry look,
    And trembles at thy rod.

Have mercy, LORD, for I am weak,
    Regard my heavy grones;
O let thy voice of comfort speak,
    And heal my broken bones!

By day my busy beating head
    Is fill'd with anxious fears;
By night, upon my restless bed,
    I weep a flood of tears.

Thus I sit desolate and mourn,
    Mine eyes grow dull with grief;
How long, my LORD, ere thou return,
    And bring my soul relief?

O come and shew thy pow'r to save,
    And spare my fainting breath;
For who can praise thee in the grave,
    Or sing thy name in death?

Satan, my cruel envious foe,
    Insults me in my pain;
He smiles to see me brought so low,
    And tells me hope is vain,

But hence, thou enemy, depart!
    Nor tempt me to despair;
My Saviour comes to cheer my heart,
    The LORD has heard my pray'r.

---

1 Book II, Hymn 34, and Book III, Hymn 68.

NONE UPON EARTH I DESIRE BESIDES THEE.

Whom have I in heaven but thee? and there is none upon earth that I desire beside thee.—PSALM 73:25.

How tedious and tasteless the hours,
    When JESUS no longer I see;
Sweet prospects, sweet birds, and sweet flow'rs,
    Have lost all their sweetness with me:
The mid-summer sun shines but dim,
    The fields strive in vain to look gay;
But when I am happy in him,
    December's as pleasant as May.

His name yields the richest perfume,
    And sweeter than music his voice;
His presence disperses my gloom,
    And makes all within me rejoice:
I should, were he always thus nigh,
    Have nothing to wish or to fear;
No mortal so happy as I,
    My summer would last all the year.

Content with beholding his face,
    My all to his pleasure resign'd;
No changes of season or place,
    Would make any change in my mind:
While bless'd with a sense of his love,
    A palace a toy would appear;
And prisons would palaces prove,
    If JESUS would dwell with me there.

Dear LORD, if indeed I am thine,
    If thou art my sun and my song;
Say, why do I languish and pine,
    And why are my winters so long?
O drive these dark clouds from my sky,
    Thy soul-cheering presence restore;
Or take me unto thee on high,
    Where winter and clouds are no more.

THE BELIEVER'S SAFETY.

Surely he shall deliver thee from the snare of the fowler, and from the noisome pestilence. He shall cover thee with his feathers, and under his wings shalt thou trust: his truth shall be thy shield and buckler. Thou shalt not be afraid for the terror by night; nor for the arrow that flieth by day; Nor for the pestilence that walketh in darkness; nor for the destruction that wasteth at noonday.
      —PSALM 91:3–6.
(The entire chapter of Psalm 91 was referenced.)

INCARNATE GOD! the soul that knows
    Thy name's mysterious pow'r;
Shall dwell in undisturb'd repose,
    Nor fear the trying hour.

Thy wisdom, faithfulness and love,
    To feeble helpless worms;
A buckler and a refuge prove,
    From enemies and storms.

In vain the fowler spreads his net,
    To draw them from thy care;
Thy timely call instructs their feet,
    To shun the artful snare.

When like a baneful pestilence,
    Sin mows its thousands down
On ev'ry side, without defence,
    Thy grace secures thine own.

No midnight terrors haunt their bed,
    No arrow wounds by day;
Unhurt on serpents they shall tread,
    If found in duty's way.

Angels, unseen, attend the saints,
    And bear them in their arms;
To cheer the spirit when it faints,
    And guard the life from harms.

The angels' LORD, himself is nigh,
    To them that love his name;
Ready to save them when they cry,
    And put their foes to shame.

Crosses and changes are their lot,
    Long as they sojourn here;
But since their Saviour changes not,
    What have the saints to fear?

THE BELIEVER'S SAFETY.

THAT man no guard or weapons needs,
Whose heart the blood of JESUS knows;
But safe may pass, if duty leads,
Thro' burning sands or mountain-snows.

Releas'd from guilt he feels no fear,
Redemption is his shield and tow'r;
He sees his Saviour always near
To help, in ev'ry trying hour.

Tho' I am weak and Satan strong,
And often to assault me tries;
When JESUS is my shield and song,
Abash'd the wolf before me flies.

His love possessing I am blest,
Secure whatever change may come;
Whether I go to East or West,
With him I still shall be at home.

If plac'd beneath the northern pole,
Tho' winter reigns with rigor there;
His gracious beams would cheer my soul,
And make a spring throughout the year.

Or if the desarts sun-burnt soil,
My lonely dwelling e'er should prove;
His presence would support my toil,
Whose smile is life, whose voice is love.

HE LED THEM BY A RIGHT WAY.

And he led them forth by the right way, that they might go to a city of habitation.—PSALM 107:7.

WHEN Israel was from Egypt freed,
    The LORD, who brought them out,
Help'd them in ev'ry time of need,
    But led them round about.[1]

To enter Canaan soon they hop'd,
    But quickly chang'd their mind;
When the Red-sea their passage stopp'd,
    And Pharaoh march'd behind.

The desart fill'd them with alarms,
    For water and for food;
And Amalek, by force of arms,
    To check their progress stood.

They often murmur'd by the way,
    Because they judg'd by sight;
But were at length constrain'd to say,
    The LORD had led them right.

In the Red-sea that stopp'd them first,
    Their enemies were drown'd;
The rocks gave water for their thirst,
    And Manna spread the ground.

By fire and cloud their way was shown,
    Across the pathless sands;
And Amalek was overthrown,
    By Moses' lifted hands.

The way was right their hearts to prove,
    To make GOD's glory known;
And shew his wisdom, pow'r and love,
    Engag'd to save his own.

Just so the true believer's path
    Thro' many dangers lies;
Tho' dark to sense, 'tis right to faith,
    And leads us to the skies.

---

1 Exodus 13:17—And it came to pass, when Pharaoh had let the people go, that God led them not through the way of the land of the Philistines, although that was near; for God said, Lest peradventure the people repent when they see war, and they return to Egypt.

WHAT SHALL I RENDER.[1]

What shall I render unto the LORD for all his benefits toward me? I will take the cup of salvation, and call upon the name of the LORD.
—PSALM 116:12–13.

FOR mercies, countless as the sands,
   Which daily I receive
From JESUS, my Redeemer's hands,
   My soul what canst thou give?

Alass! from such a heart as mine,
   What can I bring him forth?
My best is stain'd and dy'd with sin,
   My all is nothing worth.

Yet this acknowledgment I'll make
   For all he has bestow'd;
Salvation's sacred cup I'll take,
   And call upon my GOD.

The best returns for one like me,
   So wretched and so poor;
Is from his gifts to draw a plea,
   And ask him still for more.

I cannot serve him as I ought,
   No works have I to boast;
Yet would I glory in the thought
   That I shall owe him most.

DWELLING IN MESECH.

Woe is me, that I sojourn in Mesech, that I dwell in the tents of Kedar! My soul hath long dwelt with him that hateth peace. I am for peace: but when I speak, they are for war.—PSALM 120:5–7.

WHAT a mournful life is mine,
   Fill'd with crosses, pains and cares!
Ev'ry work defil'd with sin,
   Ev'ry step beset with snares!

If alone I pensive sit,
   I myself can hardly bear;
If I pass along the street,
   Sin and riot triumph there.

JESUS! how my heart is pain'd,
   How it mourns for souls deceiv'd!
When I hear thy name profan'd,
   When I see thy Spirit griev'd!

When thy childrens' griefs I view,
   Their distress becomes my own;
All I hear, or see, or do,
   Makes me tremble, weep and grone.

Mourning thus I long had been,
   When I heard my Saviour's voice;
"Thou hast cause to mourn for sin,
   But in me thou may'st rejoice."

This kind word dispell'd my grief,
   Put to silence my complaints;
Tho' of sinners I am chief,
   He his rank'd me with his saints.

Tho' constrain'd to dwell a while
   Where the wicked strive and brawl;
Let them frown; so he but smile,
   Heav'n will make amends for all.

There, believers, we shall rest,
   Free from sorrow, sin and fears;
Nothing there our peace molests,
   Thro' eternal rounds of years.

Let us then the fight endure,
   See our Captain looking down;
He will make the conquest sure,
   And bestow the promis'd crown.

---

1 Book III. Hymn 67.

A FRIEND THAT STICKETH CLOSER THAN A BROTHER.

A man that hath friends must shew himself friendly: and there is a friend that sticketh closer than a brother.—PROVERBS 18:24.

ONE there is, above all others,
Well deserves the name of friend;
His is love beyond a brother's,
Costly, free, and knows no end:
   They who once his kindness prove,
   Find it everlasting love!

Which of all our friends to save us,
Could or would have shed their blood?
But our JESUS dy'd to have us
Reconcil'd, in him to GOD:
   This was boundless love indeed!
   JESUS is a friend in need.

Men, when rais'd to lofty stations,
Often know their friends no more;
Slight and scorn their poor relations
Tho' they valu'd them before.
   But our Saviour always owns
   Those whom he redeem'd with grones.

When he liv'd on earth abased,
Friend of sinners was his name;
Now, above all glory raised,
He rejoices in the same:
   Still he calls them brethren, friends,
   And to all their wants attends.

Could we bear from one another,
What he daily bears from us?
Yet this glorious Friend and Brother,
Loves us tho' we treat him thus:
   Tho' for good we render ill,
   He accounts us brethren still.

Oh! for grace our hearts to soften!
Teach us, LORD, at length to love;
We, alass! forget too often,
What a Friend we have above:
   But when home our souls are brought,
   We will love thee as we ought.

VANITY OF LIFE.[1]

Vanity of vanities, saith the Preacher, vanity of vanities; all is vanity.—ECCLESIASTES 1:2.

THE evils that beset our path
   Who can prevent or cure?
We stand upon the brink of death
   When most we seem secure.

If we to-day sweet peace possess,
   It soon may be withdrawn;
Some change may plunge us in distress,
   Before to-morrow's dawn.

Disease and pain invade our health
   And find an easy prey;
And oft, when least expected, wealth
   Takes wings and flies away.

A fever or a blow can shake
   Our wisdom's boasted rule;
And of the brightest genius make
   A madman or a fool.

The gourds, from which we look for fruit,
   Produce us only pain;
A worm unseen attacks the root,
   And all our hopes are vain.

I pity those who seek no more
   Than such a world can give;
Wretched they are, and blind, and poor,
   And dying while they live.

Since sin has fill'd the earth with woe,
   And creatures fade and die;
LORD wean our hearts from things below,
   And fix our hopes on high.

---

1 Book II. Hymn 6.

VANITY OF THE CREATURE SANCTIFIED.

HONEY tho' the bee prepares,
An envenom'd sting he wears;
Piercing thorns a guard compose
Round the fragrant blooming rose.

Where we think to find a sweet,
Oft a painful sting we meet:
When the rose invites our eye,
We forget the thorn is nigh.

Why are thus our hopes beguil'd?
Why are all our pleasures spoil'd?
Why do agony and woe
From our choicest comforts grow?

Sin has been the cause of all!
'Twas not thus before the fall:
What but pain, and thorn, and sting,
From the root of sin can spring?

Now with ev'ry good we find
Vanity and grief entwin'd;
What we feel, or what we fear,
All our joys embitter here.

Yet, thro' the Redeemer's love,
These afflictions blessings prove;
He the wounding stings and thorns,
Into healing med'cines turns.

From the earth our hearts they wean,
Teach us on his arm to lean;
Urge us to a throne of grace,
Make us seek a resting place.

In the mansions of our King
Sweets abound without a sting;
Thornless there the roses blow,
And the joys unmingled flow.

THE NAME OF JESUS.

Because of the savour of thy good ointments thy name is as ointment poured forth, therefore do the virgins love thee.—SONG OF SOLOMON 1:3.

How sweet the name of JESUS sounds
    In a believer's ear!
It sooths his sorrows, heals his wounds,
    And drives away his fear.

It makes the wounded spirit whole,
    And calms the troubled breast;
'Tis Manna to the hungry soul,
    And to the weary rest.

Dear name! the rock on which I build,
    My shield and hiding place;
My never-failing treas'ry fill'd
    With boundless stores of grace.

By thee my pray'rs acceptance gain,
    Altho' with sin defil'd;
Satan accuses me in vain,
    And I am own'd a child.

JESUS! my Shepherd, Husband, Friend,
    My Prophet, Priest, and King;
My LORD, my Life, my Way, my End,
    Accept the praise I bring.

Weak is the effort of my heart,
    And cold my warmest thought;
But when I see thee as thou art,
    I'll praise thee as I ought.

'Till then I would thy love proclaim
    With ev'ry fleeting breath;
And may the music of thy name
    Refresh my soul in death.

THE REFUGE, RIVER, AND ROCK OF THE CHURCH.

*And a man shall be as an hiding place from the
wind, and a covert from the tempest; as rivers of
water in a dry place, as the shadow of a great rock
in a weary land.*—ISAIAH 32:2.

HE who on earth as man was known,
　　And bore our sins and pains;
Now, seated on th' eternal throne,
　　The GOD of glory reigns.

His hands the wheels of nature guide
　　With an unerring skill;
And countless worlds extended wide,
　　Obey his sov'reign will.

While harps unnumber'd sound his praise,
　　In yonder world above;
His saints on earth admire his ways,
　　And glory in his love.

His righteousness, to faith reveal'd,
　　Wrought out for guilty worms;
Affords a hiding place and shield,
　　From enemies and storms.

This land, thro' which his pilgrims go,
　　Is desolate and dry;
But streams of grace from him o'erflow
　　Their thirst to satisfy.

When troubles, like a burning sun,
　　Beat heavy on their head;
To this almighty Rock they run,
　　And find a pleasing shade.

How glorious he! how happy they
　　In such a glorious friend!
Whose love secures them all the way,
　　And crowns them at the end.

ZION, OR THE CITY OF GOD.[1]

*Look upon Zion, the city of our solemnities: thine
eyes shall see Jerusalem a quiet habitation, a tab-
ernacle that shall not be taken down; not one of the
stakes thereof shall ever be removed, neither shall
any of the cords thereof be broken. But there the glo-
rious LORD will be unto us a place of broad rivers
and streams; wherein shall go no galley with oars,
neither shall gallant ship pass thereby.*
　　　　　　　　　　　　—ISAIAH 33:20–21.

GLORIOUS things of thee are spoken,[2]
Zion, city of our GOD!
He, whose word cannot be broken,
Form'd thee for his own abode:[3]
On the rock of ages founded,[4]
What can shake thy sure repose?
With salvation's walls surrounded[5]
Thou may'st smile at all thy foes.

See! the streams of living waters
Springing from eternal love;[6]
Well supply thy sons and daughters,
And all fear of want remove:
Who can faint while such a river
Ever flows their thirst t' assuage?
Grace, which like the LORD, the giver,
Never fails from age to age.

Round each habitation hov'ring
See the cloud and fire appear![7]
　　　　　　(Continued on the next page.)

---

1 Book II. Hymn 24.
2 Psalm 87:3—Glorious things are spoken of thee, O city of God. Selah.
3 Psalm 132:14—This is my rest for ever: here will I dwell; for I have desired it.
4 Matthew 16:18—And I say also unto thee, That thou art Peter, and upon this rock I will build my church; and the gates of hell shall not prevail against it.
5 Isaiah 26:1—In that day shall this song be sung in the land of Judah; We have a strong city; salvation will God appoint for walls and bulwarks.
6 Psalm 46:4—There is a river, the streams whereof shall make glad the city of God, the holy place of the tabernacles of the most High.
7 Isaiah 4:5–6—And the LORD will create upon every dwelling place of mount Zion, and upon her assemblies, a cloud and smoke by day, and the shining of a flaming fire by night: for upon all the glory shall be a defence. And there shall be a tabernacle for a shadow in the day time from the heat, and for a place of refuge, and for a covert from storm and from rain.

For a glory and a cov'ring,
Shewing that the LORD is near:
Thus deriving from their banner
Light by night and shade by day;
Safe they feed upon the Manna
Which he gives them when they pray.

Blest inhabitants of Zion,
Wash'd in the Redeemer's blood!
JESUS, whom their souls rely on,
Makes them kings and priests to GOD:[1]
'Tis his love his people raises
Over self to reign as kings
And as priests, his solemn praises
Each for a thank-off'ring brings.

Saviour, if of Zion's city
I thro' grace a member am;
Let the world deride or pity,
I will glory in thy name:
Fading is the worldling's pleasure,
All his boasted pomp and show;
Solid joys and lasting treasure,
None but Zion's children know.

LOOK UNTO ME, AND BE YE SAVED.

Look unto me, and be ye saved, all the ends of the earth: for I am God, and there is none else.
—ISAIAH 45:22.

As the serpent rais'd by Moses[2]
Heal'd the burning serpent's bite;
JESUS thus himself discloses
To the wounded sinner's sight:
Hear his gracious invitation,
"I have life and peace to give,
I have wrought out full salvation,
Sinner, look to me and live.

Pore upon your sins no longer,
Well I know their mighty guilt;
But my love than death is stronger,
I my blood have freely spilt:
Tho' your heart has long been hard'ned,
Look on me—it soft shall grow;
Past transgressions shall be pardon'd,
And I'll wash you white as snow.

I have seen what you were doing,
Tho' you little thought of me;
You were madly bent on ruin,
But I said—It shall not be:
You had been for ever wretched,
Had I not espous'd your part;
Now behold my arms outstretched
To receive you to my heart.

Well may shame, and joy, and wonder,
All your inward passions move;
I could crush thee with my thunder,
But I speak to thee in love:
See! your sins are all forgiven,
I have paid the countless sum!
Now my death has open'd heaven,
Thither you shall shortly come."

(Continued on the next page.)

---

1 Revelation 1:6—And hath made us kings and priests unto God and his Father; to him be glory and dominion for ever and ever. Amen.

---

2 Numbers 21:9—And Moses made a serpent of brass, and put it upon a pole, and it came to pass, that if a serpent had bitten any man, when he beheld the serpent of brass, he lived.

Dearest Saviour, we adore thee
For thy precious life and death;
Melt each stubborn heart before thee,
Give us all the eye of faith:
From the law's condemning sentence,
To thy mercy we appeal;
Thou alone canst give repentance,
Thou alone our souls canst heal.

THE GOOD PHYSICIAN.

How lost was my condition
Till Jesus made me whole!
There is but one Physician
Can cure a sin-sick soul.
Next door to death he found me,
And snatch'd me from the grave,
To tell to all around me,
His wond'rous pow'r to save.

The worst of all diseases
Is light, compar'd with sin;
On ev'ry part it seizes,
But rages most within:
'Tis palsy, plague, and fever,
And madness—all combin'd;
And none but a believer
The least relief can find.

From men great skill professing
I thought a cure to gain;
But this prov'd more distressing,
And added to my pain:
Some said that nothing ail'd me,
Some gave me up for lost;
Thus ev'ry refuge fail'd me,
And all my hopes were cross'd.

At length this great Physician,
How matchless is his grace!
Accepted my petition,
And undertook my case:
First gave me sight to view him,
For sin my eyes had seal'd;
Then bid me look unto him,
I look'd, and I was heal'd.

A dying, risen Jesus,
Seen by the eye of faith;
At once from danger frees us,
And saves the soul from death:
Come then to this Physician,
His help he'll freely give;
He makes no hard condition,
'Tis only—look and live.

TO THE AFFLICTED, TOSSED WITH TEMPESTS AND NOT COMFORTED.

For thy Maker is thine husband; the LORD *of hosts is his name; and thy Redeemer the Holy One of Israel; The God of the whole earth shall he be called. For the* LORD *hath called thee as a woman forsaken and grieved in spirit, and a wife of youth, when thou wast refused, saith thy God. For a small moment have I forsaken thee; but with great mercies will I gather thee. In a little wrath I hid my face from thee for a moment; but with everlasting kindness will I have mercy on thee, saith the* LORD *thy Redeemer. For this is as the waters of Noah unto me: for as I have sworn that the waters of Noah should no more go over the earth; so have I sworn that I would not be wroth with thee, nor rebuke thee. For the mountains shall depart, and the hills be removed; but my kindness shall not depart from thee, neither shall the covenant of my peace be removed, saith the* LORD *that hath mercy on thee. O thou afflicted, tossed with tempest, and not comforted, behold, I will lay thy stones with fair colours, and lay thy foundations with sapphires.*—ISAIAH 54:5–11.

PENSIVE, doubting, fearful heart,
Hear what CHRIST the Saviour says;
Ev'ry word should joy impart,
Change thy mourning into praise:
Yes, he speaks, and speaks to thee,
May he help thee to believe!
Then thou presently wilt see,
Thou hast little cause to grieve.

"Fear thou not, nor be ashamed,
All thy sorrows soon shall end:
I who heav'n and earth have fram'd,
Am thy husband and thy friend:
I the High and Holy One,
Israel's GOD by all ador'd;
As thy Saviour will be known,
Thy Redeemer and thy LORD.

For a moment I withdrew,
And thy heart was fill'd with pain;
But my mercies I'll renew,
Thou shalt soon rejoice again:

(Continued in the next column.)

Tho' I seem to hide my face,
Very soon my wrath shall cease;
'Tis but for a moment's space,
Ending in eternal peace.

When my peaceful bow appears[1]
Painted on the wat'ry cloud;
'Tis to dissipate thy fears,
Lest the earth should be o'erflow'd:
'Tis an emblem too of grace,
Of my cov'nant love a sign;
Tho' the mountains leave their place,
Thou shalt be for ever mine.

Tho' afflicted, tempest-toss'd,
Comfortless awhile thou art,
Do not think thou canst be lost,
Thou art graven on my heart:
All thy wastes I will repair,
Thou shalt be rebuilt anew;
And in thee it shall appear,
What a GOD of love can do."

---

1 Genesis 9:13–14—I do set my bow in the cloud, and it shall be for a token of a covenant between me and the earth. And it shall come to pass, when I bring a cloud over the earth, that the bow shall be seen in the cloud.

TRUST OF THE WICKED, AND THE RIGHTEOUS COMPARED.

Thus saith the LORD; Cursed be the man that trusteth in man, and maketh flesh his arm, and whose heart departeth from the LORD. For he shall be like the heath in the desert, and shall not see when good cometh; but shall inhabit the parched places in the wilderness, in a salt land and not inhabited. Blessed is the man that trusteth in the LORD, and whose hope the LORD is. For he shall be as a tree planted by the waters, and that spreadeth out her roots by the river, and shall not see when heat cometh, but her leaf shall be green; and shall not be careful in the year of drought, neither shall cease from yielding fruit.—JEREMIAH 17:5–8.

As parched in the barren sands
    Beneath a burning sky;
The worthless bramble with'ring stands,
    And only grows to die.

Such is the sinner's awful case,
    Who makes the world his trust;
And dares his confidence to place
    In vanity and dust.

A secret curse destroys his root,
    And dries his moisture up;
He lives awhile, but bears no fruit,
    Then dies without a hope.

But happy he whose hopes depend
    Upon the LORD alone;
The soul that trusts in such a friend,
    Can ne'er be overthrown.

Tho' gourds should wither, cisterns break,
    And creature-comforts die;
No change his solid hope can shake,
    Or stop his sure supply.

So thrives and blooms the tree whose roots
    By constant streams are fed;
Array'd in green, and rich in fruits,
    It rears its branching head.

It thrives, tho' rain should be deny'd,
    And drought around prevail;
'Tis planted by a river's side
    Whose waters cannot fail.

THE LORD IS MY PORTION.

The LORD is my portion, saith my soul; therefore will I hope in him.—LAMENTATIONS 3:24.

FROM pole to pole let others roam,
    And search in vain for bliss;
My soul is satisfy'd at home,
    The LORD my portion is.

JESUS, who on his glorious throne
    Rules heav'n and earth and sea;
Is pleas'd to claim me for his own,
    And give himself to me.

His person fixes all my love,
    His blood removes my fear;
And while he pleads for me above,
    His arm preserves me here.

His word of promise is my food,
    His Spirit is my guide;
Thus daily is my strength renew'd
    And all my wants supply'd.[1]

For him I count as gain each loss,
    Disgrace, for him, renown;
Well may I glory in his cross,
    While he prepares my crown!

Let worldlings then indulge their boast,
    How much they gain or spend!
Their joys must soon give up the ghost,
    But mine shall know no end.

---

[1] Book III. Hymn 59.

HUMBLED AND SILENCED
BY MERCY.

*And when I passed by thee, and saw thee polluted in thine own blood, I said unto thee when thou wast in thy blood, Live; yea, I said unto thee when thou wast in thy blood, Live.—*EZEKIEL 16:6.

That thou mayest remember, and be confounded, and never open thy mouth any more because of thy shame, when I am pacified toward thee for all that thou hast done, saith the Lord GOD.—EZEKIEL 16:63.

ONCE perishing in blood I lay,
   Creatures no help could give,
But JESUS pass'd me in the way,
   He saw, and bid me live.

Tho' Satan still his rule maintain'd,
   And all his arts employ'd;
That mighty Word his rage restrain'd,
   I could not be destroy'd.

At length the time of love arriv'd
   When I my LORD should know;
Then Satan, of his pow'r depriv'd,
   Was forc'd to let me go.

O can I e'er that day forget
   When JESUS kindly spoke!
"Poor soul, my blood has paid thy debt,
   And now I break thy yoke.

Henceforth I take thee for my own,
   And give myself to thee;
Forsake the idols thou hast known,
   And yield thyself to me."

Ah, worthless heart! it promis'd fair,
   And said it would be thine;
I little thought it e'er would dare
   Again with idols join.

LORD, dost thou such backslidings heal,
   And pardon all that's past?
Sure, if I am not made of steel,
   Thou hast prevail'd at last.

My tongue, which rashly spoke before,
   This mercy will restrain;
Surely I now shall boast no more,
   Nor censure, nor complain.

THE POWER AND TRIUMPH
OF FAITH.

*And whoso falleth not down and worshippeth shall the same hour be cast into the midst of a burning fiery furnace.—*DANIEL 3:6.

SUPPORTED by the word,
   Tho' in himself a worm,
   The servant of the LORD
   Can wond'rous acts perform:
Without dismay he boldly treads
Where'er the path of duty leads.

   The haughty king in vain,
   With fury on his brow,
   Believers would constrain
   To golden gods to bow:
The furnace could not make them fear,
Because they knew the LORD was near.

   As vain was the decree
   Which charg'd them not to pray;
   Daniel still bow'd his knee,
   And worship'd thrice a day:
Trusting in GOD, he fear'd not men,
Tho' threatened with the lion's den.

   Secure they might refuse
   Compliance with such laws,
   For what had they to lose,
   When GOD espous'd their cause?
He made the hungry lions crouch,
Nor durst the fire *his* children touch.

   The LORD is still the same,
   A mighty shield and tow'r,
   And they who trust his name
   Are guarded by his pow'r:
He can the rage of lions tame,
And bear them harmless thro' the flame.

   Yet we too often shrink
   When trials are in view;
   Expecting we must sink,
   And never can get thro'.
But could we once believe indeed,
From all these fears we should be freed.

BELSHAZZAR.

In the same hour came forth fingers of a man's hand, and wrote over against the candlestick upon the plaister of the wall of the king's palace: and the king saw the part of the hand that wrote. Then the king's countenance was changed, and his thoughts troubled him, so that the joints of his loins were loosed, and his knees smote one against another.
—DANIEL 5:5–6.

POOR sinners! little do they think
  With whom they have to do!
But stand securely on the brink
  Of everlasting woe.

Belshazzar thus, profanely bold,
  The LORD of hosts defy'd;
But vengeance soon his boasts controll'd,
  And humbled all his pride.

He saw a hand upon the wall
  (And trembled on his throne)
Which wrote his sudden dreadful fall
  In characters unknown.

Why should he tremble at the view
  Of what he could not read?
Foreboding conscience quickly knew
  His ruin was decreed.

See him o'erwhelm'd with deep distress!
  His eyes with anguish roll;
His looks, and loosen'd joints, express
  The terrors of his soul.

His pomp and music, guests and wine,
  No more delight afford;
O sinner, ere this case be thine,
  Begin to seek the LORD.

The law like this hand-writing stands,
  And speaks the wrath of GOD;[1]
But JESUS answers its demands,
  And cancels it with blood.

THE GOURD.

But God prepared a worm when the morning rose the next day, and it smote the gourd that it withered.—JONAH 4:7.

As once for Jonah, so the LORD
To sooth and cheer my mournful hours,
Prepar'd for me a pleasing gourd,
Cool was its shade, and sweet its flow'rs.

To prize his gift was surely right;
But thro' the folly of my heart,
It hid the Giver from my sight,
And soon my joy was chang'd to smart.

While I admir'd its beauteous form,
Its pleasant shade and graceful fruit;
The LORD, displeas'd, sent forth a worm,
Unseen, to prey upon the root.

I trembled when I saw it fade,
But guilt restrain'd the murm'ring word;
My folly I confess'd, and pray'd,
Forgive my sin, and spare my gourd.

His wond'rous love can ne'er be told,
He heard me and reliev'd my pain;
His word the threat'ning worm controll'd,
And bid my gourd revive again.

Now, LORD, my gourd is mine no more,
'Tis thine, who only could'st it raise;
The idol of my heart before,
Henceforth shall flourish to thy praise.

---

[1] Colossians 2:14—Blotting out the handwriting of ordinances that was against us, which was contrary to us, and took it out of the way, nailing it to his cross.

PRAYER FOR THE LORD'S PROMISED PRESENCE.

Sing and rejoice, O daughter of Zion: for, lo, I come, and I will dwell in the midst of thee, saith the LORD.—ZECHARIAH 2:10.

SON of GOD! thy people's shield!
Must we still thine absence mourn?
Let thy promise be fulfill'd,
Thou hast said, "I will return!"

Gracious Leader now appear,
Shine upon us with thy light!
Like the spring, when thou art near,
Days and suns are doubly bright.

As a mother counts the days
Till her absent son she see;
Longs and watches, weeps and prays,
So our spirits long for thee.

Come, and let us feel thee nigh,
Then thy sheep shall feed in peace;
Plenty bless us from on high,
Evil from amongst us cease.

With thy love, and voice, and aid,
Thou canst ev'ry care assuage;
Then we shall not be afraid,
Tho' the world and Satan rage.

Thus each day for thee we'll spend,
While our callings we pursue;
And the thoughts of such a friend
Shall each night our joy renew.

Let thy light be ne'er withdrawn,
Golden days afford us long!
Thus we pray at early dawn,
This shall be our ev'ning song.

A BRAND PLUCKED OUT OF THE FIRE.

And he shewed me Joshua the high priest standing before the angel of the LORD, and Satan standing at his right hand to resist him. And the LORD said unto Satan, The LORD rebuke thee, O Satan; even the LORD that hath chosen Jerusalem rebuke thee: is not this a brand plucked out of the fire? Now Joshua was clothed with filthy garments, and stood before the angel. And he answered and spake unto those that stood before him, saying, Take away the filthy garments from him. And unto him he said, Behold, I have caused thine iniquity to pass from thee, and I will clothe thee with change of raiment. And I said, Let them set a fair mitre upon his head. So they set a fair mitre upon his head, and clothed him with garments. And the angel of the LORD stood by.—ZECHARIAH 3:1–5.

WITH Satan, my accuser near,
My spirit trembled when I saw
The LORD in majesty appear,
And heard the language of his law.

In vain I wish'd and strove to hide
The tatter'd filthy rags I wore;
While my fierce foe, insulting cry'd,
"See what you trusted in before!"

Struck dumb, and left without a plea,
I heard my gracious Saviour say,
"Know, Satan, I this sinner free,
I dy'd to take his sins away.

This is a brand which I in love,
To save from wrath and sin design;
In vain thy accusations prove,
I answer all, and claim him mine."

At his rebuke the tempter fled;
Then he remov'd my filthy dress;
"Poor sinner take this robe, he said,
It is thy Saviour's righteousness.

And see, a crown of life prepar'd!
That I might thus thy head adorn;
I thought no shame or suff'ring hard,
But wore, for thee, a crown of thorn."

(Continued on the next page.)

O how I heard these gracious words!
They broke and heal'd my heart at once;
Constrain'd me to become the LORD's,
And all my idol-gods renounce.

Now, Satan, thou hast lost thy aim,
Against this brand thy threats are vain;
JESUS has pluck'd it from the flame,
And who shall put it in again?

ON ONE STONE SHALL BE SEVEN EYES.

For behold the stone that I have laid before Joshua; upon one stone shall be seven eyes: behold, I will engrave the graving thereof, saith the LORD of hosts, and I will remove the iniquity of that land in one day.—ZECHARIAH 3:9.

JESUS CHRIST, the LORD's anointed,
Who his blood for sinners spilt;
Is the Stone by GOD appointed,
And the church is on him built:
He delivers all who trust him from their guilt.

Many eyes at once are fixed
On a person so divine;
Love, with awful justice mixed,
In his great redemption shine:
Mighty JESUS! give me leave to call thee mine.

By the Father's eye approved,
Lo, a voice is heard from heav'n,[1]
"Sinners, this is my Beloved,
For your ransom freely given:
All offences, for his sake, shall be forgiven."

Angels with their eyes pursu'd him,[2]
When he left his glorious throne;
With astonishment they view'd him
Put the form of servant on:
Angels worshipp'd him who was on earth
        unknown.

Satan and his host amazed,
Saw this stone in Zion laid;
JESUS, tho' to death abased,
Bruis'd the subtle serpent's head:[3]
When to save us, on the cross his blood he
        shed.

(Continued on the next page.)

---

1 Matthew 3:17—And lo a voice from heaven, saying, This is my beloved Son, in whom I am well pleased.

2 1 Timothy 3:16—And without controversy great is the mystery of godliness: God was manifest in the flesh, justified in the Spirit, seen of angels, preached unto the Gentiles, believed on in the world, received up into glory.

3 John 12:31—Now is the judgment of this world: now shall the prince of this world be cast out.

When a guilty sinner sees him,
While he looks his soul is heal'd;
Soon this sight from anguish frees him,
And imparts a pardon seal'd:[1]
May this Saviour be to all our hearts reveal'd!

With desire and admiration,
All his blood-bought flock behold;
Him who wrought out their salvation,
And enclos'd them in his fold:[2]
Yet their warmest love, and praises, are too
    cold.

By the eye of carnal reason
Many view him with disdain;[3]
How will they abide the season
When he'll come with all his train:
To escape him then they'll wish, but wish in
    vain.

How their hearts will melt and tremble
When they hear his awful voice;[4]
But his saints he'll then assemble,
As his portion and his choice;
And receive them to his everlasting joys.

---

1 John 3:15—That whosoever believeth in him should
  not perish, but have eternal life.
2 1 Peter 2:7—Unto you therefore which believe he is
  precious: but unto them which be disobedient, the
  stone which the builders disallowed, the same is made
  the head of the corner,
3 Psalm 118:22—The stone which the builders refused
  is become the head stone of the corner.
4 Revelation 1:7—Behold, he cometh with clouds; and
  every eye shall see him, and they also which pierced
  him: and all kindreds of the earth shall wail because
  of him. Even so, Amen

THEY SHALL BE MINE, SAITH THE LORD.

*Then they that feared the Lord spake often one to
another: and the Lord hearkened, and heard it,
and a book of remembrance was written before
him for them that feared the Lord, and that
thought upon his name. And they shall be mine,
saith the Lord of hosts, in that day when I make
up my jewels; and I will spare them, as a man
spareth his own son that serveth him. Then shall
ye return, and discern between the righteous and
the wicked, between him that serveth God and him
that serveth him not.*—Malachi 3:16–18.

When sinners utter boasting words,
    And glory in their shame;
The Lord, well-pleas'd, an ear affords
    To those who fear his name.

They often meet to seek his face,
    And what they do, or say,
Is noted in his book of grace
    Against another day.

For they, by faith, a day descry,
    And joyfully expect,
When he, descending from the sky,
    His jewels will collect.

Unnotic'd now, because unknown,
    A poor and suff'ring few;
He comes to claim them for his own,
    And bring them forth to view.

With transport then their Saviour's care
    And favor they shall prove;
As tender parents guard and spare
    The children of their love.

Assembled worlds will then discern
    The saints alone are blest;
When wrath shall like an oven burn,
    And vengeance strike the rest.

THE BEGGAR.

Ask, and it shall be given you; seek, and ye shall find; knock, and it shall be opened unto you: For every one that asketh receiveth; and he that seeketh findeth; and to him that knocketh it shall be opened.—MATTHEW 7:7–8.

Encourag'd by thy word
Of promise to the poor;
Behold, a beggar, LORD,
Waits at thy mercy's door!
No hand, no heart, O LORD, but thine,
Can help or pity wants like mine.

The beggar's usual plea
Relief from men to gain,
If offer'd unto thee,
I know thou would'st disdain:
And pleas which move thy gracious ear,
Are such as men would scorn to hear.

I have no right to say
That tho' I now am poor,
Yet once there was a day
When I possessed more:
Thou know'st that from my very birth,
I've been the poorest wretch on earth.

Nor can I dare profess,
As beggars often do,
Tho' great is my distress,
My wants have been but few:
If thou shouldst leave my soul to starve,
It would be what I well deserve.

'Twere folly to pretend
I never begg'd before;
Or if thou now befriend,
I'll trouble thee no more:
Thou often hast reliev'd my pain,
And often I must come again.

Tho' crumbs are much too good
For such a dog as I;
No less than children's food
My soul can satisfy:
O do not frown and bid me go,
I must have all thou canst bestow.

(Continued in the next column.)

Nor can I willing be
Thy bounty to conceal
From others, who like me,
Their wants and hunger feel:
I'll tell them of thy mercy's store,
And try to send a thousand more.

Thy thoughts, thou only wise!
Our thoughts and ways transcend,
Far as the arched skies
Above the earth extend:[1]
Such pleas as mine men would not bear,
But GOD receives a beggar's pray'r.

---

1 Isaiah 55:8–9—For my thoughts are not your thoughts, neither are your ways my ways, saith the LORD. For as the heavens are higher than the earth, so are my ways higher than your ways, and my thoughts than your thoughts.

THE LEPER.

And, behold, there came a leper and worshipped him, saying, Lord, if thou wilt, thou canst make me clean. And Jesus put forth his hand, and touched him, saying, I will; be thou clean. And immediately his leprosy was cleansed.
—MATTHEW 8:2–3.

OFT as the leper's case I read,
    My own describ'd I feel;
Sin is a leprosy indeed,
    Which none but CHRIST can heal.

Awhile I would have pass'd for well,
    And strove my spots to hide;
Till it broke out incurable,
    Too plain to be deny'd.

Then from the saints I sought to flee,
    And dreaded to be seen;
I thought they all would point at me,
    And cry, "Unclean, unclean!"

What anguish did my soul endure,
    Till hope and patience ceas'd?
The more I strove myself to cure,
    The more the plague increas'd.

While thus I lay distress'd, I saw
    The Saviour passing by;
To him, tho' fill'd with shame and awe,
    I rais'd my mournful cry.

LORD, thou canst heal me if thou wilt,
    For thou canst all things do;
O cleanse my leprous soul from guilt,
    My filthy heart renew!

He heard, and with a gracious look,
    Pronounc'd the healing word;
"I will, be clean"—and while he spoke
    I felt my health restor'd.

Come lepers, seize the present hour,
    The Saviour's grace to prove;
He *can* relieve, for he is pow'r,
    He *will*, for he is love.

A SICK SOUL.

But when Jesus heard that, he said unto them, They that be whole need not a physician, but they that are sick.—MATTHEW 9:12.

PHYSICIAN of my sin-sick soul,
    To thee I bring my case;
My raging malady controll,
    And heal me by thy grace.

Pity the anguish I endure,
    See how I mourn and pine;
For never can I hope a cure
    From any hand but thine.

I would disclose my whole complaint,
    But where shall I begin?
No words of mine can fully paint
    That worst distemper, sin.

It lies not in a single part,
    But thro' my frame is spread;
A burning fever in my heart,
    A palsy in my head.

It makes me deaf, and dumb, and blind,
    And impotent and lame;
And overclouds, and fills my mind,
    With folly, fear, and shame.

A thousand evil thoughts intrude
    Tumultuous in my breast;
Which indispose me for my food,
    And rob me of my rest.

LORD I am sick, regard my cry,
    And set my spirit free;
Say, canst thou let a sinner die,
    Who longs to live to thee?

SATAN RETURNING.

When the unclean spirit is gone out of a man, he walketh through dry places, seeking rest, and findeth none. Then he saith, I will return into my house from whence I came out; and when he is come, he findeth it empty, swept, and garnished. Then goeth he, and taketh with himself seven other spirits more wicked than himself, and they enter in and dwell there: and the last state of that man is worse than the first. Even so shall it be also unto this wicked generation.—MATTHEW 12:43–45.

WHEN JESUS claims the sinner's heart,
   Where Satan rul'd before;
The evil spirit must depart,
   And dares return no more.

But when he goes without constraint,
   And wanders from his home;
Altho' withdrawn, 'tis but a feint,
   He means again to come.

Some outward change perhaps is seen
   If Satan quit the place;
But tho' the house seem swept and clean,
   'Tis destitute of grace.

Except the Saviour dwell and reign
   Within the sinner's mind;
Satan, when he returns again,
   Will easy entrance find.

With rage and malice sevenfold,
   He then resumes his sway;
No more by checks to be controll'd,
   No more to go away.

The sinner's former state was bad,
   But worse the latter far;
He lives possess'd, and blind, and mad,
   And dies in dark despair.

LORD save me from this dreadful end!
   And from this heart of mine,
O drive and keep away the fiend
   Who fears no voice but thine.

THE WHEAT AND TARES.

He answered and said unto them, He that soweth the good seed is the Son of man; The field is the world; the good seed are the children of the kingdom; but the tares are the children of the wicked one; The enemy that sowed them is the devil; the harvest is the end of the world; and the reapers are the angels. As therefore the tares are gathered and burned in the fire; so shall it be in the end of this world. The Son of man shall send forth his angels, and they shall gather out of his kingdom all things that offend, and them which do iniquity; And shall cast them into a furnace of fire: there shall be wailing and gnashing of teeth.—MATTHEW 13:37–42.

THO' in the outward church below
The wheat and tares together grow;
JESUS ere long will weed the crop,
And pluck the tares, in anger, up.

Will it relieve their horrors there,
To recollect their stations here?
How much they heard, how much they knew,
How long amongst the wheat they grew!

Oh! this will aggravate their case!
They perish'd under means of grace;
To them the word of life and faith,
Became an instrument of death.

We seem alike when thus we meet,
Strangers might think we all are wheat;
But to the LORD's all-searching eyes,
Each heart appears without disguise.

The tares are spar'd for various ends,
Some, for the sake of praying friends;
Others, the LORD, against their will,
Employs his counsels to fulfill.

But tho' they grow so tall and strong,
His plan will not require them long;
In harvest, when he saves his own,
The tares shall into hell be thrown.

PETER WALKING UPON THE WATER.

And Peter answered him and said, Lord, if it be thou, bid me come unto thee on the water. And he said, Come. And when Peter was come down out of the ship, he walked on the water, to go to Jesus. But when he saw the wind boisterous, he was afraid; and beginning to sink, he cried, saying, Lord, save me. And immediately Jesus stretched forth his hand, and caught him, and said unto him, O thou of little faith, wherefore didst thou doubt?
—MATTHEW 14:28–31.

A WORD from JESUS calms the sea,
　The stormy wind controls;
And gives repose and liberty
　To tempest-tossed souls.

To Peter on the waves he came,
　And gave him instant peace;
Thus he to me reveal'd his name,
　And bid my sorrows cease.

Then fill'd with wonder, joy and love,
　Peter's request was mine;
LORD, call me down, I long to prove
　That I am wholly thine.

Unmov'd at all I have to meet
　On life's tempestuous sea;
Hard, shall be easy; bitter, sweet,
　So I may follow thee.

He heard and smil'd, and bid me try,
　I eagerly obey'd;
But when from him I turn'd my eye,
　How was my soul dismay'd!

The storm increas'd on ev'ry side,
　I felt my spirit shrink;
And soon, with Peter, loud I cry'd,
　"LORD, save me, or I sink."

Kindly he caught me by the hand,
　And said, "Why dost thou fear?
Since thou art come at my command,
　And I am always near.

Upon my promise rest thy hope,
　And keep my love in view;
I stand engag'd to hold thee up,
　And guide thee safely thro'."

WOMAN OF CANAAN.

And, behold, a woman of Canaan came out of the same coasts, and cried unto him, saying, Have mercy on me, O Lord, thou son of David; my daughter is grievously vexed with a devil. But he answered her not a word. And his disciples came and besought him, saying, Send her away; for she crieth after us. But he answered and said, I am not sent but unto the lost sheep of the house of Israel. Then came she and worshipped him, saying, Lord, help me. But he answered and said, It is not meet to take the children's bread, and to cast it to dogs. And she said, Truth, Lord: yet the dogs eat of the crumbs which fall from their masters' table. Then Jesus answered and said unto her, O woman, great is thy faith: be it unto thee even as thou wilt. And her daughter was made whole from that very hour.—MATTHEW 15:22–28.

PRAY'R an answer will obtain,
　Tho' the LORD awhile delay;
None shall seek his face in vain,
　None be empty sent away.

When the woman came from Tyre,
　And for help to JESUS sought;
Tho' he granted her desire,
　Yet at first he answer'd not.

Could she guess at his intent,
　When he to his follow'rs said,
"I to Israel's sheep am sent,
　Dogs must not have children's bread."

She was not of Israel's seed,
　But of Canaan's wretched race;
Thought herself a dog indeed;
　Was not this a hopeless case?

Yet altho' from Canaan sprung,
　Tho' a dog herself she stil'd;
She had Israel's faith and tongue,
　And was own'd for Abraham's child.

From his words she draws a plea;
　Tho' unworthy children's bread,
'Tis enough for one like me,
　If with crumbs I may be fed.

(Continued on the next page.)

Jesus then his heart reveal'd,
"Woman canst thou thus believe?
I to thy petition yield,
All that thou canst wish, receive."

'Tis a pattern set for us,
How we ought to wait and pray;
None who plead and wrestle thus,
Shall be empty sent away.

WHAT THINK YE OF CHRIST?

Saying, What think ye of Christ? whose son is he?
They say unto him, The son of David.
—Matthew 22:42.

What think you of Christ? is the test
To try both your state and your scheme;
You cannot be right in the rest,
Unless you think rightly of him.
As Jesus appears in your view,
As he is beloved or not;
So God is disposed to you,
And mercy or wrath are your lot.

Some take him a creature to be,
A man, or an angel at most;
Sure these have not feelings like me,
Nor know themselves wretched and lost:
So guilty, so helpless, am I,
I durst not confide in his blood,
Nor on his protection rely,
Unless I were sure he is God.

Some call him a Saviour, in word,
But mix their own works with his plan;
And hope he his help will afford,
When they have done all that they can:
If doings prove rather too light
(A little, they own, they may fail)
They purpose to make up full weight,
By casting his name in the scale.

Some stile him the pearl of great price,
And say he's the fountain of joys;
Yet feed upon folly and vice,
And cleave to the world and its toys:
Like Judas, the Saviour they kiss,
And, while they salute him, betray;
Ah! what will profession like this
Avail in his terrible day?

If ask'd what of Jesus I think?
Tho' still my best thoughts are but poor;
I say, he's my meat and my drink,
My life, and my strength, and my store,
My Shepherd, my Husband, my Friend,
My Saviour from sin and from thrall;
My hope from beginning to end,
My Portion, my Lord, and my All.

THE FOOLISH VIRGINS.[1]

Then shall the kingdom of heaven be likened unto ten virgins, which took their lamps, and went forth to meet the bridegroom.—MATTHEW 25:1.

WHEN descending from the sky
　　The Bridegroom shall appear;
And the solemn midnight cry,
　　Shall call professors near:
How the sound our hearts will damp!
How will shame o'erspread each face!
If we only have a lamp,
　　Without the oil of grace.

Foolish virgins then will wake
　　And seek for a supply;
But in vain the pains they take
　　To borrow or to buy:
Then with those they now despise,
Earnestly they'll wish to share;
But the best, among the wise,
　　Will have no oil to spare.

Wise are they, and truly blest,
　　Who then shall ready be!
But despair will seize the rest,
　　And dreadful misery:
Once, they'll cry, we scorn'd to doubt,
Tho' in lies our trust we put;
Now our lamp of hope is out,
　　The door of mercy shut.

If they then presume to plead,
　　"LORD open to us now;
We on earth have hear'd and pray'd,
　　And with thy saints did bow:"
He will answer from his throne,
"Tho' you with my people mix'd,
Yet to me you ne'er were known,
　　Depart, your doom is fix'd."

O that none who worship here
　　May hear that word, Depart!
LORD impress a godly fear
　　On each professor's heart:
Help us, LORD, to search the camp,
Let us not ourselves beguile;
Trusting to a dying lamp
　　Without a stock of oil.

1 Book III. Hymn 72.

PETER SINNING AND REPENTING.

And after a while came unto him they that stood by, and said to Peter, Surely thou also art one of them; for thy speech bewrayeth thee.—MATTHEW 26:73.

WHEN Peter boasted, soon he fell,
　　Yet was by grace restor'd;
His case should be regarded well
　　By all who fear the LORD.

A voice it has, and helping hand,
　　Backsliders to recall;
And cautions those who think they stand,
　　Lest suddenly they fall.

He said, "Whatever others do,
　　With JESUS I'll abide;"
Yet soon amidst a murd'rous crew
　　His suff'ring LORD deny'd.

He who had been so bold before,
　　Now trembled like a leaf;
Not only ly'd, but curs'd and swore,
　　To gain the more belief.

While he blasphem'd he heard the cock,
　　And JESUS look'd in love;
At once, as if by light'ning struck,
　　His tongue forbore to move.

Deliver'd thus from Satan's snare
　　He starts, as from a sleep;
His Saviour's look he could not bear,
　　But hasted forth to weep.

But sure the faithful cock had crow'd
　　A hundred times in vain;
Had not the LORD that look bestow'd,
　　The meaning to explain.

As I, like Peter, vows have made,
　　Yet acted Peter's part;
So conscience, like the cock, upbraids
　　My base, ungrateful heart.

LORD JESUS, hear a sinner's cry,
　　My broken peace renew;
And grant one pitying look, that I
　　May weep with Peter too.

THE LEGION DISPOSSESSED.

And when he was come into the ship, he that had been possessed with the devil prayed him that he might be with him. Howbeit Jesus suffered him not, but saith unto him, Go home to thy friends, and tell them how great things the Lord hath done for thee, and hath had compassion on thee.—MARK 5:18–19.

LEGION was my name by nature,
Satan rag'd within my breast;
Never misery was greater,
Never sinner more possess'd:
Mischievous to all around me,
To myself the greatest foe;
Thus I was, when JESUS found me,
Fill'd with madness, sin and woe.

Yet in this forlorn condition,
When he came to set me free;
I reply'd, to my Physician,
"What have I to do with thee?"
But he would not be prevented,
Rescu'd me against my will;
Had he staid till I consented,
I had been a captive still.

"Satan, tho' thou fain wouldst have it,
Know this soul is none of thine;
I have shed my blood to save it,
Now I challenge it for mine:[1]
Tho' it long has thee resembled,
Henceforth it shall me obey;"
Thus he spoke while Satan trembled,
Gnash'd his teeth and fled away.

Thus my frantic soul he healed,
Bid my sins and sorrows cease;
"Take, said he, my pardon sealed,
I have sav'd thee, go in peace:"
Rather take me, LORD, to heaven,
Now thy love and grace I know;
Since thou hast my sins forgiven,
Why should I remain below?

(Continued in the next column.)

"Love, he said, will sweeten labors,
Thou hast something yet to do;
Go and tell your friends and neighbors,
What my love has done for you:
Live to manifest my glory,
Wait for heav'n a little space;
Sinners, when they hear thy story,
Will repent and seek my face."

---

1 Book III. Hymn 54.

THE RULER'S DAUGHTER RAISED.

And when he was come in, he saith unto them,
Why make ye this ado, and weep? the damsel is not
dead, but sleepeth. And they laughed him to scorn.
But when he had put them all out, he taketh the fa-
ther and the mother of the damsel, and them that
were with him, and entereth in where the damsel
was lying. And he took the damsel by the hand,
and said unto her, Talitha cumi; which is, being
interpreted, Damsel, I say unto thee, arise. And
straightway the damsel arose, and walked; for she
was of the age of twelve years. And they were aston-
ished with a great astonishment.—MARK 5:39–42.

COULD the creatures help or ease us
Seldom should we think of pray'r;
Few, if any, come to JESUS,
Till reduc'd to self-dispair:
Long we either slight or doubt him,
But when all the means we try,
Prove we cannot do without him,
Then at last to him we cry.

Thus the ruler when his daughter
Suffer'd much, tho' CHRIST was nigh,
Still deferr'd it, till he thought her
At the very point to die:
Tho' he mourn'd for her condition,
He did not entreat the LORD,
Till he found that no physician
But himself, could help afford.

JESUS did not once upbraid him,
That he had no sooner come;
But a gracious answer made him,
And went straitway with him home:
Yet his faith was put to trial
When his servants came, and said,
"Tho' he gave thee no denial,
'Tis too late, the child is dead."

JESUS, to prevent his grieving,
Kindly spoke and eas'd his pain;
"Be not fearful, but believing,
Thou shalt see her live again:"

(Continued in the next column.)

When he found the people weeping,
"Cease, he said, no longer mourn;
For she is not dead, but sleeping,"
Then they laughed him to scorn.

O thou meek and lowly Saviour,
How determin'd is thy love!
Not this rude unkind behaviour,
Could thy gracious purpose move:
Soon as he the room had enter'd,
Spoke, and took her by the hand;
Death at once his prey surrender'd,
And she liv'd at his command.

Fear not then, distress'd believer,
Venture on his mighty name;
He is able to deliver,
And his love is still the same:
Can his pity or his power,
Suffer thee to pray in vain;
Wait but his appointed hour,
And thy suit thou shalt obtain.

BUT ONE LOAF.[1]

Now the disciples had forgotten to take bread,
neither had they in the ship with them more than
one loaf.—MARK 8:14.

WHEN the disciples cross'd the lake
    With but one loaf on board;
How strangely did their hearts mistake
    The caution of their LORD.

"The leaven of the Pharisees
    Beware," the Saviour said;
They thought, it is because he sees
    We have forgotten bread.

It seems they had forgotten too,
    What their own eyes had view'd;
How with what scarce suffic'd for few,
    He fed a multitude.

If five small loaves, by his command,
    Could many thousands serve;
Might they not trust his gracious hand,
    That they should never starve?

They oft his pow'r and love had known,
    And doubtless were to blame;
But we have reason good to own
    That we are just the same.

How often has he brought relief,
    And ev'ry want supply'd!
Yet soon, again, our unbelief
    Says, "Can the LORD provide?"

Be thankful for one loaf to-day,
    Tho' that be all your store;
To-morrow, if you trust and pray,
    Shall timely bring you more.

BARTIMEUS.

And when he heard that it was Jesus of Nazareth,
he began to cry out, and say, Jesus, thou son of
David, have mercy on me. And many charged him
that he should hold his peace: but he cried the
more a great deal, Thou son of David, have mercy
on me.—MARK 10:47–48.

MERCY, O thou Son of David!
Thus blind Bartimeus pray'd;
Others by thy word are saved,
Now to me afford thine aid:
Many for his crying chid him,
But he call'd the louder still;
Till the gracious Saviour bid him
"Come, and ask me what you will."

Money was not what he wanted,
Tho' by begging us'd to live;
But he ask'd, and JESUS granted
Alms, which none but he could give:
LORD remove this grievous blindness,
Let my eyes behold the day;
Strait he saw, and won by kindness,
Follow'd JESUS in the way.

Oh! methinks I hear him praising,
Publishing to all around;
"Friends, is not my case amazing?
What a Saviour I have found:
Oh! that all the blind but knew him,
And would be advis'd by me!
Surely, would they hasten to him,
He would cause them all to see."

---

1 Book III. Hymn 57.

THE BLASTED FIG-TREE.

*And in the morning, as they passed by, they saw the fig tree dried up from the roots.—*MARK 11:20.

ONE awful word which JESUS spoke,
Against the tree which bore no fruit;
More piercing than the light'nings stroke,
Blasted and dry'd it to the root.

But could a tree the LORD offend,
To make him shew his anger thus?
He surely had a farther end,
To be a warning word to us.

The fig-tree by its leaves was known,
But having not a fig to show;
It brought a heavy sentence down,
"Let none hereafter on thee grow."

Too many, who the gospel hear,
Whom Satan blinds and sin deceives;
We to this fig-tree may compare,
They yield no fruit, but only leaves.

Knowledge, and zeal, and gifts, and talk,
Unless combin'd with faith and love,
And witness'd by a gospel walk,
Will not a true profession prove.

Without the fruit the LORD expects
Knowledge will make our state the worse;
The barren trees he still rejects,
And soon will blast them with his curse.

O LORD, unite our hearts in pray'r!
On each of us thy Spirit send;
That we the fruits of grace may bear,
And find acceptance in the end.

THE TWO DEBTORS.

*Wherefore I say unto thee, Her sins, which are many, are forgiven; for she loved much: but to whom little is forgiven, the same loveth little.—*LUKE 7:47.

ONCE a woman silent stood
    While JESUS sat at meat;
From her eyes she pour'd a flood
    To wash his sacred feet:
Shame and wonder, joy and love,
All at once possess'd her mind;
That she ere so vile could prove,
    Yet now forgiveness find.

"How came this vile woman here,
    Will JESUS notice such?
Sure, if he a prophet were,
    He would disdain her touch!"
Simon thus, with scornful heart,
Slighted one whom JESUS lov'd;
But her Saviour took her part,
    And thus his pride reprov'd.

"If two men in debt were bound,
    One less, the other more;
Fifty, or five hundred pound,
    And both alike were poor;
Should the lender both forgive,
When he saw them both distress'd;
Which of them would you believe
    Engag'd to love him best?"

"Surely he who most did owe,"
    The Pharisee reply'd;
Then our LORD, by judging so,
    "Thou dost for her decide:
Simon if like her you knew
How much you forgiveness need;
You like her had acted too,
    And welcom'd me indeed!

When the load of sin is felt,
    And much forgiveness known;
Then the heart of course will melt,
    Tho' hard before as stone:

(Continued on the next page.)

Blame not then her love and tears,
Greatly she in debt has been;
But I have remov'd her fears,
    And pardon'd all her sin."

When I read this woman's case,
    Her love and humble zeal;
I confess, with shame of face,
    My heart is made of steel.
Much has been forgiv'n to me,
JESUS paid my heavy score;
What a creature must I be
    That I can love no more!

THE GOOD SAMARITAN.

But a certain Samaritan, as he journeyed, came where he was: and when he saw him, he had compassion on him, And went to him, and bound up his wounds, pouring in oil and wine, and set him on his own beast, and brought him to an inn, and took care of him. And on the morrow when he departed, he took out two pence, and gave them to the host, and said unto him, Take care of him; and whatsoever thou spendest more, when I come again, I will repay thee.—LUKE 10:33–35.

How kind the good Samaritan
To him who fell among the thieves!
Thus JESUS pities fallen man,
And heals the wounds the soul receives.

Oh! I remember well the day,
When sorely wounded, nearly slain;
Like that poor man I bleeding lay,
And gron'd for help, but gron'd in vain.

Men saw me in this helpless case,
And pass'd without compassion by;
Each neighbour turn'd away his face,
Unmoved by my mournful cry.

But he whose name had been my scorn,
(As Jews Samaritans despise)
Came, when he saw me thus forlorn,
With love and pity in his eyes.

Gently he rais'd me from the ground,
Press'd me to lean upon his arm;
And into ev'ry gaping wound
He pour'd his own all-healing balm.

Unto his church my steps he led,
The house prepar'd for sinners lost;
Gave charge I should be cloth'd and fed;
And took upon him all the cost.

Thus sav'd from death, from want secur'd,
I wait till he again shall come,
(When I shall be completely cur'd)
And take me to his heav'nly home.

There thro' eternal boundless days,
When nature's wheel no longer rolls;
How shall I love, adore, and praise,
This good Samaritan to souls!

MARTHA AND MARY.

Now it came to pass, as they went, that he entered into a certain village: and a certain woman named Martha received him into her house. And she had a sister called Mary, which also sat at Jesus' feet, and heard his word. But Martha was cumbered about much serving, and came to him, and said, Lord, dost thou not care that my sister hath left me to serve alone? bid her therefore that she help me. And Jesus answered and said unto her, Martha, Martha, thou art careful and troubled about many things: But one thing is needful: and Mary hath chosen that good part, which shall not be taken away from her.—LUKE 10:38–42.

MARTHA her love and joy express'd
By care to entertain her guest;
While Mary sat to hear her LORD,
And could not bear to lose a word.

The principle in both the same,
Produc'd in each a diff'rent aim;
The one to feast the LORD was led,
The other waited to be fed.

But Mary chose the better part,
Her Saviour's words refresh'd her heart;
While busy Martha angry grew,
And lost her time and temper too.

With warmth she to her sister spoke,
But brought upon herself rebuke;
"One thing is needful, and but one,
Why do thy thoughts on many run?"

How oft are we like Martha vex'd,
Encumber'd, hurried, and perplex'd?
While trifles so engross our thought,
The one thing needful is forgot.

LORD teach us this one thing to choose,
Which they who gain can never lose;
Sufficient in itself alone,
And needful, were the world our own.

Let groveling hearts the world admire,
Thy love is all that I require!
Gladly I may the rest resign,
If the one needful thing be mine!

THE HEART TAKEN.

When a strong man armed keepeth his palace, his goods are in peace: But when a stronger than he shall come upon him, and overcome him, he taketh from him all his armour wherein he trusted, and divideth his spoils.—LUKE 11:21–22.

THE castle of the human heart
    Strong in its native sin;
Is guarded well, in ev'ry part,
    By him who dwells within.

For Satan there, in arms, resides,
    And calls the place his own;
With care against assaults provides,
    And rules, as on a throne.

Each traitor thought on him, as chief,
    In blind obedience waits;
And pride, self-will, and unbelief,
    Are posted at the gates.

Thus Satan for a season reigns,
    And keeps his goods in peace;
The soul is pleas'd to wear his chains,
    Nor wishes a release.

But JESUS, stronger far than he,
    In his appointed hour
Appears, to set his people free
    From the usurper's pow'r.

"This heart I bought with blood, he says,
    And now it shall be mine;"
His voice the strong one arm'd dismays,
    He knows he must resign.

In spite of unbelief and pride,
    And self, and Satan's art;
The gates of brass fly open wide,
    And JESUS wins the heart.

The rebel soul that once withstood
    The Saviour's kindest call;
Rejoices now, by grace subdu'd,
    To serve him with her all.

THE WORLDLING.

And he spake a parable unto them, saying, The ground of a certain rich man brought forth plenti-fully: And he thought within himself, saying, What shall I do, because I have no room where to bestow my fruits? And he said, This will I do: I will pull down my barns, and build greater; and there will I bestow all my fruits and my goods. And I will say to my soul, Soul, thou hast much goods laid up for many years; take thine ease, eat, drink, and be merry. But God said unto him, Thou fool, this night thy soul shall be required of thee: then whose shall those things be, which thou hast provided? So is he that layeth up treasure for himself, and is not rich toward God.—LUKE 12:16–21.

MY barns are full, my stores increase,
    And now, for many years,
Soul, eat and drink, and take thine ease,
    Secure from wants and fears.

Thus while a worldling boasted once,
    As many now presume;
He heard the LORD himself pronounce
    His sudden, awful doom.

"This night, vain fool, thy soul must pass
    Into a world unknown;
And who shall then the stores possess
    Which thou hast call'd thine own."

Thus blinded mortals fondly scheme
    For happiness below;
Till death disturbs the pleasing dream,
    And they awake to woe.

Ah! who can speak the vast dismay
    That fills the sinner's mind;
When torn, by death's strong hand, away,
    He leaves his all behind.

Wretches, who cleave to earthly things,
    But are not rich to GOD;
Their dying hour is full of stings,
    And hell their dark abode.

Dear Saviour, make us timely wise,
    Thy gospel to attend;
That we may live above the skies,
    When this poor life shall end.

THE BARREN FIG-TREE.

He spake also this parable; A certain man had a fig tree planted in his vineyard; and he came and sought fruit thereon, and found none. Then said he unto the dresser of his vineyard, Behold, these three years I come seeking fruit on this fig tree, and find none: cut it down; why cumbereth it the ground? And he answering said unto him, Lord, let it alone this year also, till I shall dig about it, and dung it: And if it bear fruit, well: and if not, then after that thou shalt cut it down.—LUKE 13:6–9.

THE church a garden is
    In which believers stand,
    Like ornamental trees
    Planted by GOD's own hand:
His Spirit waters all their roots,
And ev'ry branch abounds with fruits.

But other trees there are,
    In this enclosure grow;
    Which, tho' they promise fair,
    Have only leaves to show:
No fruits of grace are on them found,
They stand but cumb'rers of the ground.

The under gard'ner grieves,
    In vain his strength he spends,
    For heaps of useless leaves,
    Afford him small amends:
He hears the LORD his will make known,
To cut the barren fig-trees down.

How difficult his post,
    What pangs his bowels move,
    To find his wishes crost,
    His labors useless prove!
His last relief is earnest pray'r,
LORD, spare them yet another year.

Spare them, and let me try
    What farther means may do;
    I'll fresh manure apply,
    My digging I'll renew:
Who knows but yet they fruit may yield!
If not—'tis just, they must be fell'd.

(Continued on the next page.)

If under means of grace,
No gracious fruits appear;
It is a dreadful case,
Tho' GOD may long forbear:
At length he'll strike the threatened blow,[1]
And lay the barren fig-tree low.

THE PRODIGAL SON.

And he said, A certain man had two sons: And the younger of them said to his father, Father, give me the portion of goods that falleth to me. And he divided unto them his living. And not many days after the younger son gathered all together, and took his journey into a far country, and there wasted his substance with riotous living. And when he had spent all, there arose a mighty famine in that land; and he began to be in want. And he went and joined himself to a citizen of that country; and he sent him into his fields to feed swine. And he would fain have filled his belly with the husks that the swine did eat: and no man gave unto him. And when he came to himself, he said, How many hired servants of my father's have bread enough and to spare, and I perish with hunger! I will arise and go to my father, and will say unto him, Father, I have sinned against heaven, and before thee, And am no more worthy to be called thy son: make me as one of thy hired servants. And he arose, and came to his father. But when he was yet a great way off, his father saw him, and had compassion, and ran, and fell on his neck, and kissed him. And the son said unto him, Father, I have sinned against heaven, and in thy sight, and am no more worthy to be called thy son. But the father said to his servants, Bring forth the best robe, and put it on him; and put a ring on his hand, and shoes on his feet: And bring hither the fatted calf, and kill it; and let us eat, and be merry: For this my son was dead, and is alive again; he was lost, and is found. And they began to be merry.—LUKE 15:11–24.

AFFLICTIONS, tho' they seem severe;
　　In mercy oft are sent;
They stopp'd the prodigal's career,
　　And forc'd him to repent.

Altho' he no relentings felt
　　Till he had spent his store;
His stubborn heart began to melt
　　When famine pinch'd him sore.

"What have I gain'd by sin, he said,
　　But hunger, shame, and fear;
My father's house abounds with bread,
　　While I am starving here.

(Continued on the next page.)

---

1 Book II. Hymn 26.

I'll go, and tell him all I've done,
   And fall before his face;
Unworthy to be call'd his son,
   I'll seek a servant's place."

His father saw him coming back,
   He saw, and ran, and smil'd;
And threw his arms around the neck
   Of his rebellious child.

"Father, I've sinn'd—but O forgive!"
   "I've heard enough, he said,
Rejoice my house, my son's alive,
   For whom I mourn'd as dead.

Now let the fatted calf be slain,
   And spread the news around;
My son was dead, but lives again,
   Was lost, but now is found."

'Tis thus the LORD his love reveals,
   To call poor sinners home;
More than a father's love he feels,
   And welcomes all that come.

THE RICH MAN AND LAZARUS.

*There was a certain rich man, which was clothed in purple and fine linen, and fared sumptuously every day: And there was a certain beggar named Lazarus, which was laid at his gate, full of sores, And desiring to be fed with the crumbs which fell from the rich man's table: moreover the dogs came and licked his sores. And it came to pass, that the beggar died, and was carried by the angels into Abraham's bosom: the rich man also died, and was buried; And in hell he lift up his eyes, being in torments, and seeth Abraham afar off, and Lazarus in his bosom. And he cried and said, Father Abraham, have mercy on me, and send Lazarus, that he may dip the tip of his finger in water, and cool my tongue; for I am tormented in this flame. But Abraham said, Son, remember that thou in thy lifetime receivedst thy good things, and likewise Lazarus evil things: but now he is comforted, and thou art tormented.—*LUKE 16:19–25.

A WORLDLING spent each day
   In luxury and state;
   While a believer lay,
   A beggar at his gate:
Think not the LORD's appointments strange,
Death made a great and lasting change.

   Death brought the saint release
   From want, disease, and scorn;
   And to the land of peace,
   His soul, by angels borne,
In Abraham's bosom safely plac'd,
Enjoys an everlasting feast.

   The rich man also dy'd,
   And in a moment fell
   From all his pomp and pride
   Into the flames of hell:
The beggar's bliss from far beheld,
His soul with double anguish fill'd.

   "O Abra'm send, he cries,
   (But his request was vain)
   The beggar from the skies
   To mitigate my pain!
One drop of water I entreat,
To sooth my tongue's tormenting heat."

(Continued on the next page.)

Let all who worldly pelf,
And worldly spirits have,
Observe, each for himself,
The answer Abra'm gave:
"Remember, thou wast fill'd with good,
While the poor beggar pin'd for food.

Neglected at thy door
With tears he begg'd his bread;
But now, he weeps no more,
His griefs and pains are fled:
His joys eternally will flow,
While thine expire in endless woe."

LORD, make us truly wise,
To choose thy peoples lot;
And earthly joys despise,
Which soon will be forgot:
The greatest evil we can fear,
Is to possess our portion here!

THE IMPORTUNATE WIDOW.[1]

*And he spake a parable unto them to this end, that men ought always to pray, and not to faint; Saying, There was in a city a judge, which feared not God, neither regarded man: And there was a widow in that city; and she came unto him, saying, Avenge me of mine adversary. And he would not for a while: but afterward he said within himself, Though I fear not God, nor regard man; Yet because this widow troubleth me, I will avenge her, lest by her continual coming she weary me. And the Lord said, Hear what the unjust judge saith. And shall not God avenge his own elect, which cry day and night unto him, though he bear long with them?—*LUKE 18:1–7.

OUR LORD, who knows full well
The heart of ev'ry saint;
Invites us, by a parable,
To pray and never faint.

He bows his gracious ear,
We never plead in vain;
Yet we must wait, till he appear,
And pray, and pray again.

Tho' unbelief suggest,
Why should we longer wait?
He bids us never give him rest,
But be importunate.

'Twas thus a widow poor,
Without support or friend,
Beset the unjust judge's door,
And gain'd, at last, her end.

For her he little car'd,
As little for the laws;
Nor GOD, nor man, did he regard,
Yet he espous'd her cause.

She urg'd him day and night,
Would no denial take;
At length he said, "I'll do her right,
For my own quiet sake."

(Continued on the next page.)

---

1 Book II. Hymn 60.

And shall not JESUS hear
His chosen, when they cry?
Yes, tho' he may awhile forbear,
He'll help them from on high.

His nature, truth and love,
Engage him on their side;
When they are griev'd, his bowels move,
And can they be deny'd?

Then let us earnest be,
And never faint in pray'r;
He loves our importunity,
And makes our cause his care.

ZACCHEUS.

*And Jesus entered and passed through Jericho.
And, behold, there was a man named Zacchaeus,
which was the chief among the publicans, and he
was rich. And he sought to see Jesus who he was;
and could not for the press, because he was little
of stature. And he ran before, and climbed up into
a sycomore tree to see him: for he was to pass that
way. And when Jesus came to the place, he looked
up, and saw him, and said unto him, Zacchaeus,
make haste, and come down; for to day I must
abide at thy house.*—LUKE 19:1–6.

ZACCHEUS climb'd the tree,
And thought himself unknown;
But how surpriz'd was he
When JESUS call'd him down!
The LORD beheld him, tho' conceal'd,
And by a word his pow'r reveal'd.

Wonder and joy at once
Were painted in his face;
Does he my name pronounce?
And does he know my case?
Will JESUS deign with me to dine?
LORD, I, with all I have, am thine!

Thus where the gospel's preach'd,
And sinners come to hear;
The hearts of some are reach'd
Before they are aware:
The word directly speaks to them,
And seems to point them out by name.

'Tis curiosity
Oft brings them in the way,
Only the man to see,
And hear what he can say;
But how the sinner starts to find
The preacher knows his inmost mind.

His long forgotten faults
Are brought again in view,
And all his secret thoughts
Reveal'd in public too:
Tho' compass'd with a crowd about,
The searching word has found him out.

(Continued on the next page.)

While thus distressing pain
And sorrow fills his heart;
He hears a voice again,
That bids his fears depart:
Then like Zaccheus he is blest,
And JESUS deigns to be his guest.

THE BELIEVER'S DANGER, SAFETY, AND DUTY.

And the Lord said, Simon, Simon, behold, Satan hath desired to have you, that he may sift you as wheat: But I have prayed for thee, that thy faith fail not: and when thou art converted, strengthen thy brethren.—LUKE 22:31–32.

"SIMON, beware! the Saviour said,
   Satan, your subtle foe,
Already has his measures laid
   Your soul to overthrow.

He wants to sift you all, as wheat,
   And thinks his vict'ry sure;
But I his malice will defeat,
   My pray'r shall faith secure."

Believers, tremble and rejoice,
   Your help and danger view;
This warning has to you a voice,
   This promise speaks to you.

Satan beholds, with jealous eye,
   Your privilege and joy;
He's always watchful, always nigh,
   To tear and to destroy.

But JESUS lives to intercede,
   That faith may still prevail,
He will support in time of need,
   And Satan's arts shall fail.

Yet, let us not the warning slight,
   But watchful still be found;
Though faith cannot be slain in fight,
   It may receive a wound.

While Satan watches, dare we sleep?
   We must our guard maintain;
But, LORD, do thou the city keep,
   Or else we watch in vain.[1]

---

1 Psalm 127:1—Except the LORD build the house, they labour in vain that build it: except the LORD keep the city, the watchman waketh but in vain.

FATHER FORGIVE THEM.

And Pilate gave sentence that it should be as they required.—LUKE 23:34.

"FATHER, forgive (the Saviour said)
    They know not what they do:"
His heart was mov'd when thus he pray'd
    For me, my friends, and you.

He saw, that as the Jews abus'd
    And crucify'd his flesh;
So he, by us, would be refus'd,
    And crucify'd afresh.

Thro' love of sin, we long were prone
    To act as Satan bid;
But now, with grief and shame we own,
    We knew not what we did.

We knew not the desert of sin,
    Nor whom we thus defy'd;
Nor where our guilty souls had been,
    If JESUS had not dy'd.

We knew not what a law we broke,
    How holy, just and pure!
Nor what a GOD we durst provoke,
    But thought ourselves secure.

But JESUS all our guilt foresaw,
    And shed his precious blood
To satisfy the holy law,
    And make our peace with GOD.

My sin, dear Saviour, made thee bleed,
    Yet didst thou pray for me!
I knew not what I did, indeed,
    When ignorant of thee.

THE TWO MALEFACTORS.

And one of the malefactors which were hanged railed on him, saying, If thou be Christ, save thyself and us. But the other answering rebuked him, saying, Dost not thou fear God, seeing thou art in the same condemnation? And we indeed justly; for we receive the due reward of our deeds: but this man hath done nothing amiss. And he said unto Jesus, Lord, remember me when thou comest into thy kingdom. And Jesus said unto him, Verily I say unto thee, Today shalt thou be with me in paradise.—LUKE 23:39–43.

SOVEREIGN grace has pow'r alone
To subdue a heart of stone;
And the moment grace is felt,
Then the hardest heart will melt.

When the LORD was crucify'd,
Two transgressors with him dy'd;
One with vile blaspheming tongue,
Scoff'd at JESUS as he hung.

Thus he spent his wicked breath,
In the very jaws of death;
Perish'd, as too many do,
With the Saviour in his view.

But the other, touch'd with grace,
Saw the danger of his case;
Faith receiv'd to own the LORD,
Whom the scribes and priests abhorr'd.

"LORD, he pray'd, remember me,
When in glory thou shalt be:"
"Soon with me, the LORD replies,
Thou shalt rest in paradise."

This was wond'rous grace indeed,
Grace vouchsaf'd in time of need!
Sinners trust in JESU's name,
You shall find him still the same.

But beware of unbelief,
Think upon the hard'ned thief;
If the gospel you disdain,
CHRIST, to you, will die in vain.

THE WOMAN OF SAMARIA.

The woman then left her waterpot, and went her
way into the city, and saith to the men.—JOHN 4:28.

JESUS, to what didst thou submit
To save thy dear-bought flock from hell!
Like a pour trav'ller see him sit,
Athirst, and weary, by the well.

The woman who for water came,
(What great events on small depend)
Then learnt the glory of his name,
The Well of life, the sinner's Friend!

Taught from her birth to hate the Jews,
And fill'd with party-pride; at first
Her zeal induc'd her to refuse
Water, to quench the Saviour's thirst.

But soon she knew the gift of GOD,
And JESUS, whom she scorn'd before,
Unask'd, that drink on her bestow'd,
Which whoso tastes shall thirst no more.

His words her prejudice remov'd,
Her sin she felt, relief she found;
She saw and heard, believ'd and lov'd,
And ran to tell her neighbours round.

O come, this wond'rous man behold!
The promis'd Saviour! this is he,
Whom ancient prophecies foretold,
Born, from our guilt to set us free.

Like her, in ignorance content,
I worshipp'd long I knew not what;
Like her, on other things intent,
I found him, when I sought him not.

He told me all that e'er I did,
And told me all was pardon'd too;
And now, like her, as he has bid,
I live to point him out to you.

THE POOL OF BETHESDA.[1]

Now there is at Jerusalem by the sheep market
a pool, which is called in the Hebrew tongue
Bethesda, having five porches. In these lay a great
multitude of impotent folk, of blind, halt, withered,
waiting for the moving of the water. For an angel
went down at a certain season into the pool, and
troubled the water: whosoever then first after the
troubling of the water stepped in was made whole
of whatsoever disease he had.—JOHN 5:2–4.

BESIDE the gospel pool
　Appointed for the poor;
From year to year, my helpless soul
　Has waited for a cure.

How often have I seen
　The healing waters move;
And others, round me, stepping in
　Their efficacy prove.

But my complaints remain,
　I feel the very same;
As full of guilt, and fear, and pain,
　As when at first I came.

O would the LORD appear
　My malady to heal;
He knows how long I've languish'd here,
　And what distress I feel.

How often have I thought
　Why should I longer lie?
Surely the mercy I have sought
　Is not for such as I.

But whither can I go?
　There is no other pool
Where streams of sov'reign virtue flow
　To make a sinner whole.

Here then, from day to day,
　I'll wait, and hope, and try;
Can JESUS hear a sinner pray,
　Yet suffer him to die?

No: he is full of grace;
　He never will permit
A soul, that fain would see his face,
　To perish at his feet.

1 Book III. Hymn 7.

THE POOL OF BETHESDA.

HERE at Bethesda's pool, the poor,
 The wither'd, halt, and blind;
With waiting hearts expect a cure,
 And free admittance find.

Here streams of wond'rous virtue flow
 To heal a sin-sick soul;
To wash the filthy white as snow,
 And make the wounded whole.

The dumb break forth in songs of praise,
 The blind their sight receive;
The cripple runs in wisdom's ways,
 The dead revive, and live!

Restrain'd to no one case, or time,
 These waters always move;
Sinners, in ev'ry age and clime,
 Their vital influence prove.

Yet numbers daily near them lie,
 Who meet with no relief;
With life in view they pine and die
 In hopeless unbelief.

'Tis strange they should refuse to bathe,
 And yet frequent the pool;
But none can even wish for faith,
 While love of sin bears rule.

Satan their consciences has seal'd,
 And stupefy'd their thought;
For were they willing to be heal'd,
 The cure would soon be wrought.

Do thou, dear Saviour, interpose,
 Their stubborn wills constrain;
Or else to them the water flows,
 And grace is preach'd in vain.

THE DISCIPLES AT SEA.[1]

And when even was now come, his disciples went down unto the sea, And entered into a ship, and went over the sea toward Capernaum. And it was now dark, and Jesus was not come to them. And the sea arose by reason of a great wind that blew. So when they had rowed about five and twenty or thirty furlongs, they see Jesus walking on the sea, and drawing nigh unto the ship: and they were afraid. But he saith unto them, It is I; be not afraid. Then they willingly received him into the ship: and immediately the ship was at the land whither they went.—JOHN 6:16–21.

CONSTRAIN'D by their LORD to embark,
And venture, without him, to sea;
The season tempestuous and dark,
How griev'd the disciples must be!
But tho' he remain'd on the shore,
He spent the night for them in pray'r;
They still were as safe as before,
And equally under his care.

They strove, tho' in vain, for a while,
The force of the waves to withstand;
But when they were weary'd with toil,
They saw their dear Saviour at hand:
They gladly receiv'd him on board,
His presence their spirits reviv'd;
The sea became calm at his word,
And soon at their port they arriv'd.

We, like the disciples, are toss'd
By storms, on a perilous deep;
But cannot be possibly lost,
For JESUS has charge of the ship:
Tho' billows and winds are enrag'd,
And threaten to make us their sport;
This pilot his word has engag'd
To bring us, in safety, to port.

If sometimes we struggle alone,
And he is withdrawn from our view;
It makes us more willing to own,
We nothing, without him, can do:

(Continued on the next page.)

---

1 Book II. Hymn 87.

Then Satan our hopes would assail,
But JESUS is still within call;
And when our poor efforts quite fail,
He comes in good time and does all.

Yet, LORD, we are ready to shrink
Unless we thy presence perceive;
O save us (we cry) or we sink,
We would, but we cannot believe:
The night has been long and severe,
The winds and the seas are still high;
Dear Saviour, this moment appear,
And say to our souls, "It is I!"[1]

WILL YE ALSO GO AWAY?

Then said Jesus unto the twelve, Will ye also go away? Then Simon Peter answered him, Lord, to whom shall we go? thou hast the words of eternal life. And we believe and are sure that thou art that Christ, the Son of the living God.—JOHN 6:67–69.

WHEN any turn from Zion's way,
    (Alass! what numbers do!)
Methinks I hear my Saviour say,
    "Wilt thou forsake me too?"

Ah LORD! with such a heart as mine,
    Unless thou hold me fast;
I feel I must, I shall decline,
    And prove like them at last.

Yet thou alone hast pow'r, I know,
    To save a wretch like me;
To whom, or whither, could I go,
    If I should turn from thee?

Beyond a doubt I rest assur'd
    Thou art the CHRIST of GOD;
Who hast eternal life secur'd
    By promise and by blood.

The help of men and angels join'd,
    Could never reach my case;
Nor can I hope relief to find,
    But in thy boundless grace.

No voice but thine can give me rest,
    And bid my fears depart;
No love but thine can make me bless'd,
    And satisfy my heart.

What anguish has that question stirr'd,
    If I will also go?
Yet, LORD, relying on thy word,
    I humbly answer, No!

---

1 Book III. Hymn 18.

THE RESURRECTION AND THE LIFE.

*Jesus said unto her, I am the resurrection, and the life: he that believeth in me, though he were dead, yet shall he live:—*JOHN 11:25.

"I AM, saith CHRIST our glorious head,
    (May we attention give)
The resurrection of the dead,
    The life of all that live.

By faith in me, the soul receives
    New life, tho' dead before;
And he that in my name believes,
    Shall live, to die no more.

The sinner, sleeping in his grave,
    Shall at my voice awake;
And when I once begin to save,
    My work I ne'er forsake."

Fulfill thy promise, gracious LORD,
    On us assembled here;
Put forth thy Spirit with the word,
    And cause the dead to hear.

Preserve the pow'r of faith alive,
    In those who love thy name;
For sin and Satan daily strive
    To quench the sacred flame.

Thy pow'r and mercy first prevail'd
    From death to set us free;
And often since our life had fail'd,
    If not renew'd by thee.

To thee we look, to thee we bow;
    To thee, for help, we call;
Our life and resurrection thou,
    Our hope, our joy, our all.

WEEPING MARY.

*But Mary stood without at the sepulchre weeping: and as she wept, she stooped down, and looked into the sepulchre, And seeth two angels in white sitting, the one at the head, and the other at the feet, where the body of Jesus had lain. And they say unto her, Woman, why weepest thou? She saith unto them, Because they have taken away my LORD, and I know not where they have laid him. And when she had thus said, she turned herself back, and saw Jesus standing, and knew not that it was Jesus. Jesus saith unto her, Woman, why weepest thou? whom seekest thou? She, supposing him to be the gardener, saith unto him, Sir, if thou have borne him hence, tell me where thou hast laid him, and I will take him away. Jesus saith unto her, Mary. She turned herself, and saith unto him, Rabboni; which is to say, Master.—*JOHN 20:11–16.

MARY to her Saviour's tomb
Hasted at the early dawn;
Spice she brought, and sweet perfume,
But the LORD, she lov'd, was gone.
For awhile she weeping stood,
Struck with sorrow and surprize;
Shedding tears, a plenteous flood,
For her heart supply'd her eyes.

JESUS, who is always near,
Tho' too often unperceiv'd;
Came, his drooping child to chear,
And enquired, Why she griev'd?
Tho' at first she knew him not,
When he call'd her by her name,
Then her griefs were all forgot,
For she found he was the same.

Grief and sighing quickly fled
When she heard his welcome voice;
Just before she thought him dead,
Now he bids her heart rejoice:
What a change his word can make,
Turning darkness into day!
You who weep for JESUS' sake;
He will wipe your tears away.

(Continued on the next page.)

He who came to comfort her,
When she thought her all was lost;
Will for your relief appear,
Tho' you now are tempest-toss'd:
On his word your burden cast,
On his love your thoughts employ;
Weeping for awhile may last,
But the morning brings the joy.

LOVEST THOU ME?

He saith to him again the second time, Simon, son of Jonas, lovest thou me? He saith unto him, Yea, Lord; thou knowest that I love thee. He saith unto him, Feed my sheep.—JOHN 21:16.

'TIS a point I long to know,
Oft it causes anxious thought;
Do I love the LORD, or no?
Am I his, or am I not?

If I love, why am I thus?
Why this dull and lifeless frame?
Hardly, sure, can they be worse,
Who have never heard his name!

Could my heart so hard remain,
Pray'r a task and burden prove;
Ev'ry trifle give me pain,
If I knew a Saviour's love?

When I turn my eyes within,
All is dark, and vain, and wild;
Fill'd with unbelief and sin,
Can I deem myself a child?

If I pray, or hear, or read,
Sin is mix'd with all I do;
You that love the LORD indeed,
Tell me, Is it thus with you?

Yet I mourn my stubborn will,
Find my sin, a grief, and thrall;
Should I grieve for what I feel,
If I did not love at all?

Could I joy his saints to meet
Choose the ways I once abhorr'd,
Find, at times, the promise sweet,
If I did not love the LORD?

LORD decide the doubtful case!
Thou who art thy people's sun;
Shine upon thy work of grace,
If it be indeed begun.

Let me love thee more and more,
If I love at all, I pray;
If I have not lov'd before,
Help me to begin to-day.

THE DEATH OF STEPHEN.

When they heard these things, they were cut to the heart, and they gnashed on him with their teeth. But he, being full of the Holy Ghost, looked up stedfastly into heaven, and saw the glory of God, and Jesus standing on the right hand of God, And said, Behold, I see the heavens opened, and the Son of man standing on the right hand of God. Then they cried out with a loud voice, and stopped their ears, and ran upon him with one accord, And cast him out of the city, and stoned him: and the witnesses laid down their clothes at a young man's feet, whose name was Saul. And they stoned Stephen, calling upon God, and saying, Lord Jesus, receive my spirit. And he kneeled down, and cried with a loud voice, Lord, lay not this sin to their charge. And when he had said this, he fell asleep.—ACTS 7:54–60.

As some tall rock amidst the waves,
The fury of the tempest braves;
While the fierce billows tossing high,
Break at its foot and murm'ring die:

Thus they, who in the LORD confide,
Tho' foes assault on ev'ry side;
Cannot be mov'd or overthrown,
For JESUS makes their cause his own.

So faithful Stephen, undismay'd,
The malice of the Jews survey'd;
The holy joy which fill'd his breast
A lustre on his face impress'd.

"Behold! he said, the world of light
Is open'd to my strengthen'd sight;
My glorious LORD appears in view,
That JESUS, whom ye lately slew."

With such a friend and witness near,
No form of death could make him fear;
Calm, amidst show'rs of stones, he kneels,
And only for his murd'rers feels.

May we, by faith, perceive thee thus,
Dear Saviour, ever near to us!
This sight our peace, thro' life, shall keep,
And death be fear'd no more than sleep.

THE REBEL'S SURRENDER TO GRACE. LORD, WHAT WILT THOU HAVE ME TO DO?

And he trembling and astonished said, Lord, what wilt thou have me to do? And the Lord said unto him, Arise, and go into the city, and it shall be told thee what thou must do.—ACTS 9:6.

LORD, thou hast won, at length I yield,
My heart, by mighty grace compell'd,
    Surrenders all to thee;
Against thy terrors long I strove,
But who can stand against thy love?
    Love conquers even me.

All that a wretch could do, I try'd,
Thy patience scorn'd, thy pow'r defy'd,
    And trampled on thy laws;
Scarcely thy martyrs at the stake,
Could stand more steadfast for thy sake,
    Than I in Satan's cause.

But since thou hast thy love reveal'd,
And shewn my soul a pardon seal'd,
    I can resist no more:
Couldst thou for such a sinner bleed?
Canst thou for such a rebel plead?
    I wonder and adore!

If thou hadst bid thy thunders roll,
And light'nings flash to blast my soul,
    I still had stubborn been:
But mercy has my heart subdu'd,
A bleeding Saviour I have view'd,
    And now, I hate my sin.

Now, LORD, I would be thine alone,
Come take possession of thine own,
    For thou hast set me free;
Releas'd from Satan's hard command,
See all my powers waiting stand,
    To be employ'd by thee.

My will conform'd to thine would move,
On thee my hope, desire, and love,
    In fix'd attention join;

(Continued on the next page.)

My hands, my eyes, my ears, my tongue,
Have Satan's servants been too long,
    But now they shall be thine.

And can I be the very same,
Who lately durst blaspheme thy name;
    And on thy gospel tread?
Surely each one, who hears my case,
Will praise thee, and confess thy grace
    Invincible indeed!

PETER RELEASED FROM PRISON.

Peter therefore was kept in prison: but prayer was made without ceasing of the church unto God for him. And when Herod would have brought him forth, the same night Peter was sleeping between two soldiers, bound with two chains: and the keepers before the door kept the prison. And, behold, the angel of the Lord came upon him, and a light shined in the prison: and he smote Peter on the side, and raised him up, saying, Arise up quickly. And his chains fell off from his hands. And the angel said unto him, Gird thyself, and bind on thy sandals. And so he did. And he saith unto him, Cast thy garment about thee, and follow me.
        —Acts 12:5–8.

Fervent persevering pray'rs
    Are faith's assur'd resource;
Brazen gates, and iron bars,
    In vain withstand their force:
Peter when in prison cast,
Tho' by soldiers kept with care;
Tho' the doors were bolted fast,
    Was soon releas'd by pray'r.

While he slept an angel came
    And spread a light around;
Touch'd, and call'd him by his name,
    And rais'd him from the ground:
All his chains and fetters burst,
Ev'ry door wide open flew;
Peter thought he dream'd, at first,
    But found the vision true.

Thus the Lord can make a way
    To bring his saints relief;
'Tis their part, to wait and pray,
    In spite of unbelief:
He can break thro' walls of stone,
Sink the mountain to a plain;
They, to whom his name is known,
    Can never pray in vain.

Thus in chains of guilt and sin,
    Poor sinners sleeping lie;
No alarm is felt within,
    Altho' condemn'd to die:

(Continued on the next page.)

Till descending from above
(Mercy smiling in his eyes)
JESUS, with a voice of love,
 Awakes, and bids them rise.

Glad the summons they obey,
 And liberty desire;
Strait their fetters melt away,
 Like wax before the fire:
By the word of him who dy'd,
Guilty pris'ners to release;
Ev'ry door flies open wide,
 And they depart in peace.

THE TREMBLING GOALER.

Then he called for a light, and sprang in, and came trembling, and fell down before Paul and Silas, And brought them out, and said, Sirs, what must I do to be saved?—ACTS 16:29–30.

A BELIEVER, free from care,
May in chains, or dungeons, sing,
If the LORD be with him there;
And he happier than a king:
Paul and Silas thus confin'd,
Tho' their backs were torn by whips,
Yet possessing peace of mind,
Sung his praise with joyful lips.

Suddenly the prison shook,
Open flew the iron doors;
And the goaler, terror-struck,
Now his captives' help implores:
Trembling at their feet he fell,
"Tell me, Sirs, what must I do
To be sav'd from guilt and hell?
None can tell me this but you."

"Look to JESUS, they reply'd,
If on Him thou canst believe;
By the death which he has dy'd,
Thou salvation shalt receive:"
While the living word he heard,
Faith sprung up within his heart;
And releas'd from all he fear'd,
In their joy his soul had part.

Sinners, CHRIST is still the same,
O that you could likewise fear!
Then the mention of his name
Would be music to your ear:
JESUS rescues Satan's slaves,
His dear wounds still plead, "Forgive!"
JESUS to the utmost saves;
Sinners, look to him and live.

THE EXORCISTS.

*Then certain of the vagabond Jews, exorcists, took upon them to call over them which had evil spirits the name of the Lord Jesus, saying, We adjure you by Jesus whom Paul preacheth. And there were seven sons of one Sceva, a Jew, and chief of the priests, which did so. And the evil spirit answered and said, Jesus I know, and Paul I know; but who are ye? And the man in whom the evil spirit was leaped on them, and overcame them, and prevailed against them, so that they fled out of that house naked and wounded.—*ACTS 19:13–16.

WHEN the apostle wonders wrought,
And heal'd the sick, in JESUS' name;
The sons of Sceva vainly thought
That they had pow'r to do the same.

On one possess'd they try'd their art,
And naming JESUS preach'd by Paul,
They charg'd the spirit to depart
Expecting he'd obey their call.

The spirit answer'd, with a mock,
"JESUS I know; and Paul I know;
I must have gone if Paul had spoke,
But who are ye that bid me go?"

With fury then the man he fill'd,
Who on the poor pretenders flew;
Naked and wounded, almost kill'd,
They fled in all the peoples view.

JESUS! that name, pronounc'd by faith,
Is full of wonder-working pow'r;
It conquers Satan, sin and death,
And cheers in troubles darkest hour.

But they, who are not born again,
Know nothing of it but the sound;
They do but take his name in vain
When most their zeal and pains abound.

Satan their vain attempts derides,
Whether they talk, or pray, or preach;
Long as the love of sin abides,
His pow'r is safe beyond their reach.

But you, believers, may rejoice,
Satan well knows your mighty Friend;
He trembles at your Saviour's voice,
And owns he cannot gain his end.

PAUL'S VOYAGE.

*And when it was determined that we should sail into Italy, they delivered Paul and certain other prisoners unto one named Julius, a centurion of Augustus' band. And entering into a ship of Adramyttium, we launched, meaning to sail by the coasts of Asia; one Aristarchus, a Macedonian of Thessalonica, being with us.—*ACTS 27:1–2.

(The entire chapter of Acts 27 was referenced.)

IF Paul in Caesar's court must stand,
He need not fear the sea;
Secur'd from harm, on ev'ry hand,
By the divine decree.

Altho' the ship, in which he sail'd,
By dreadful storms was toss'd;
The promise over all prevail'd,
And not a life was lost.

JESUS! the GOD whom Paul ador'd,
Who saves in time of need;
Was then confess'd, by all on board,
A present help indeed!

Tho' neither sun nor stars were seen
Paul knew the LORD was near;
And faith preserv'd his soul serene,
When others shook for fear.

Believers thus are toss'd about
On life's tempestuous main;
But grace assures, beyond a doubt,
They shall their port attain.

They must, they shall appear one day,
Before their Saviour's throne;
The storms they meet with by the way,
But make his power known.

Their passage lies across the brink
Of many a threat'ning wave;
The world expects to see them sink,
But JESUS lives to save.

LORD, tho' we are but feeble worms,
Yet since thy word is past;
We'll venture thro' a thousand storms,
To see thy face at last.

THE GOOD THAT I WOULD I DO NOT.

For the good that I would I do not: but the evil which I would not, that I do.—ROMANS 7:19.
    (The entire chapter of Romans 7 was referenced.)

I WOULD, but cannot sing,
    Guilt has untun'd my voice;
The serpent sin's envenom'd sting
    Has poison'd all my joys.

I know the LORD is nigh,
    And would, but cannot, pray;
For Satan meets me when I try,
    And frights my soul away.

I would but can't repent
    Tho' I endeavour oft;
This stony heart can ne'er relent
    Till JESUS make it soft.

I would but cannot love,
    Tho' woo'd by love divine;
No arguments have pow'r to move
    A soul so base as mine.

I would, but cannot rest
    In GOD's most holy will;
I know what he appoints is best,
    Yet murmur at it still.

Oh could I but believe!
    Then all would easy be;
I would, but cannot, LORD relieve,
    My help must come from thee!

But if indeed I *would*,
    Tho' I can nothing do;
Yet the desire is something good,
    For which my praise is due.

By nature prone to ill,
    Till thine appointed hour
I was as destitute of will,
    As now I am of pow'r.

Wilt thou not crown, at length,
    The work thou hast begun?
And with a will, afford me strength
    In all thy ways to run.

SALVATION DRAWING NEARER.

And that, knowing the time, that now it is high time to awake out of sleep: for now is our salvation nearer than when we believed. The night is far spent, the day is at hand: let us therefore cast off the works of darkness, and let us put on the armour of light.—ROMANS 13:11–12.
    (The entire chapter of Romans 13 was referenced.)

DARKNESS overspreads us here,
But the night wears fast away;
Jacob's star will soon appear,
Leading on eternal day!
Now 'tis time to rouse from sleep,
Trim our lamps and stand prepar'd;
For our LORD strict watch to keep,
Lest he find us off our guard.

Let his people courage take,
Bear with a submissive mind
All they suffer for his sake,
Rich amends they soon will find:
He will wipe away their tears,
Near himself appoint their lot;
All their sorrows, pains and fears,
Quickly then will be forgot.

Tho' already sav'd, by grace,
From the hour we first believ'd;
Yet while sin and war have place,
We have but a part receiv'd:
Still we for salvation wait,
Ev'ry hour it nearer comes!
Death will break the prison gate,
And admit us to our homes.

Sinners, what can you expect?
You who now the Saviour dare;
Break his laws, his grace reject,
You must stand before his bar!
Tremble, lest he say, Depart!
Oh the horrors of that sound!
LORD, make ev'ry careless heart,
Seek thee while thou may'st be found.

THAT ROCK WAS CHRIST.

And did all drink the same spiritual drink: for they drank of that spiritual Rock that followed them: and that Rock was Christ.—1 CORINTHIANS 10:4.

WHEN Israel's tribes were parch'd with thirst,
Forth from the Rock the waters burst;
And all their future journey thro',
Yielded them drink and gospel too!

In Moses' rod, a type they saw,
Of his severe and fiery law;
The smitten rock prefigur'd him,
From whose pierc'd side all blessings stream.

But ah! the types were all too faint,
His sorrows or his worth to paint;
Slight was the stroke of Moses' rod,
But he endur'd the wrath of GOD.

Their outward rock could feel no pain,
But ours was wounded, torn and slain;
The rock gave but a watry flood,
But JESUS pour'd forth streams of blood.

The earth is like their wilderness,
A land of drought and sore distress;
Without one stream from pole to pole,
To satisfy a thirsty soul.

But let the Saviour's praise resound!
In him refreshing streams are found;
Which pardon, strength, and comfort give,
And thirsty sinners drink and live.

MY GRACE IS SUFFICIENT FOR THEE.

And he said unto me, My grace is sufficient for thee: for my strength is made perfect in weakness. Most gladly therefore will I rather glory in my infirmities, that the power of Christ may rest upon me.—2 CORINTHIANS 12:9.

OPPRESS'D with unbelief and sin,
Fightings without, and fears within;
While earth and hell, with force combin'd,
Assault and terrify my mind.

What strength have I against such foes,
Such hosts and legions to oppose?
Alass! I tremble, faint, and fall,
LORD save me, or I give up all.

Thus sorely prest I sought the LORD,
To give me some sweet cheering word;
Again I sought, and yet again,
I waited long, but not in vain.

Oh! 'twas a cheering word indeed!
Exactly suited to my need;
"Sufficient for thee is my grace,
Thy weakness my great pow'r displays."

Now despond and mourn no more,
I welcome all I fear'd before;
Tho' weak I'm strong, tho' troubled blest,
For CHRIST's own pow'r shall on me rest.

My grace would soon exhausted be,
But his is boundless as the sea;
Then let me boast with holy Paul,
That I am nothing, CHRIST is all.

THE INWARD WARFARE.

For the flesh lusteth against the Spirit, and the Spirit against the flesh: and these are contrary the one to the other: so that ye cannot do the things that ye would.—GALATIANS 5:17.

STRANGE and mysterious is my life,
What opposites I feel within!
A stable peace, a constant strife,
The rule of grace, the pow'r of sin:
    Too often I am captive led,
    Yet daily triumph in my Head.

I prize the privilege of pray'r,
But oh! what backwardness to pray!
Tho' on the LORD I cast my care,
I feel its burden ev'ry day:
    I seek *his* will in all I do,
    Yet find my own is working too.

I call the promises my own,
And prize them more than mines of gold;
Yet tho' their sweetness I have known,
They leave me unimpress'd and cold:
    One hour upon the truth I feed,
    The next I know not what I read.

I love the holy day of rest,
When JESUS meets his gather'd saints;
Sweet day, of all the week the best!
For its return my spirit pants:
    Yet often, thro' my unbelief,
    It proves a day of guilt and grief.

While on my Saviour I rely,
I know my foes shall loose their aim;
And therefore dare their pow'r defy,
Assur'd of conquest thro' his name:
    But soon my confidence is slain,
    And all my fears return again.

Thus diff'rent pow'rs within me strive,
And grace, and sin, by turns prevail;
I grieve, rejoice, decline, revive,
And vict'ry hangs in doubtful scale:
    But JESUS has his promise pass'd,
    That grace shall overcome at last.

THE WORD QUICK AND POWERFUL.

For the word of God is quick, and powerful, and sharper than any twoedged sword, piercing even to the dividing asunder of soul and spirit, and of the joints and marrow, and is a discerner of the thoughts and intents of the heart. Neither is there any creature that is not manifest in his sight: but all things are naked and opened unto the eyes of him with whom we have to do.—HEBREWS 4:12–13.

THE word of CHRIST, our LORD,
    With whom we have to do;
Is sharper than a two-edg'd sword,
    To pierce the sinner thro'!

Swift as the light'nings blaze
    When awful thunders roll,
It fills the conscience with amaze,
    And penetrates the soul.

No heart can be conceal'd
    From his all-piercing eyes;
Each thought and purpose stands reveal'd,
    Naked, without disguise.

He sees his peoples fears,
    He notes their mournful cry;
He counts their sighs and falling tears,
    And helps them from on high.

Tho' feeble is their good,
    It has his kind regard;
Yea, all they would do, if they could,[1]
    Shall find a sure reward.

He sees the wicked too,
    And will repay them soon,
For all the evil deeds they do,
    And all they would have done.[2]

Since all our secret ways
    Are mark'd and known by thee;
Afford us, LORD, thy light of grace
    That we ourselves may see.

1 1 Kings 8:18—And the LORD said unto David my father, Whereas it was in thine heart to build an house unto my name, thou didst well that it was in thine heart.

2 Matthew 5:28—But I say unto you, That whosoever looketh on a woman to lust after her hath committed adultery with her already in his heart.

LOOKING UNTO JESUS.

Looking unto Jesus the author and finisher of our faith; who for the joy that was set before him endured the cross, despising the shame, and is set down at the right hand of the throne of God.
—HEBREWS 12:2.

By various maxims, forms and rules,
That pass for wisdom in the schools,
I strove my passion to restrain;
But all my efforts prov'd in vain.

But since the Saviour I have known
My rules are all reduc'd to one;
To keep my LORD, by faith, in view,
This strength supplies and motives too.

I see him lead a suff'ring life,
Patient, amidst reproach and strife;
And from his pattern courage take
To bear, and suffer, for his sake.

Upon the cross I see him bleed,
And by the sight from guilt am freed;
This sight destroys the life of sin,
And quickens heav'nly life within.

To look to JESUS as he rose
Confirms my faith, disarms my foes;
Satan I shame and overcome,
By pointing to my Saviour's tomb.

Exalted on his glorious throne,
I see him make my cause his own;
Then all my anxious cares subside,
For JESUS lives, and will provide.

I see him look with pity down,
And hold in view the conqu'ror's crown;
If press'd with griefs and cares before,
My soul revives, nor asks for more.

By faith I see the hour at hand
When in his presence I shall stand;
Then it will be my endless bliss,
To see him where, and as he is.

LOVE-TOKENS.

And ye have forgotten the exhortation which speaketh unto you as unto children, My son, despise not thou the chastening of the Lord, nor faint when thou art rebuked of him: For whom the Lord loveth he chasteneth, and scourgeth every son whom he receiveth. If ye endure chastening, God dealeth with you as with sons; for what son is he whom the father chasteneth not? But if ye be without chastisement, whereof all are partakers, then are ye bastards, and not sons. Furthermore we have had fathers of our flesh which corrected us, and we gave them reverence: shall we not much rather be in subjection unto the Father of spirits, and live? For they verily for a few days chastened us after their own pleasure; but he for our profit, that we might be partakers of his holiness. Now no chastening for the present seemeth to be joyous, but grievous: nevertheless afterward it yieldeth the peaceable fruit of righteousness unto them which are exercised thereby.—HEBREWS 12:5–11.

AFFLICTIONS do not come alone,
    A voice attends the rod;
By both he to his saints is known,
    A Father and a GOD!

Let not my children slight the stroke
    I for chastisement send;
Nor faint beneath my kind rebuke,
    For still I am their friend.

The wicked I perhaps may leave
    Awhile, and not reprove;
But all the children I receive
    I scourge, because I love.

If therefore you were left without
    This needful discipline;
You might, with cause, admit a doubt,
    If you, indeed, were mine.

Shall earthly parents then expect
    Their children to submit?
And will not you, when I correct,
    Be humbled at my feet?

(Continued on the next page.)

To please themselves they oft chastise,
    And put their sons to pain;
But you are precious in my eyes,
    And shall not smart in vain.

I see your hearts, at present, fill'd
    With grief, and deep distress;
But soon these bitter seeds shall yield
    The fruits of righteousness.

Break thro' the clouds, dear LORD, and shine!
    Let us perceive thee nigh!
And to each mourning child of thine
    These gracious words apply.

EPHESUS.

Unto the angel of the church of Ephesus write; These things saith he that holdeth the seven stars in his right hand, who walketh in the midst of the seven golden candlesticks.—REVELATION 2:1.

He that hath an ear, let him hear what the Spirit saith unto the churches; To him that overcometh will I give to eat of the tree of life, which is in the midst of the paradise of God.—REVELATION 2:7.

THUS saith the LORD to Ephesus,
And thus he speaks to some of us;
"Amidst my churches, lo, I stand,
And hold the pastors in my hand.

Thy works, to me, are fully known,
Thy patience, and thy toil, I own;
Thy views of gospel truth are clear,
Nor canst thou other doctrine bear.

Yet I must blame while I approve,
Where is thy first, thy fervent love?
Dost thou forget my love to thee,
That thine is grown so faint to me?

Recall to mind the happy days
When thou wast fill'd with joy and praise;
Repent, thy former works renew,
Then I'll restore thy comforts too.

Return at once, when I reprove,
Lest I thy candlestic remove;
And thou, too late, thy loss lament,
I warn before I strike, Repent."

Hearken to what the Spirit saith,
To him that overcomes by faith;
"The fruit of life's unfading tree,
In paradise his food shall be."

SMYRNA.

He that hath an ear, let him hear what the Spirit saith unto the churches; He that overcometh shall not be hurt of the second death.—REVELATION 2:11.

THE message first to Smyrna sent,
    A message full of grace;
To all the Saviour's flock is meant,
    In ev'ry age and place.

Thus to his church, his chosen bride,
    Saith the great First and Last;
"Who ever lives, tho' once he dy'd,
    Hold thy profession fast.

Thy works and sorrows well I know,
    Perform'd and borne for me;
Poor tho' thou art, despis'd and low,
    Yet who is rich like thee?

I know thy foes, and what they say,
    How long they have blasphem'd;
The synagogue of Satan, they,
    Tho' they would Jews be deem'd.

Tho' Satan for a season rage,
    And prisons be your lot;
l am your friend, and I engage
    You shall not be forgot.

Be faithful unto death, nor fear
    A few short days of strife;
Behold! the prize you soon shall wear,
    A crown of endless life!"

Hear what the holy Spirit saith
    Of all who overcome;
"They shall escape the second death,
    The sinner's awful doom!"

PHILADELPHIA.

And to the angel of the church in Philadelphia write; These things saith he that is holy, he that is true, he that hath the key of David, he that openeth, and no man shutteth; and shutteth, and no man openeth; I know thy works: behold, I have set before thee an open door, and no man can shut it: for thou hast a little strength, and hast kept my word, and hast not denied my name. Behold, I will make them of the synagogue of Satan, which say they are Jews, and are not, but do lie; behold, I will make them to come and worship before thy feet, and to know that I have loved thee. Because thou hast kept the word of my patience, I also will keep thee from the hour of temptation, which shall come upon all the world, to try them that dwell upon the earth. Behold, I come quickly: hold that fast which thou hast, that no man take thy crown. Him that overcometh will I make a pillar in the temple of my God, and he shall go no more out: and I will write upon him the name of my God, and the name of the city of my God, which is new Jerusalem, which cometh down out of heaven from my God: and I will write upon him my new name. He that hath an ear, let him hear what the Spirit saith unto the churches.—REVELATION 3:7–13.

THUS saith the holy One, and true,
    To his beloved faithful few;
"Of heav'n and hell I hold the keys,
    To shut, or open, as I please.

I know thy works, and I approve,
    Tho' small thy strength, sincere thy love;
Go on, my word and name to own,
    For none shall rob thee of thy crown.

Before thee see my mercy's door
    Stands open wide to shut no more;
Fear not temptation's fiery day,
    For I will be thy strength and stay.

Thou hast my promise, hold it fast,
    The trying hour will soon be past;
Rejoice, for lo! I quickly come,
    To take thee to my heav'nly home.

(Continued on the next page.)

A pillar there, no more to move,
Inscrib'd with all my names of love;
A monument of mighty grace,
Thou shalt for ever have a place."

Such is the conqueror's reward,
Prepar'd and promis'd by the LORD!
Let him that has the ear of faith,
Attend to what the Spirit saith.

LAODICEA.

And unto the angel of the church of the Laodiceans write; These things saith the Amen, the faithful and true witness, the beginning of the creation of God; I know thy works, that thou art neither cold nor hot: I would thou wert cold or hot. So then because thou art lukewarm, and neither cold nor hot, I will spue thee out of my mouth. Because thou sayest, I am rich, and increased with goods, and have need of nothing; and knowest not that thou art wretched, and miserable, and poor, and blind, and naked: I counsel thee to buy of me gold tried in the fire, that thou mayest be rich; and white raiment, that thou mayest be clothed, and that the shame of thy nakedness do not appear; and anoint thine eyes with eyesalve, that thou mayest see. As many as I love, I rebuke and chasten: be zealous therefore, and repent. Behold, I stand at the door, and knock: if any man hear my voice, and open the door, I will come in to him, and will sup with him, and he with me.—REVELATION 3:14-20.

HEAR what the LORD, the great Amen,
The true and faithful Witness says!
He form'd the vast creation's plan,
And searches all our hearts and ways.

To some he speaks as once of old,
"I know thee, thy profession's vain;
Since thou art neither hot nor cold,
I'll spit thee from me with disdain.

Thou boasteth, "I am wise and rich,
Encreas'd in goods and nothing need;"
And dost not know thou art a wretch,
Naked and poor, and blind and dead.

Yet while I thus rebuke, I love,
My message is in mercy sent;
That thou may'st my compassion prove,
I can forgive, if thou repent.

Wouldst thou be truly rich and wise?
Come, buy my gold in fire well try'd,
My ointment to anoint thine eyes,
My robe, thy nakedness to hide.

(Continued on the next page.)

See at thy door I stand and knock!
Poor sinner, shall I wait in vain?
Quickly thy stubborn heart unlock,
That I may enter with my train.

Thou canst not entertain a king,
Unworthy thou of such a guest!
But I my own provisions bring,
To make thy soul a heavenly feast."

THE LITTLE BOOK.[1]

*And I went unto the angel, and said unto him,
Give me the little book. And he said unto me, Take
it, and eat it up; and it shall make thy belly bitter,
but it shall be in thy mouth sweet as honey.*
—REVELATION 10:9.
(The entire chapter of Revelation 10 was referenced.)

WHEN the belov'd disciple took
The angels' little open book,
Which by the LORD's command he eat,
It tasted bitter after sweet.

Thus when the gospel is embrac'd,
At first 'tis sweeter to the taste
Than honey, or the honey-comb,
But there's a bitterness to come.

What sweetness does the promise yield,
When by the Spirit's power seal'd?
The longing soul is fill'd with good,
Nor feels a wish for other food.

By these inviting tastes allur'd,
We pass to what must be endur'd;
For soon we find it is decreed,
That bitter must to sweet succeed.

When sin revives and shews its pow'r,
When Satan threatens to devour,
When GOD afflicts and men revile,
We drag our steps with pain and toil.

When thus deserted, tempest-toss'd,
The sense of former sweetness lost;
We tremble lest we were deceiv'd
In thinking that we once believ'd.

The LORD first makes the sweetness known,
To win and fix us for his own;
And tho' we now some bitter meet,
We hope for everlasting sweet.

---

1 Book III. Hymn 27.

TIME HOW SWIFT.

WHILE with ceaseless course the sun
Hasted thro' the former year,
Many souls their race have run,
Never more to meet us here:
Fix'd in an eternal state,
They have done with all below;
We a little longer wait,
But how little—none can know.

As the winged arrow flies
Speedily the mark to find;
As the light'ning from the skies
Darts, and leaves no trace behind;
Swiftly thus our fleeting days
Bear us down life's rapid stream;
Upwards, LORD, our spirits raise,
All below is but a dream.

Thanks for mercies past receive,
Pardon of our sins renew;
Teach us, henceforth, how to live
With eternity in view:
Bless thy word to young and old,
Fill us with a Saviour's love;
And when life's short tale is told,
May we dwell with thee above.

TIME HOW SHORT.

TIME, with an unweary'd hand,
Pushes round the seasons past;
And in life's frail glass, the sand
Sinks apace, not long to last:
Many, well as you or I,
Who last year assembled thus;
In their silent graves now lie,
Graves will open soon for us!

Daily sin, and care, and strife,
While the LORD prolongs our breath,
Make it but a dying life,
Or a kind of living death:
Wretched they, and most forlorn,
Who no better portion know;
Better ne'er to have been born,
Than to have our all below.

When constrain'd to go alone,
Leaving all you love behind;
Ent'ring on a world unknown,
What will then support your mind?
When the LORD his summons sends,[1]
Earthly comforts lose their pow'r;
Honors, riches, kindred, friends,
Cannot cheer a dying hour.

Happy souls who fear the LORD!
Time is not too swift for you;
When your Saviour gives the word,
Glad you'll bid the world adieu:
Then he'll wipe away your tears,
Near himself appoint your place;
Swifter fly, ye rolling years,
LORD, we long to see thy face.

---

1 Isaiah 10:3—And what will ye do in the day of visitation, and in the desolation which shall come from far? to whom will ye flee for help? and where will ye leave your glory?

UNCERTAINTY OF LIFE.

SEE! another year is gone!
Quickly have the seasons past!
This we enter now upon
May to many prove our last:
Mercy hitherto has spar'd,
But have mercies been improv'd?
Let us ask, am I prepar'd
Should I be this year remov'd?

Some we now no longer see,
Who their mortal race have run;
Seem'd as fair for life as we,
When the former year begun:
Some, but who GOD only knows,
Who are here assembled now;
Ere the present year shall close,
To the stroke of death must bow.

Life a field of battle is,
Thousands fall within our view;
And the next death-bolt that flies,
May be sent to me or you:
While we preach, and while we hear,
Help us, LORD, each one, to think,
Vast eternity is near,
I am standing on the brink.

If from guilt and sin set free,
By the knowledge of thy grace;
Welcome, then, the call will be
To depart and see thy face:
To thy saints, while here below,
With new years, new mercies come;
But the happiest year they know
Is their last, which leads them home.

A NEW-YEAR'S THOUGHT AND PRAYER.

TIME, by moments, steals away,
First the hour, and then the day;
Small the daily loss appears,
Yet it soon amounts to years:
Thus another year is flown,
Now it is no more our own;
If it brought or promis'd good,
Than the years before the flood.

But (may none of us forget)
It has left us much in debt;
Favors from the LORD receiv'd,
Sins that have his Spirit griev'd;
Mark'd by an unerring hand
In his book recorded stand;
Who can tell the vast amount,
Plac'd to each of our account?

Happy, the believing soul!
CHRIST for you has paid the whole;
While you own the debt is large,
You may plead a full discharge:
But poor careless sinner, say,
What can you to justice pay?
Tremble, lest when life is past,
Into prison you be cast!

Will you still increase the score?
Still be careless, as before?
Oh, forbid it, gracious LORD,
Touch their spirits by thy word!
Now, in mercy, to them show
What a mighty debt they owe!
All their unbelief subdue,
Let *them* find forgiveness too.

Spar'd to see another year,
Let thy blessing meet us here;
Come, thy dying work revive,
Bid thy drooping garden thrive:
Sun of righteousness arise!
Warm our hearts, and bless our eyes;
Let our pray'r thy bowels move,
Make this year a time of love!

DEATH AND WAR. 1778.

Hark! how time's wide sounding bell
Strikes on each attentive ear!
Tolling loud the solemn knell
Of the late departed year:
Years, like mortals, wear away,
Have their birth, and dying day;
Youthful spring, and wintry age,
Then to others quit the stage.

Sad experience may relate
What a year the last has been!
Crops of sorrow have been great,
From the fruitful seeds of sin:
Oh! what numbers gay and blithe,
Fell by death's unsparing scythe?
While they thought the world their own,
Suddenly he mow'd them down.

See how war, with dreadful stride,
Marches at the Lord's command;
Spreading desolation wide,
Thro' a once much-favour'd land:
War, with heart and arms of steel,
Preys on thousands at a meal;
Daily drinking human gore,
Still he thirsts, and calls for more.

If the God, whom we provoke,
Hither should his way direct;
What a sin-avenging stroke
May a land, like this, expect!
They who now securely sleep,
Quickly then, would wake and weep;
And too late would learn to fear,
When they saw the danger near.

You are safe, who know his love,
He will all his truth perform;
To your souls a refuge prove
From the rage of ev'ry storm:
But we tremble for the youth;
Teach them, Lord, thy saving truth;
Join them to thy faithful few,
Be to them a refuge too.

EARTHLY PROSPECTS DECEITFUL.

Oft in vain the voice of truth,
Solemnly and loudly warns;
Thoughtless, inexperienc'd youth,
Tho' it hears, the warning scorns:
Youth in fancy's glass surveys
Life prolong'd to distant years;
While the vast, imagin'd space,
Fill'd with sweets and joys appears.

Awful disappointment, soon
Overclouds the prospect gay!
Some their sun goes down at noon,
Torn by death's strong hand away:
Where are then their pleasing schemes?
Where the joys they hop'd to find?
Gone for ever, like their dreams,
Leaving not a trace behind.

Others, who are spar'd awhile,
Live to weep o'er fancy's cheat;
Find distress, and pain, and toil,
Bitter things instead of sweet:
Sin has spread a curse around,
Poison'd all things here below;
On this base polluted ground,
Peace and joy can never grow.

Grace alone can cure our ills,
Sweeten life, with all its cares;
Regulate our stubborn wills,
Save us from surrounding snares:
Tho' you oft have heard in vain,
Former years in folly spent;
Grace invites you yet again,
Once more calls you to repent.

Call'd again, at length, beware,
Hear the Saviour's voice, and live;
Lest he in his wrath should swear,
He no more will warning give:
Pray, that you may hear and feel,
Ere the day of grace be past;
Lest your hearts grow hard as steel,
Or this year should prove your last.

PRAYER FOR A BLESSING.

Now, gracious LORD, thine arm reveal,
 And make thy glory known;
Now let us all thy presence feel,
 And soften hearts of stone!

Help us to venture near thy throne,
 And plead a Saviour's name;
For all that we can call our own,
 Is vanity and shame.

From all the guilt of former sin
 May mercy set us free;
And let the year we now begin,
 Begin and end with thee.

Send down thy Spirit from above
 That saints may love thee more;
And sinners now may learn to love
 Who never lov'd before.

And when before thee we appear
 In our eternal home;
May growing numbers worship here,
 And praise thee in our room.

PRAYER FOR A BLESSING.

Now may fervent pray'r arise
Wing'd with faith, and pierce the skies;
Fervent pray'r shall bring us down
Gracious answers from the throne.

Bless, O LORD, the op'ning year
To each soul assembled here;
Clothe thy word with pow'r divine,
Make us willing to be thine.

Shepherd of thy blood-bought sheep!
Teach the stony heart to weep;
Let the blind have eyes to see,
See themselves, and look on thee!

Let the minds of all our youth
Feel the force of sacred truth;
While the gospel-call they hear
May they learn to love and fear!

Shew them what their ways have been,
Shew them the desert of sin;
Then thy dying love reveal,
This shall melt a heart of steel.

Where thou hast thy work begun,
Give new strength the race to run;
Scatter darkness, doubts and fears,
Wipe away the mourners tears.

Bless us all, both old and young;
Call forth praise from ev'ry tongue;
Let the whole assembly prove
All thy pow'r, and all thy love!

CASTING THE GOSPEL NET.

WHEN Peter thro' the tedious night[1]
Had often cast his net in vain;
Soon as his LORD appear'd in sight
He gladly let it down again.

Once more the gospel net we cast,
Do thou, O LORD, the effort own;
We learn from disappointments past,
To rest our hope on thee alone.

Upheld by thy supporting hand,
We enter on another year;
And now we meet, at thy command,
To seek thy gracious presence here.

May this be a much favour'd hour,
To souls in Satan's bondage led!
O clothe thy word with sovereign pow'r
To break the rocks, and raise the dead!

Have mercy on our num'rous youth,
Who young in years, are old in sin;
And by thy Spirit, and thy truth,
Shew them the state their souls are in.

Then, by a Saviour's dying love
To ev'ry wounded heart reveal'd,
Temptations, fears, and guilt remove,
And be their Sun, and Strength, and Shield.

To mourners speak a cheering word,
On seeking souls vouchsafe to shine;
Let poor backsliders be restor'd,
And all thy saints in praises join.

O hear our pray'r and give us hope,
That when thy voice shall call us home,
Thou still wilt raise a people up,
To love and praise thee in our room.

THE SHUNAMITE.[2]

THE Shunamite, oppress'd with grief,
When she had lost the son she lov'd,
Went to Elisha for relief,
Nor vain her application prov'd.

He sent his servant on before
To lay a staff upon his head;
This *he* could do, but do no more,
He left him, as he found him, dead.

But when the LORD's almighty pow'r
Wrought with the prophet's prayer, and faith,
The mother saw a joyful hour,
She saw her child restor'd from death.

Thus, like the weeping Shunamite,
For many, dead in sin we grieve;
Now, LORD, display thine arm of might,
Cause them to hear thy voice and live.

Thy preachers bear the staff in vain,
Tho' at thine own command we go;
LORD, we have try'd, and try'd again,
We find them dead, and leave them so.

Come then thyself—to ev'ry heart
The glory of thy name make known;
The means are our appointed part,
The pow'r and grace are thine alone.

---

1 Luke 5:4—Now when he had left speaking, he said
unto Simon, Launch out into the deep, and let down
your nets for a draught.

2 2 Kings 4:31—And Gehazi passed on before them,
and laid the staff upon the face of the child; but there
was neither voice, nor hearing. Wherefore he went
again to meet him, and told him, saying, The child is
not awaked.

ELIJAH'S PRAYER.[1]

DOES it not grief, and wonder move,
To think of Israel's shameful fall?
Who needed miracles to prove
Whether the LORD was GOD, or Baal!

Methinks I see Elijah stand,
His features glow with love and zeal,
In faith and pray'r he lifts his hand,
And makes to heav'n his great appeal,

"O GOD! if I thy servant am,
If 'tis thy message fills my heart;
Now glorify thy holy name,
And shew this people who thou art!"

He spake, and lo! a sudden flame
Consum'd the wood, the dust, the stone;
The people struck, at once proclaim
"The LORD is GOD, the LORD alone."

Like him we mourn an awful day,
When more for Baal, than GOD appear;
Like him, believers, let us pray,
And may the GOD of Israel hear!

LORD, if thy servant speaks thy truth,
If he indeed is sent by thee;
Confirm the word to all our youth,
And let them thy salvation see.

Now may thy Spirit's holy fire
Pierce ev'ry heart that hears thy word;
Consume each hurtful vain desire,
And make them know thou art the LORD.

PREACHING TO THE DRY BONES.[2]

PREACHERS may, from Ezekiel's case,
Draw hope in this declining day;
A proof, like this, of sovereign grace
Should chase our unbelief away.

When sent to preach to mold'ring bones,
Who could have thought he would succeed?
But well he knew, the LORD from stones
Could raise up Abra'ms chosen seed.

Can these be made a num'rous host,
And such dry bones new life receive?
The prophet answer'd, "LORD thou knowst
They shall, if thou commandment give."

Like him, around I cast my eye,
And oh! what heaps of bones appear!
Like him, by JESUS sent, I'll try,
For he can cause the dead to hear.

Hear, ye dry bones, the Saviour's word!
He, who when dying, gasp'd, "Forgive,"
That gracious, sinner-loving LORD,
Says, "Look to me, dry bones, and live."

Thou heav'nly wind awake and blow,
In answer to the pray'r of faith;
Now thine almighty influence show,
And fill dry bones with living breath.

O make them hear, and feel, and shake,
And, at thy call, obedient move;
The bonds of death and Satan break,
And bone to bone unite in love.

---

1 1 Kings 18:36–39—And it came to pass at the time of the offering of the evening sacrifice, that Elijah the prophet came near, and said, LORD God of Abraham, Isaac, and of Israel, let it be known this day that thou art God in Israel, and that I am thy servant, and that I have done all these things at thy word. Hear me, O LORD, hear me, that this people may know that thou art the LORD God, and that thou hast turned their heart back again. Then the fire of the LORD fell, and consumed the burnt sacrifice, and the wood, and the stones, and the dust, and licked up the water that was in the trench. And when all the people saw it, they fell on their faces: and they said, The LORD, he is the God; the LORD, he is the God.

(The entire chapter of 1 Kings 18 was referenced.)

---

2 Ezekiel 37:4–7—Again he said unto me, Prophesy upon these bones, and say unto them, O ye dry bones, hear the word of the LORD. Thus saith the Lord GOD unto these bones; Behold, I will cause breath to enter into you, and ye shall live: And I will lay sinews upon you, and will bring up flesh upon you, and cover you with skin, and put breath in you, and ye shall live; and ye shall know that I am the LORD. So I prophesied as I was commanded: and as I prophesied, there was a noise, and behold a shaking, and the bones came together, bone to his bone.

(The entire chapter of Ezekiel 37 was referenced.)

THE ROD OF MOSES.

WHEN Moses wav'd his mystic rod
What wonders follow'd while he spoke?
Firm as a wall the waters stood,[1]
Or gush'd in rivers from the rock![2]

At his command the thunders roll'd,
Light'ning and hail his voice obey'd;[3]
And Pharaoh trembled, to behold
His land in desolation laid.

But what could Moses' rod have done
Had he not been divinely sent?
The pow'r was from the LORD alone,
And Moses but the instrument.

O LORD, regard thy peoples pray'rs!
Assist a worm to preach aright;
And since thy gospel-rod he bears,
Display thy wonders in our sight.

Proclaim the thunders of thy law,
Like light'ning let thine arrows fly,
That careless sinners, struck with awe,
For refuge may to JESUS cry!

Make streams of godly sorrow flow
From rocky hearts, unus'd to feel;
And let the poor in spirit know
That thou art near, their griefs to heal.

But chiefly, we would now look up
To ask a blessing for our youth,
The rising generations hope,
That they may know and love thy truth.

Arise, O LORD, afford a sign,
Now shall our pray'rs success obtain;
Since both the means and pow'r are thine,
How can the rod be rais'd in vain!

1 Exodus 14:21—And Moses stretched out his hand
   over the sea; and the LORD caused the sea to go back
   by a strong east wind all that night, and made the sea
   dry land, and the waters were divided.
2 Numbers 20:11—And Moses lifted up his hand, and
   with his rod he smote the rock twice: and the water
   came out abundantly, and the congregation drank,
   and their beasts also.
3 Exodus 9:23—And Moses stretched forth his rod
   toward heaven: and the LORD sent thunder and hail,
   and the fire ran along upon the ground; and the LORD
   rained hail upon the land of Egypt.

GOD SPEAKING FROM MOUNT ZION.

THE GOD who once to Israel spoke
From Sinai's top, in fire and smoke,
In gentler strains of gospel grace
Invites us, now, to seek his face.

He wears no terrors on his brow,
He speaks, in love, from Zion, now;
It is the voice of JESUS' blood
Calling poor wand'rers home to GOD.

The holy Moses quak'd and fear'd
When Sinai's thundring *law* he heard;
But reigning grace, with accents mild,
Speaks to the sinner, as a child.

Hark! how from Calvary it sounds;
From the Redeemer's bleeding wounds!
"Pardon and grace, I freely give,
Poor sinner, look to me, and live."

What other arguments can move
The heart, that slights a Saviour's love!
Yet till Almighty pow'r constrain,
This matchless love is preach'd in vain.

O Saviour let that pow'r be felt,
And cause each stony heart to melt!
Deeply impress upon our youth
The light, and force, of gospel truth.

With this new-year may they begin
To live to thee, and die to sin;
To enter by the narrow way
Which leads to everlasting day.

How will they else thy presence bear
When as a Judge thou shalt appear!
When slighted love, to wrath shall turn,
And the whole earth like Sinai burn!

A PRAYER FOR POWER ON THE MEANS OF GRACE.

O THOU, at whose almighty word,
The glorious light from darkness sprung!
Thy quick'ning influence afford,
And clothe with pow'r the preacher's tongue.

Tho' 'tis thy truth he hopes to speak,
He cannot give the hearing ear;
'Tis thine, the stubborn heart to break,
And make the careless sinner fear.

As when of old, the water flow'd
Forth from the rock at thy command;[1]
Moses in vain had wav'd the rod,
Without thy wonder-working hand.

As when the walls of Jericho[2]
Down to the earth at once were cast;
It was thy pow'r that brought them low,
And not the trumpets feeble blast.

Thus we would in the means be found,
And thus, on thee alone, depend;
To make the gospel's joyful sound
Effectual, to the promis'd end.

Now, while we hear thy word of grace,
Let self and pride before it fall;
And rocky hearts dissolve apace,
In streams of sorrow at thy call.

On all our youth assembled here
The unction of thy Spirit pour;
Nor let them lose another year,
Lest thou shouldst strive and call no more.

ELIJAH'S MANTLE.

And it came to pass, as they still went on, and talked, that, behold, there appeared a chariot of fire, and horses of fire, and parted them both asunder; and Elijah went up by a whirlwind into heaven. And Elisha saw it, and he cried, My father, my father, the chariot of Israel, and the horsemen thereof. And he saw him no more: and he took hold of his own clothes, and rent them in two pieces. He took up also the mantle of Elijah that fell from him, and went back, and stood by the bank of Jordan; And he took the mantle of Elijah that fell from him, and smote the waters, and said, Where is the LORD *God of Elijah? and when he also had smitten the waters, they parted hither and thither: and Elisha went over.*—2 KINGS 2:11–14.

ELISHA, struck with grief and awe,
Cry'd, "Ah! where now is Israel's stay?"
When he his honour'd master saw
Borne by a fiery carr away.

But while he look'd a last adieu,
His mantle, as it fell, he caught;
The Spirit rested on him too,
And equal miracles he wrought.

"Where is Elijah's GOD," he cry'd,
And with the mantle smote the flood;
His word controll'd the swelling tide,
Th' obedient waters upright stood.

The wonder-working gospel, thus
From hand to hand, has been convey'd;
We have the mantle still with us,
But where, O where, the Spirit's aid.

When Peter first this mantle wav'd,[3]
How soon it melted hearts of steel!

(Continued on the next page)

---

1 Numbers 20:11—And Moses lifted up his hand, and with his rod he smote the rock twice: and the water came out abundantly, and the congregation drank, and their beasts also.

2 Joshua 6:20—So the people shouted when the priests blew with the trumpets: and it came to pass, when the people heard the sound of the trumpet, and the people shouted with a great shout, that the wall fell down flat, so that the people went up into the city, every man straight before him, and they took the city.

---

3 Acts 2:38–41—Then Peter said unto them, Repent, and be baptized every one of you in the name of Jesus Christ for the remission of sins, and ye shall receive the gift of the Holy Ghost. For the promise is unto you, and to your children, and to all that are afar off, even as many as the LORD our God shall call. And with many other words did he testify and exhort, saying, Save yourselves from this untoward generation. Then they that gladly received his word were baptized: and the same day there were added unto them about three thousand souls.

(The entire chapter of Acts 2 was referenced.)

Sinners, by thousands, then were sav'd,
But now how few its virtues feel?

Where is Elijah's GOD, the LORD,
Thine Israel's hope, and joy, and boast!
Reveal thine arm, confirm thy word,
Give us another Pentecost!

Assist thy messenger to speak,
And while he aims to lisp thy truth,
The bonds of sin and Satan break,
And pour thy blessing on our youth.

For them we now approach thy throne,
Teach them to know and love thy name;
Then shall thy thankful people own
Elijah's GOD is still the same.

DAVID'S CHARGE TO SOLOMON.

And thou, Solomon my son, know thou the God of thy father, and serve him with a perfect heart and with a willing mind: for the LORD searcheth all hearts, and understandeth all the imaginations of the thoughts: if thou seek him, he will be found of thee; but if thou forsake him, he will cast thee off for ever.—1 CHRONICLES 28:9.

O DAVID's Son, and David's LORD!
From age to age thou art the same;
Thy gracious presence now afford,
And teach our youth to know thy name!

Thy people, LORD, tho' oft distrest,
Upheld by thee, thus far are come;
And now we long to see thy rest,
And wait thy word to call us home.

Like David, when this life shall end,
We trust in thee sure peace to find;
Like him, to thee we now commend
The children we must leave behind.

Ere long, we hope to be, where care,
And sin, and sorrow, never come;
But oh! accept our humble pray'r,
That these may praise thee in our room.

Shew them how vile they are by sin,
And wash them in thy cleansing blood;
Oh, make them willing to be thine,
And be, to them, a cov'nant GOD.

Long may thy light and truth remain
To bless this place, when we are gone;
And numbers here be born again,
To dwell for ever near thy throne.

THE LORD'S CALL TO HIS CHILDREN.

Wherefore come out from among them, and be ye separate, saith the Lord, and touch not the unclean thing; and I will receive you. And will be a Father unto you, and ye shall be my sons and daughters, saith the Lord Almighty.—2 Corinthians 6:17–18.

Let us adore the grace that seeks
  To draw our hearts above!
Attend, 'tis God the Saviour speaks,
  And ev'ry word is love.

Tho' fill'd with awe, before his throne
  Each angel veils his face;
He claims a people for his own
  Amongst our sinful race.

Careless, awhile, they live in sin,
  Enslav'd to Satan's pow'r;
But they obey the call divine,
  In his appointed hour.

"Come forth, he says, no more pursue
  The paths that lead to death;
Look up, a bleeding Saviour view,
  Look, and be sav'd by faith.

My sons and daughters you shall be
  Thro' the atoning blood;
And you shall claim, and find, in me,
  A Father, and a God."

Lord, speak these words to ev'ry heart,
  By thine all-powerful voice;
That we may now from sin depart,
  And make thy love our choice.

If now, we learn to seek thy face
  By Christ, the living way;
We'll praise thee for this hour of grace,
  Thro' an eternal day.

THE PRAYER OF JABEZ.

And Jabez was more honourable than his brethren: and his mother called his name Jabez, saying, Because I bare him with sorrow. And Jabez called on the God of Israel, saying, Oh that thou wouldest bless me indeed, and enlarge my coast, and that thine hand might be with me, and that thou wouldest keep me from evil, that it may not grieve me! And God granted him that which he requested.—1 Chronicles 4:9–10.

Jesus, who bought us with his blood,
  And makes our souls his care;
Was known of old as Israel's God,
  And answer'd Jabez' pray'r.

Jabez! a child of grief! the name
  Befits poor sinners well;
For Jesus bore the cross and shame,
  To save our souls from hell.

Teach us, O Lord, like him, to plead
  For mercies from above;
O come, and bless our souls indeed,
  With light, and joy, and love.

The gospel's promis'd land is wide,
  We fain would enter in;
But we are press'd, on ev'ry side,
  With unbelief and sin.

Arise, O Lord, enlarge our coast,
  Let us possess the whole;
That Satan may no longer boast
  He can thy work controll.

Oh, may thine hand be with us still,
  Our Guide and Guardian be;
To keep us safe from ev'ry ill,
  Till death shall set us free.

Help us on thee to cast our care,
  And on thy word to rest;
That Israel's God, who heareth pray'r,
  Will grant us our request.

WAITING AT WISDOM'S GATES.

Blessed is the man that heareth me, watching daily at my gates, waiting at the posts of my doors. For whoso findeth me findeth life, and shall obtain favour of the LORD.—PROVERBS 8:34–35.

ENSNAR'D, too long, my heart has been
   In folly's hurtful ways;
Oh, may I now, at length, begin
   To hear what Wisdom says!

'Tis JESUS, from the mercy-seat,
   Invites me to his rest;
He calls poor sinners to his feet
   To make them truly blest.

Approach my soul to Wisdom's gates
   While it is call'd to-day;
No one who watches there and waits
   Shall e'er be turn'd away.

He will not let me seek in vain,
   For all, who trust his word,
Shall everlasting life obtain,
   And favor from the LORD.

LORD, I have hated thee too long,
   And dar'd thee to thy face;
I've done my soul exceeding wrong
   In slighting all thy grace.

Now I would break my league with death,
   And live to thee alone;
Oh let thy Spirit's seal of faith,
   Secure me for thine own.

Let all the saints assembled here,
   Yea, let all heav'n rejoice;
That I begin with this new-year,
   To make the LORD my choice.

ASKING THE WAY TO ZION.

They shall ask the way to Zion with their faces thitherward, saying, Come, and let us join ourselves to the LORD in a perpetual covenant that shall not be forgotten.—JEREMIAH 50:5.

ZION! the city of our GOD,
   How glorious is the place!
The Saviour there has his abode,
   And sinners see his face!

Firm, against ev'ry adverse shock,
   Its mighty bulwarks prove;
'Tis built upon the living Rock,
   And wall'd around with love.

There, all the fruits of glory grow,
   And joys that never die;
And streams of grace, and knowledge flow,
   The soul to satisfy.

Come, set your faces Zion-ward,
   The sacred road enquire;
And let a union to the LORD
   Be henceforth your desire!

The gospel shines to give you light,
   No longer, then, delay;
The Spirit waits to guide you right,
   And JESUS is the way.

O LORD, regard thy peoples pray'r,
   Thy promise now fulfill;
And young and old, by grace prepare,
   To dwell on Zion's hill.

WE WERE PHARAOH'S BONDMEN.

And when thy son asketh thee in time to come, say-ing, What mean the testimonies, and the statutes, and the judgments, which the LORD our God hath commanded you? Then thou shalt say unto thy son, We were Pharaoh's bondmen in Egypt; and the LORD brought us out of Egypt with a mighty hand: And the LORD shewed signs and wonders, great and sore, upon Egypt, upon Pharaoh, and upon all his household, before our eyes: And he brought us out from thence, that he might bring us in, to give us the land which he sware unto our fathers.—DEUTERONOMY 6:20–23.

BENEATH the tyrant Satan's yoke
   Our souls were long opprest;
Till grace our galling fetters broke,
   And gave the weary rest.

JESUS, in that important hour,
   His mighty arm made known;
He ransom'd us by price, and pow'r,
   And claim'd us for his own.

Now, freed from bondage, sin, and death,
   We walk in Wisdom's ways;
And wish to spend our ev'ry breath,
   In wonder, love, and praise.

Ere long, we hope with him to dwell
   In yonder world above;
And now, we only live to tell
   The riches of his love.

O might we, ere we hence remove,
   Prevail upon our youth
To seek, that they may likewise prove,
   His mercy and his truth.

Like Simeon, we shall gladly go,[1]
   When JESUS calls us home;
If they are left a seed below,
   To serve him in our room.

LORD hear our pray'r, indulge our hope,
   On these thy Spirit pour;
That they may take our story up,
   When we can speak no more.

---

[1] Luke 2:29—Lord, now lettest thou thy servant depart in peace, according to thy word.

TRAVAILING IN BIRTH FOR SOULS.

My little children, of whom I travail in birth again until Christ be formed in you—GALATIANS 4:19.

WHAT contradictions meet
   In ministers employ!
   It is a bitter sweet,
   A sorrow full of joy:
No other post affords a place
For equal honor, or disgrace!

Who can describe the pain
   Which faithful preachers feel;
   Constrain'd to speak, in vain,
   To hearts as hard as steel?
Or who can tell the pleasures felt,
When stubborn hearts begin to melt?

The Saviour's dying love,
   The soul's amazing worth;
   Their utmost efforts move,
   And draw their bowels forth:
They pray and strive, their rest departs,
Till CHRIST be form'd in sinners hearts.

If some small hope appear,
   They still are not content;
   But, with a jealous fear,
   They watch for the event:
Too oft they find their hopes deceiv'd,
Then, how their inmost souls are griev'd!

But when their pains succeed,
   And from the tender blade
   The rip'ning ears proceed,
   Their toils are overpaid:
No harvest-joy can equal theirs,
To find the fruit of all their cares.

On what has now been sown
   Thy blessing, LORD, bestow;
   The pow'r is thine alone,
   To make it spring and grow:
Do thou the gracious harvest raise,
And thou, alone, shalt have the praise.

WE ARE AMBASSADORS FOR CHRIST.

*Now then we are ambassadors for Christ, as
though God did beseech you by us: we pray you in
Christ's stead, be ye reconciled to God.*
—2 CORINTHIANS 5:20.

THY message, by the preacher, seal,
   And let thy pow'r be known;
That ev'ry sinner here, may feel
   The word is not his own.

Amongst the foremost of the throng
   Who dare thee to thy face,
He in rebellion stood too long,
   And fought against thy grace.

But grace prevail'd, he mercy found,
   And now by thee is sent,
To tell his fellow-rebels round,
   And call them to repent.

In JESUS, GOD is reconcil'd,
   The worst may be forgiv'n;
Come, and he'll own you as a child,
   And make you heirs of heav'n.

Oh, may the word of gospel truth
   Your chief desires engage;
And JESUS be your guide in youth,
   Your joy in hoary age.

Perhaps the year, that's now begun,
   May prove to some their last;
The sands of life may soon be run,
   The day of grace be past.

Think, if you slight this embassy,
   And will not warning take;
When JESUS in the clouds you see,
   What answer will you make?

PAUL'S FAREWEL CHARGE.

*Wherefore I take you to record this day, that I am
pure from the blood of all men. For I have not
shunned to declare unto you all the counsel of
God.*—ACTS 20:26–27.

WHEN Paul was parted from his friends
   It was a weeping day;
But JESUS made them all amends,
   And wip'd their tears away.

Ere long they met again, with joy,
   (Secure no more to part)
Where praises ev'ry tongue employ,
   And pleasure fills each heart.

Thus all the preachers of his grace
   Their children soon shall meet;
Together see their Saviour's face,
   And worship at his feet.

But they who heard the word in vain,
   Tho' oft, and plainly, warn'd;
Will tremble, when they meet again
   The ministers they scorn'd.

On your own heads your blood will fall
   If any perish here;
The preachers, who have told you *all*,
   Shall stand approv'd, and clear.

Yet, LORD, to save themselves alone,
   Is not their utmost view;
Oh! hear their pray'r, thy message own,
   And save their hearers too.

HOW SHALL I PUT THEE AMONG THE CHILDREN?

But I said, How shall I put thee among the children, and give thee a pleasant land, a goodly heritage of the hosts of nations? and I said, Thou shalt call me, My father; and shalt not turn away from me.—JEREMIAH 3:19.

ALASS! by nature how deprav'd,
   How prone to ev'ry ill!
Our lives, to Satan, how enslav'd,
   How obstinate our will!

And can such sinners be restor'd,
   Such rebels reconcil'd?
Can grace itself the means afford
   To make a foe a child?

Yes, grace has found the wond'rous means
   Which shall effectual prove;
To cleanse us from our countless sins,
   And teach our hearts to love.

JESUS for sinners undertakes,
   And dy'd that we may live;
His blood a full atonement makes,
   And cries aloud, "Forgive."

Yet one thing more must grace provide,
   To bring us home to GOD;
Or we shall slight the LORD, who dy'd,
   And trample on his blood.

The holy Spirit must reveal
   The Saviour's work and worth;
Then the hard heart begins to feel
   A new and heavenly birth.

Thus bought with blood, and born again,
   Redeem'd, and sav'd, by grace;
Rebels, in GOD's own house obtain
   A son's and daughter's place.

WINTER.[1]

SEE, how rude winter's icy hand
Has stripp'd the trees, and seal'd the ground!
But spring shall soon his rage withstand,
And spread new beauties all around.

My soul, a sharper winter mourns,
Barren and fruitless I remain;
When will the gentle spring return,
And bid my graces grow again?

JESUS, my glorious Sun arise!
'Tis thine, the frozen heart to move;
Oh! hush these storms and clear my skies,
And let me feel thy vital love!

Dear LORD, regard my feeble cry,
I faint and droop till thou appear;
Wilt thou permit thy plant to die?
Must it be winter all the year?

Be still, my soul, and wait his hour,
With humble pray'r, and patient faith;
Till he reveals his gracious pow'r,
Repose on what his promise saith.

He, by whose all-commanding word,[2]
Seasons this changing course maintain;
In ev'ry change a pledge affords,
That none shall seek his face in vain.

---

1 Book III. Hymn 31.
2 Genesis 8:22—While the earth remaineth, seedtime and harvest, and cold and heat, and summer and winter, and day and night shall not cease.

WAITING FOR SPRING.

THO' cloudy skies, and northern blasts,
Retard the gentle spring awhile;
The sun will conqu'ror prove at last,
And nature wear a vernal smile.

The promise, which from age to age,
Has brought the changing seasons round;
Again shall calm the winter's rage,
Perfume the air, and paint the ground.

The virtue of that first command,
I know still does, and will prevail;
That while the earth itself shall stand,
The spring and summer shall not fail.

Such changes are for us decreed;
Believers have their winters too;
But spring shall certainly succeed,
And all their former life renew.

Winter and spring have each their use,
And each, in turn, his people know;
One kills the weeds their hearts produce,
The other makes their graces grow.

Tho' like dead trees awhile they seem,
Yet having life within their root,
The welcome spring's reviving beam
Draws forth their blossoms, leaves, and fruit.

But if the tree indeed be dead,
It feels no change, tho' spring return,
Its leafless, naked, barren head,
Proclaims it only fit to burn.

Dear LORD, afford our souls a spring,
Thou know'st our winter has been long;
Shine forth, and warm our hearts to sing,
And thy rich grace shall be our song.

SPRING.

BLEAK winter is subdu'd at length,
    And forc'd to yield the day;
The sun has waited all his strength,
    And driven him away.

And now long wish'd for spring is come,
    How alter'd is the scene!
The trees and shrubs are drest in bloom,
    The earth array'd in green.

Where'er we tread, beneath our feet
    The clust'ring flowers spring;
The artless birds, in concert sweet,
    Invite our hearts to sing.

But ah! in vain I strive to join,
    Oppress'd with sin and doubt;
I feel 'tis winter still, within,
    Tho' all is spring without.

Oh! would my Saviour from on high,
    Break thro' these clouds and shine!
No creature then, more blest than I,
    No song more loud than mine.

Till then—no softly warbling thrush,
    Nor cowslip's sweet perfume;
Nor beauties of each painted bush,
    Can dissipate my gloom.

To Adam, soon as he transgress'd,
    Thus Eden bloom'd in vain;
Not paradise could give him rest,
    Or sooth his heart-felt pain.

Yet here an emblem I perceive
    Of what the LORD can do;
Dear Saviour, help me to believe
    That I may flourish too.

Thy word can soon my hopes revive,
    Can overcome my foes;
And make my languid graces thrive,
    And blossom like the rose.

SPRING.

PLEASING spring again is here!
Trees and fields in bloom appear;
Hark! the birds, with artless lays,
Warble their Creator's praise!
Where, in winter, all was snow,
Now the flow'rs in clusters grow;
And the corn, in green array,
Promises a harvest-day.

What a change has taken place!
Emblem of the spring of grace;
How the soul, in winter, mourns
Till the LORD, the Sun, returns;
Till the Spirit's gentle rain,
Bids the heart revive again;
Then the stone is turn'd to flesh,
And each grace springs forth afresh.

LORD, afford a spring to me!
Let me feel like what I see;
Ah! my winter has been long,
Chill'd my hopes, and stopp'd my song!
Winter threat'ned to destroy
Faith, and love, and ev'ry joy;
If thy life was in the root,
Still I could not yield thee fruit.

Speak, and by thy gracious voice
Make my drooping soul rejoice;
O beloved Saviour, haste,
Tell me all the storms are past:
On thy garden deign to smile,
Raise the plants, enrich the soil;
Soon thy presence will restore
Life, to what seem'd dead before.

LORD, I long to be at home,
Where these changes never come!
Where the saints no winter fear,
Where 'tis spring throughout the year:
How unlike this state below!
There the flow'rs unwith'ring blow;
There no chilling blasts annoy,
All is love, and bloom, and joy.

SUMMER-STORMS.[1]

THO' the morn may be serene,
Not a threatning cloud be seen;
Who can undertake to say
'Twill be pleasant all the day?
Tempests suddenly may rise,
Darkness overspread the skies;
Light'nings flash, and thunders roar,
Ere a short-liv'd day be o'er.

Often thus, the child of grace,
Enters on his christian race;
Guilt and fear are overborne,
'Tis with him a summer's morn:
While his new-felt joys abound,
All things seem to smile around;
And he hopes it will be fair,
All the day, and all the year.

Should we warn him of a change,
He would think the caution strange;
He no change or trouble fears,
Till the gath'ring storm appears;[2]
Till dark clouds his sun conceal,
Till temptation's pow'r he feel;
Then he trembles, and looks pale,
All his hopes and courage fail.

But the wonder-working LORD
Sooths the tempest by his word;
Stills the thunder, stops the rain,
And his sun breaks forth again:
Soon the cloud again returns,
Now he joys, and now he mourns;
Oft his sky is overcast,
Ere the day of life be past.

Try'd believers too can say,
In the course of one short day,
Tho' the morning has been fair,
Prov'd a golden hour of pray'r:
Sin, and Satan, long ere night,
Have their comforts put to flight;
Ah! what heart-felt peace and joy,
Unexpected storms destroy.

(Continued on the next page.)

_____

1 Book III. Hymn 68.
2 Book I. Hymn 44.

Dearest Saviour, call us soon
To thine high eternal noon;
Never there shall tempest rise
To conceal thee from our eyes:
Satan shall no more deceive,
We no more thy Spirit grieve;
But thro' cloudless, endless days,
Sound, to golden harps, thy praise.

HAY-TIME.

THE grass, and flow'rs, which clothe the field,
 And look so green and gay;
Touch'd by the scythe, defenceless yield,
 And fall, and fade away.

Fit emblem of our mortal state!
 Thus in the scripture glass,
The young, the strong, the wise, the great,
 May see themselves but grass.[1]

Ah! trust not to your fleeting breath,
 Nor call your time your own;
Around you, see, the scythe of death
 Is mowing thousands down.

And you, who hitherto are spar'd,
 Must shortly yield your lives;
Your wisdom is to be prepar'd,
 Before the stroke arrives.

The grass, when dead, revives no more,
 You die, to live again;
But oh! if death should prove the door
 To everlasting pain.

LORD, help us to obey thy call,
 That from our sins set free;
When like the grass our bodies fall,
 Our souls may spring to thee.

---

1 Isaiah 40:7—The grass withereth, the flower fadeth:
because the spirit of the LORD bloweth upon it: surely
the people is grass.

HARVEST.

SEE! the corn again in ear!
How the fields and valleys smile!
Harvest now is drawing near
To repay the farmer's toil:
Gracious LORD, secure the crop,
Satisfy the poor with food;
In thy mercy is our hope,
We have sinn'd but thou art good.

While I view the plenteous grain
As it ripens on the stalk;
May I not instruction gain,
Helpful, to my daily walk?
All this plenty of the field
Was produc'd from foreign seeds;
For the earth itself would yield
Only crops of useless weeds.

THO', when newly sown, it lay
Hid awhile beneath the ground,
(Some might think it thrown away)
Now a large increase is found:
Tho' conceal'd, it was not lost,
Tho' it dy'd, it lives again;
Eastern storms, and nipping frosts
Have oppos'd its growth in vain.

Let the praise be all the LORD's,
As the benefit is ours!
He, in seasons, still affords
Kindly heat, and gentle show'rs:
By his care the produce thrives
Waving o'er the furrow'd lands;
And when harvest-time arrives,
Ready for the reaper stands.

Thus in barren hearts he sows
Precious seeds of heav'nly joy;[1]
Sin, and hell, in vain oppose,
None can grace's crop destroy:
Threat'ned oft, yet still it blooms,
After many changes past,
Death, the reaper, when he comes,
Finds it fully ripe at last.

---

1 Hosea 14:7—They that dwell under his shadow shall
  return; they shall revive as the corn, and grow as the

(Footnote continued in the next column.)

PRAISE FOR THE INCARNATION.

SWEETER sounds than music knows
    Charm me, in EMMANUEL's name;
All her hopes my spirit owes
    To his birth, and cross, and shame.

When he came the angels sung
    "Glory be to GOD on high;"
LORD, unloose my stamm'ring tongue,
    Who should louder sing than I.

Did the LORD a man become
    That he might the law fulfil,
Bleed and suffer in my room,
    And canst thou, my tongue, be still.

No, I must my praises bring,
    Tho' they worthless are, and weak;
For should I refuse to sing
    Sure the very stones would speak.

O my Saviour, Shield, and Sun,
    Shepherd, Brother, Husband, Friend,
Ev'ry precious name in one,
    I will love thee without end.

---

vine: the scent thereof shall be as the wine of Lebanon.
Mark 4:26–29—And he said, So is the kingdom of
God, as if a man should cast seed into the ground;
And should sleep, and rise night and day, and the
seed should spring and grow up, he knoweth not how.
For the earth bringeth forth fruit of herself; first the
blade, then the ear, after that the full corn in the ear.
But when the fruit is brought forth, immediately he
putteth in the sickle, because the harvest is come.

MAN HONOURED ABOVE ANGELS.

Now let us join with hearts and tongues,
And emulate the angels' songs;
Yea, sinners may address their King
In songs that angels cannot sing.

They praise the Lamb who once was slain,
But we can add a higher strain;[1]
Not only say, "He suffer'd thus,"
But, that he suffer'd all for *us*.

When angels by transgression fell,
Justice consign'd them all to hell;
But mercy form'd a wond'rous plan,
To save, and honor fallen man.

Jesus, who pass'd the angels by,[2]
Assum'd our flesh to bleed and die;
And still he makes it his abode,
As man, he fills the throne of God.

Our next of kin, our Brother now,
Is he to whom the angels bow;
They join with us to praise his name,
But *we* the nearest interest claim.

But ah! how faint our praises rise!
Sure, 'tis the wonder of the skies;
That we, who share his richest love,
So cold and unconcern'd should prove.

Oh glorious hour it comes with speed!
When we from sin and darkness freed,
Shall see the God who dy'd for man,
And praise him more than angels can.[3]

---

1 Revelation 5:11–13—And I beheld, and I heard the
voice of many angels round about the throne and the
beasts and the elders: and the number of them was ten
thousand times ten thousand, and thousands of thou-
sands; Saying with a loud voice, Worthy is the Lamb
that was slain to receive power, and riches, and wis-
dom, and strength, and honour, and glory, and bless-
ing. And every creature which is in heaven, and on the
earth, and under the earth, and such as are in the sea,
and all that are in them, heard I saying, Blessing, and
honour, and glory, and power, be unto him that sitteth
upon the throne, and unto the Lamb for ever and ever.
    (The entire chapter of Revelation 5 was referenced.)
2 Hebrews 2:16—For verily he took not on him the
nature of angels; but he took on him the seed of
Abraham.
3 Book III. Hymn 88.

SATURDAY EVENING.

Safely thro' another week,
   God has brought us on our way;
Let us now a blessing seek
   On th' approaching sabbath-day:
     Day, of all the week, the best;
     Emblem of eternal rest!

Mercies, multiply'd each hour,
   Thro' the week our praise demand;
Guarded by almighty pow'r,
   Fed and guided by his hand:
     Tho' ungrateful we have been,
     Only made returns of sin.

While we pray for pard'ning grace,
   Thro' the dear Redeemer's name;
Shew thy reconciled face,
   Shine away our sin and shame:
     From our worldly cares set free,
     May we rest, this night, with thee.

When the morn shall bid us rise,
   May we feel thy presence near;
May thy glory meet our eyes,
   When we in thy house appear!
     There afford us, Lord, a taste
     Of our everlasting feast.

May thy gospel's joyful sound
   Conquer sinners, comfort saints;
Make the fruits of grace abound,
   Bring relief for all complaints:
     Thus may all our sabbaths prove
     Till we join the church above!

EBENEZER.[1]

THE LORD, our salvation and light,
The guide and the strength of our days;
Has brought us together, to-night,
A new Ebenezer to raise:
The year, we have now passed thro',
His goodness with blessings has crown'd;
Each morning his mercies were new,
Then let our thanksgivings abound.

Encompass'd with dangers and snares,
Temptations, and fears, and complaints;
His ear he inclin'd to our pray'rs,
His hand open'd wide to our wants:
We never besought him in vain,
When burden'd with sorrow or sin,
He help'd us again and again,
Or where, before now, had we been?

His gospel, throughout the long year,
From sabbath to sabbath he gave;
How oft has he met with us here,
And shewn himself mighty to save?
His candlestic has been remov'd
From churches once privileg'd thus;
But, tho' we unworthy have prov'd,
It still is continu'd to us.

For so many mercies receiv'd,
Alass! what returns have we made?
His Spirit we often have griev'd,
And evil, for good, have repaid:
How well it becomes us to cry,
"Oh, who is a GOD like to thee?
Who passest iniquities by,
And plungest them deep in the sea!"

To JESUS, who sits on the throne,
Our best hallelujahs we bring;
To thee it is owing alone,
That we are permitted to sing:
Assist us, we pray, to lament
The sins of the year that is past;
And grant that the next may be spent
Far more to thy praise than the last.

EBENEZER.

LET hearts and tongues unite
And loud thanksgivings raise;
'Tis duty, mingled with delight,
The Saviour's name to praise.

To him we owe our breath,
He took us from the womb,
Which else had shut us up in death,
And prov'd an early tomb.

When on the breast we hung
Our help was in the LORD;
'Twas he first taught our infant tongue
To form the lisping word.

When in our blood we lay
He would not let us die;
Because his love had fix'd a day
To bring salvation nigh.

In childhood and in youth
His eye was on us still;
Tho' strangers to his love and truth,
And prone to cross his will.

And since his name we knew,
How gracious has he been!
What dangers has he led us thro',
What mercies have we seen!

Now thro' another year
Supported by his care;
We raise our Ebenezer here,
"The LORD has help'd thus far."

Our lot in future years
Unable to foresee;
He, kindly to prevent our fears,
Says, "Leave it all to me."

Yea, LORD, we wish to cast
Our cares upon thy breast!
Help us to praise thee for the past,
And trust thee for the rest.

---

1 1 Samuel 7:12—Then Samuel took a stone, and set it
between Mizpeh and Shen, and called the name of it
Ebenezer, saying, Hitherto hath the LORD helped us.

ON OPENING A PLACE FOR SOCIAL PRAYER.

O LORD, our languid souls inspire,
  For here, we trust, thou art!
Send down a coal of heav'nly fire,
  To warm each waiting heart.

Dear Shepherd of thy people, hear,
  Thy presence now display;
As thou hast giv'n a place for pray'r,
  So give us hearts to pray.

Shew us some token of thy love,
  Our fainting hope to raise;
And pour thy blessings from above,
  That we may render praise.

Within these walls let holy peace,
  And love, and concord dwell;
Here give the troubled conscience ease,
  The wounded spirit heal.

The feeling heart, the melting eye,
  The humble mind bestow;
And shine upon us from on high,
  To make our graces grow!

May we in faith receive thy word,
  In faith present our pray'rs;
And, in the presence of our LORD,
  Unbosom all our cares.

And may the gospel's joyful sound
  Enforc'd by mighty grace,
Awaken many sinners round,
  To come and fill the place.

THE LORD'S DAY.

How welcome to the saints, when press'd
With six days noise, and care, and toil,
Is the returning day of rest,
Which hides them from the world awhile?

Now, from the throng withdrawn away,
They seem to breathe a diff'rent air;
Compos'd and soft'ned by the day,
All things another aspect wear.

How happy if their lot is cast,
Where stately the gospel sounds!
The word is honey to their taste,
Renews their strength, and heals their
    wounds!

Tho' pinch'd with poverty at home,
With sharp afflictions daily fed;
It makes amends, if they can come
To GOD's own house for heav'nly bread!

With joy they hasten to the place,
Where they their Saviour oft have met;
And while they feast upon his grace,
Their burdens and their griefs forget.

This favor'd lot, my friends, is ours,
May we the privilege improve;
And find these consecrated hours,
Sweet earnests of the joys above!

We thank thee for thy day, O LORD,
Here we thy promis'd presence seek;
Open thine hand, with blessings stor'd,
And give us Manna for the week.

GOSPEL PRIVILEGES.

O HAPPY they who know the LORD,
 With whom he deigns to dwell!
He feeds and cheers them by his word,
 His arm supports them well.

To them, in each distressing hour,
 His throne of grace is near;
And when they plead his love and pow'r,
 He stands engag'd to hear.

He help'd his saints in ancient days
 Who trusted in his name;
And we can witness, to his praise,
 His love is still the same.

Wand'ring in sin, our souls he found,
 And bid us seek his face;
Gave us to hear the gospel sound,
 And taste the gospel grace.

Oft in his house his glory shines
 Before our wond'ring eyes;
We wish not, then, for golden mines,
 Or ought beneath the skies.

His presence sweetens all our cares,
 And makes our burdens light;
A word from him dispels our fears,
 And gilds the gloom of night.

LORD, we expect to suffer here,
 Nor would we dare repine;
But give us, still, to find thee near;
 And own us, still, for thine.

Let us enjoy, and highly prize
 These tokens of thy love;
Till thou shalt bid our spirits rise,
 To worship thee above.

GOSPEL PRIVILEGES.

HAPPY are they, to whom the LORD
 His gracious name makes known!
And by his Spirit, and his word,
 Adopts them for his own!

He calls them to his mercy-seat,
 And hears their humble pray'r;
And when within his house they meet,
 They find his presence near.

The force of their united cries
 No pow'r can long withstand;
For JESUS helps them from the skies,
 By his almighty hand.

Then mountains sink at once to plains,
 And light from darkness springs;
Each seeming loss improves their gains,
 Each trouble comfort brings.

Tho' men despise them, or revile,
 They count the trial small;
Whoever frowns, if JESUS smile,
 It makes amends for all.

Tho' meanly clad, and coarsely fed,
 And, like their Saviour, poor;
They would not change their gospel bread
 For all the worldling's store.

When chear'd with faith's sublimer joys,
 They mount on eagle's wings;
They can disdain, as children's toys,
 The pride and pomp of kings.

Dear LORD, assist our souls to pay
 The debt of praise we owe;
That we enjoy a gospel day,
 And heav'n begun below.

PRAISE FOR THE CONTINUANCE OF THE GOSPEL.[1]

ONCE, while we aim'd at Zion's songs,
A sudden mourning check'd our tongues!
Then we were call'd to sow in tears,
The seeds of joy for future years.

Oft as that memorable hour
The changing year brings round again;
We meet to praise the love and pow'r
Which heard our cries, and eas'd our pain.

Come, ye who trembled for the ark,
Unite in praise for answer'd pray'r!
Did not the LORD our sorrows mark?
Did not our sighing reach his ear?

Then smaller griefs were laid aside,
And all our cares summ'd up in one;
"Let us but have thy word, we cry'd,
In other things, thy will be done."

Since he has granted our request,
And we still hear the gospel voice;
Altho' by many trials prest,
In this we can, and will rejoice.

Tho' to our lot temptations fall,
Tho' pain and want, and cares annoy;
The precious gospel sweetens all,
And yields us med'cine, food, and joy.

A FAMINE OF THE WORD.

GLADNESS was spread thro' Israel's host
     When first they Manna view'd;
They labour'd who should gather most,
     And thought it pleasant food.

But when they had it long enjoy'd
     From day to day, the same;
Their hearts were by the plenty cloy'd,
     Altho' from heav'n it came.

Thus gospel bread at first is priz'd,
     And makes a people glad;
But afterwards too much despis'd,
     When easy to be had.

But should the LORD, displeas'd, withhold
     The bread his mercy sends;
To have our houses fill'd with gold
     Would make but poor amends.

How tedious would the week appear,
     How dull the sabbath prove?
Could we no longer meet to hear
     The precious truths we love!

How would believing parents bear
     To leave their heedless youth,
Expos'd to ev'ry fatal snare,
     Without the light of truth?

The gospel, and a praying few
     Our bulwark long have prov'd;
But OLNEY sure the day will rue
     When these shall be remov'd.

Then sin, in this once favour'd town,
     Will triumph unrestrain'd;
And wrath and vengeance hasten down,
     No more by pray'r detain'd.

Preserve us from this judgment, LORD,
     For JESUS' sake we plead;
A famine of the gospel word
     Would be a stroke indeed!

---

1 Wherever a separation is threatened between a
  minister and people who dearly love each other, this
  hymn may be as seasonable as it was once in Olney.

PRAYER FOR MINISTERS.

CHIEF Shepherd of thy chosen sheep,
   From death and sin set free;
May ev'ry under-shepherd keep
   His eye, intent on thee!

With plenteous grace their hearts prepare,
   To execute thy will;
Compassion, patience, love and care,
   And faithfulness and skill.

Enflame their minds with holy zeal
   Their flocks to feed and teach;
And let them live, and let them feel
   The sacred truths they preach.

Oh, never let the sheep complain
   That toys, which fools amuse;
Ambition, pleasure, praise or gain,
   Debase the shepherd's views.

He, that for these, forbears to feed
   The souls whom JESUS loves;
Whate'er he may profess, or plead,
   An idol-shepherd proves.[1]

The sword of GOD shall break his arm,
   A blast shall blind his eye;
His word shall have no pow'r to warm,
   His gifts shall all grow dry.

O LORD, avert this heavy woe,
   Let all thy shepherds say!
And grace, and strength, on each bestow,
   To labor while 'tis day.

---

1 Zechariah 11:17—Woe to the idol shepherd that
  leaveth the flock! the sword shall be upon his arm,
  and upon his right eye: his arm shall be clean dried
  up, and his right eye shall be utterly darkened.

PRAYER FOR A REVIVAL.

SAVIOUR, visit thy plantation,
   Grant us, LORD, a gracious rain!
All will come to desolation,
   Unless thou return again:
Keep no longer at a distance,
   Shine upon us from on high;
Lest, for want of thine assistance;
   Ev'ry plant would droop and die.

Surely, once thy garden flourish'd,
   Ev'ry part look'd gay and green;
Then thy word our spirits nourish'd,
   Happy seasons we have seen!
But a drought has since succeeded,
   And a sad decline we see;
LORD, thy help is greatly needed,
   Help can only come from thee.

Where are those we counted leaders,
   Fill'd with zeal, and love, and truth?
Old professors, tall as cedars,
   Bright examples to our youth!
Some, in whom we once delighted,
   We shall meet no more below;
Some, alass! we fear are blighted,
   Scarce a single leaf they show.

Younger plants—the sight how pleasant,
   Cover'd thick with blossoms stood;
But they cause us grief at present,
   Frosts have nipp'd them in the bud!
Dearest Saviour, hasten hither,
   Thou canst make them bloom again;
Oh, permit them not to wither,
   Let not all our hopes be vain!

Let our mutual love be fervent,
   Make us prevalent in pray'rs;
Let each one esteem'd thy servant,
   Shun the world's bewitching snares:
Break the tempter's fatal power,
   Turn the stony heart to flesh;
And begin, from this good hour,
   To revive thy work afresh.

HOPING FOR A REVIVAL.

My harp untun'd, and laid aside,
(To cheerful hours the harp belongs)
My cruel foes, insulting cry'd,
"Come, sing us one of Zion's songs."

Alass! when sinners, blindly bold,
At Zion scoff, and Zion's King;
When zeal declines, and love grows cold,
Is this a day for me to sing?

Time was, whene'er the saints I met,
With joy and praise my bosom glow'd;
But now, like Eli, sad I sit,
And tremble for the ark of GOD.

While thus to grief my soul gave way,
To see the work of GOD decline;
Methought I heard my Saviour say,
"Dismiss thy fears, the ark is mine.

Tho' for a time I hide my face,
Rely upon my love and pow'r;
Still wrestle at a throne of grace,
And wait for a reviving hour.

Take down thy long neglected harp,
I've seen thy tears, and heard thy pray'r;
The winter season has been sharp,
But spring shall all its wastes repair."

LORD, I obey, my hopes revive,
Come join with me, ye saints, and sing;
Our foes in vain against us strive;
For GOD will help and healing bring.

CHRIST CRUCIFIED.

WHEN on the cross, my LORD I see
Bleeding to death, for wretched me;
Satan and sin no more can move,
For I am all transform'd to love.

His thorns, and nails, pierce thro' my heart,
In ev'ry grone I bear a part;
I view his wounds with streaming eyes,
But see! he bows his head and dies!

Come, sinners, view the Lamb of GOD,
Wounded and dead, and bath'd in blood!
Behold his side, and venture near,
The well of endless life is here.

Here I forget my cares and pains;
I drink, yet still my thirst remains;
Only the fountain-head above,
Can satisfy the thirst of love.

Oh, that I thus could always feel!
LORD, more and more thy love reveal!
Then my glad tongue shall loud proclaim
The grace and glory of thy name.

Thy name dispels my guilt and fear,
Revives my heart, and charms my ear;
Affords a balm for ev'ry wound,
And Satan trembles at the sound.

IT IS GOOD TO BE HERE.

LET me dwell on Golgotha,
Weep and love my life away!
While I see him on the tree
Weep and bleed, and die for me!

That dear blood, for sinners spilt,
Shews my sin in all its guilt:
Ah, my soul, he bore thy load,
Thou hast slain the Lamb of GOD.

Hark! his dying words; "Forgive,
Father, let the sinner live;
Sinner, wipe thy tears away,
I thy ransom freely pay."

While I hear this grace reveal'd,
And obtain a pardon seal'd;
All my soft affections move,
Waken'd by the force of love.

Farewel world, thy gold is dross,
Now I see the bleeding cross;
JESUS dy'd to set me free
From the law, and sin, and thee!

He has dearly bought my soul
LORD, accept, and claim the whole!
To thy will I all resign,
Now, no more my own, but thine.

LOOKING AT THE CROSS.

IN evil long I took delight,
    Unaw'd by shame or fear;
Till a new object struck my sight,
    And stopp'd my wild career.

I saw one hanging on a tree,
    In agonies and blood;
Who fix'd his languid eyes on me,
    As near his cross I stood.

Sure, never till my latest breath,
    Can I forget that look;
It seem'd to charge me with his death,
    Tho' not a word he spoke.

My conscience felt, and own'd the guilt,
    And plung'd me in despair;
I saw my sins his blood had spilt,
    And help'd to nail him there.

Alass! I knew not what I did,
    But now my tears are vain;
Where shall my trembling soul be hid?
    For I the LORD have slain.

A second look he gave, which said,
    "I freely all forgive;
This blood is for thy ransom paid,
    I die, that thou may'st live."

Thus, while his death my sin displays,
    In all its blackest hue;
(Such is the mystery of grace)
    It seals my pardon too.

With pleasing grief and mournful joy,
    My spirit now is fill'd;
That I should such a life destroy,
    Yet live by him I kill'd.

SUPPLIES IN THE WILDERNESS.

WHEN Israel by divine command
    The pathless desart trod;
They found, tho' 'twas a barren land,
    A sure resource in GOD.

A cloudy pillar mark'd their road,
    And screen'd them from the heat;
From the hard rocks their water flow'd,
    And Manna was their meat.

Like them we have a rest in view,
    Secure from adverse pow'rs;
Like them we pass a desart too,
    But Israel's GOD is ours.

Yes, in this barren wilderness
    He is to us the same;
By his appointed means of grace,
    As once he was to them.

His word a light before us spreads
    By which our path we see;
His love a banner o'er our heads,
    From harm preserves us free.

LORD, 'tis enough; I ask no more,
    These blessings are divine;
I envy not the worldling's store,
    If CHRIST and heav'n are mine.

COMMUNION WITH THE SAINTS IN GLORY.

REFRESHED by the bread and wine,
    The pledges of our Saviour's love;
Now let our hearts and voices join
    In songs of praise with those above.

Do they sing, "Worthy is the Lamb?"
    Altho' we cannot reach their strains,
Yet we, thro' grace, can sing the same,
    For us he dy'd, for us he reigns.

If they behold him face to face,
    While we a glimpse can only see;
Yet equal debtors to his grace,
    As safe and as belov'd are we.

They had, like us a suff'ring time,
    Our cares and fears, and griefs they knew;
But they have conquer'd all thro' him,
    And we, ere long, shall conquer too.

Tho' all the songs of saints in light,
    Are far beneath his matchless worth;
His grace is such, he will not slight
    The poor attempts of worms on earth.

POWER OF PRAYER.

In themselves, as weak as worms,
How can poor believers stand;
When temptations, foes, and storms,
Press them close on ev'ry hand?

Weak, indeed, they feel they are,
But they know the throne of grace;
And the GOD, who answers pray'r,
Helps them when they seek his face.

Tho' the LORD awhile delay,
Succour they at length obtain;
He who taught their hearts to pray,
Will not let them cry in vain.

Wrestling pray'r can wonders do,
Bring relief in deepest straits;
Pray'r can force a passage thro'
Iron bars and brazen gates.

Hezekiah on his knees
Proud Assyria's host subdu'd;
And when smitten with disease,
Had his life by pray'r renew'd.

Peter, though confin'd and chain'd,
Pray'r prevail'd and brought him out;
When Elijah pray'd, it rain'd,
After three long years of drought.

We can likewise witness bear,
That the LORD is still the same;
Tho' we fear'd he would not hear,
Suddenly deliverance came.

For the wonders he has wrought,
Let us now our praises give;
And, by sweet experience taught,
Call upon him while we live.

THE WORD MORE PRECIOUS THAN GOLD.

PRECIOUS Bible! what a treasure
Does the word of GOD afford?
All I want for life or pleasure,
FOOD and MED'CINE, SHIELD and SWORD:
 Let the world account me poor,
 Having this I need no more.

FOOD to which the world's a stranger,
Here my hungry soul enjoys;
Of excess there is no danger,
Tho' it fills, it never cloys:
 On a dying CHRIST I feed,
 He is meat and drink indeed!

When my faith is faint and sickly,
Or when Satan wounds my mind,
Cordials, to revive me quickly,
Healing MED'CINES here I find:
 To the promises I flee,
 Each affords a remedy.

In the hour of dark temptation
Satan cannot make me yield;
For the word of consolation
Is to me a mighty SHIELD:
 While the scripture-truths are sure,
 From his malice I'm secure.

Vain his threats to overcome me,
When I take the Spirits' SWORD;
Then with ease I drive him from me,
Satan trembles at the word:
 'Tis a sword for conquest made,
 Keen the edge, and strong the blade.

Shall I envy then the miser
Doating on his golden store?
Sure I am, or should be, wiser,
I am Rich, 'tis he is Poor:
 JESUS gives me in his word,
 FOOD and MED'CINE, SHIELD and SWORD.

ON THE COMMENCEMENT OF HOSTILITIES IN AMERICA.

THE gath'ring clouds, with aspect dark,
   A rising storm presage;
Oh! to be hid within the ark,
   And shelter'd from its rage!

See the commission'd angel frown![1]
   That vial in his hand,
Fill'd with fierce wrath, is pouring down
   Upon our guilty land!

Ye saints, unite in wrestling pray'r,
   If yet there may be hope;
Who knows but Mercy yet may spare,
   And bid the angel stop?[2]

Already is the plague begun,[3]
   And fir'd with hostile rage;
Brethren, by blood and int'rest one,
   With brethren now engage.

Peace spreads her wings, prepar'd for flight,
   And war, with flaming sword,
And hasty strides draws nigh, to fight
   The battles of the LORD.

The first alarm, alas, how few,
   While distant, seem to hear!
But they will hear, and tremble too,
   When GOD shall send it near.

So thunder, o'er the distant hills,
   Gives but a murm'ring sound;
But as the tempest spreads, it fills,
   And makes the welkin[4] round.

(Continued in the next column.)

May we, at least, with one consent,
   Fall low before the throne;
With tears the nation's sins lament,
   The churches, and our own.

The humble souls who mourn and pray,
   The LORD approves and knows;
His mark secures them in the day
   When vengeance strikes his foes.

---

1 Revelation 16:1—And I heard a great voice out of the temple saying to the seven angels, Go your ways, and pour out the vials of the wrath of God upon the earth.

2 2 Samuel 24:16—And when the angel stretched out his hand upon Jerusalem to destroy it, the LORD repented him of the evil, and said to the angel that destroyed the people, It is enough: stay now thine hand. And the angel of the LORD was by the threshingplace of Araunah the Jebusite.

3 Numbers 16:46—And Moses said unto Aaron, Take a censer, and put fire therein from off the altar, and put on incense, and go quickly unto the congregation, and make an atonement for them: for there is wrath gone out from the LORD; the plague is begun.

4 Firmament, or atmosphere.

CONFESSION AND PRAYER.

December 13, 1776.

OH, may the pow'r which melts the rock
Be felt by all assembled here!
Or else our service will but mock
The GOD whom we profess to fear!

LORD, while thy judgments shake the land,
Thy peoples eyes are fix'd on thee!
We own thy just, uplifted hand,
Which thousands cannot, will not see.

How long hast thou bestow'd thy care
On this indulg'd ungrateful spot?
While other nations, far and near,
Have envy'd and admir'd our lot.

Here peace and liberty have dwelt,
The glorious gospel brightly shone;
And oft our enemies have felt
That GOD has made our cause his own.

But ah! both heav'n and earth have heard
Our vile requital of his love!
We, whom like children he has rear'd,
Rebels against his goodness prove.[1]

His grace despis'd, his pow'r defy'd,
And legions of the blackest crimes,
Profaneness, riot, lust, and pride,
Are signs that mark the present times.

The LORD, displeas'd, has rais'd his rod;
Ah, where are now the faithful few
Who tremble for the ark of GOD,
And know what Israel ought to do?[2]

LORD, hear thy people ev'ry where,
Who meet to mourn, confess and pray;
The nation and thy churches spare,
And let thy wrath be turn'd away.

MOSES AND AMALEK.[3]

February 27, 1778.

WHILE Joshua led the armed bands
    Of Israel forth to war;
Moses apart with lifted hands
    Engag'd in humble pray'r.

The armed bands had quickly fail'd,
    And perish'd in the fight;
If Moses' pray'r had not prevail'd
    To put the foes to flight.

When Moses' hands thro' weakness dropp'd,
    The warriors fainted too;
Israel's success at once was stopp'd,
    And Am'lek bolder grew.

A people, always prone to boast,
    Were taught by this suspense,
That not a num'rous armed host,
    But GOD was their defence.

We now of fleets and armies vaunt,
    And ships and men prepare;
But men like Moses most we want,
    To save the state by pray'r.

Yet, LORD, we hope thou hast prepar'd
    A hidden few to-day;
(The nation's secret strength and guard)
    To weep, and mourn, and pray.

O hear their pray'rs and grant us aid,
    Bid war and discord cease;
Heal the sad breach which sin has made,
    And bless us all with peace.

---

1 Isaiah 1:2—Hear, O heavens, and give ear, O earth: for the LORD hath spoken, I have nourished and brought up children, and they have rebelled against me.

2 1 Chronicles 12:32—And of the children of Issachar, which were men that had understanding of the times, to know what Israel ought to do; the heads of them were two hundred; and all their brethren were at their commandment.

---

3 Exodus 17:9—And Moses said unto Joshua, Choose us out men, and go out, fight with Amalek: to morrow I will stand on the top of the hill with the rod of God in mine hand.

THE HIDING PLACE.

February 10, 1779.

SEE the gloomy gath'ring cloud
Hanging o'er a sinful land!
Sure the LORD proclaims aloud,
Times of trouble are at hand:
Happy they, who love his name!
They shall always find him near;
Tho' the earth were wrapp'd in flame,
They have no just cause for fear.

Hark! his voice in accents mild,
(Oh, how comforting and sweet!)
Speaks to ev'ry humble child,
Pointing out a sure retreat!
Come, and in my chambers hide,[1]
To my saints of old well known;
There you safely may abide,
Till the storm be overblown.

You have only to repose
On my wisdom, love, and care;
Where my wrath consumes my foes,
Mercy shall my children spare:
While *they* perish in the flood,
You that bear my holy mark,[2]
Sprinkled with atoning blood,
Shall be safe within the ark.

Sinners, see the ark prepar'd!
Haste to enter while there's room;
Tho' the LORD his arm has bar'd,
Mercy still retards your doom:
Seek him while there yet is hope,
Ere the day of grace be past;
Lest in wrath he give you up,
And this call should prove your last.

ON THE EARTHQUAKE.

September 8, 1775.

ALTHO' on massy pillars built,
    The earth has lately shook;
It trembled under Britain's guilt,
    Before its Maker's look.

Swift as the shock amazement spreads,
    And sinners tremble too;
What flight can screen their guilty heads,
    If earth itself pursue.

But mercy spar'd us while it warn'd,
    The shock is felt no more;
And mercy, now, alass! is scorn'd
    By sinners, as before.

But if these warnings prove in vain,
    Say, sinner, canst thou tell,
How soon the earth may quake again,
    And open wide to hell.

Repent before the Judge draws nigh;
    Or else when he comes down,
Thou wilt in vain for earthquakes cry,
    To hide thee from his frown.[3]

But happy they who love the LORD
    And his salvation know;
The hope that's founded on his word,
    No change can overthrow.

Should the deep-rooted hills be hurl'd,
    And plung'd beneath the seas;
And strong convulsions shake the world,
    Your hearts may rest in peace.

JESUS, your Shepherd, LORD, and Chief,
    Shall shelter you from ill;
And not a worm or shaking leaf
    Can move, but at his will.

---

1 Isaiah 26:20—Come, my people, enter thou into thy chambers, and shut thy doors about thee: hide thyself as it were for a little moment, until the indignation be overpast.

2 Ezekiel 9:4—And the LORD said unto him, Go through the midst of the city, through the midst of Jerusalem, and set a mark upon the foreheads of the men that sigh and that cry for all the abominations that be done in the midst thereof.

---

3 Revelation 6:16—And said to the mountains and rocks, Fall on us, and hide us from the face of him that sitteth on the throne, and from the wrath of the Lamb.

ON THE FIRE AT OLNEY.

September 22, 1777.

WEARIED by day with toils and cares,
How welcome is the peaceful night!
Sweet sleep our wasted strength repairs,
And fits us for returning light.

Yet when our eyes in sleep are clos'd,
Our rest may break ere well begun;
To dangers ev'ry hour expos'd
We neither can foresee nor shun.

'Tis of the LORD that we can sleep
A single night without alarms;
His eye alone our lives can keep
Secure, amidst a thousand harms.

For months and years of safety past,
Ungrateful, we, alass! have been;
Tho' patient long, he spoke at last,
And bid the fire rebuke our sin.

The shout of fire! a dreadful cry,
Imprest each heart with deep dismay;
While the fierce blaze and red'ning sky,
Made midnight wear the face of day.

The throng and terror who can speak?
The various sounds that fill'd the air!
The infant's wail, the mother's shriek,
The voice of blasphemy and pray'r!

But pray'r prevail'd, and sav'd the town;
The few, who lov'd the Saviour's name,
Were hear'd, and mercy hasted down
To change the wind, and stop the flame.

Oh, may that night be ne'er forgot!
LORD, still increase thy praying few!
Were OLNEY left without a Lot,
Ruin, like Sodom's, would ensue.

A WELCOME TO CHRISTIAN FRIENDS.

KINDRED in CHRIST, for his dear sake,
A hearty welcome here receive;
May we together now partake
The joys which only he can give!

To you and us by grace 'tis giv'n,
To know the Saviour's precious name;
And shortly we shall meet in heav'n,
Our hope, our way, our end, the same.

May he, by whose kind care we meet,
Send his good Spirit from above,
Make our communications sweet,
And cause our hearts to burn with love!

Forgotten be each worldly theme,
When christians see each other thus;
We only wish to speak of him,
Who liv'd, and dy'd, and reigns for us.

We'll talk of all he did and said,
And suffer'd for us here below;
The path he mark'd for us to tread,
And what he's doing for us now.

Thus, as the moments pass away,
We'll love, and wonder, and adore;
And hasten on the glorious day,
When we shall meet to part no more.

AT PARTING.

As the sun's enliv'ning eye
Shines on ev'ry place the same;
So the LORD is always nigh
To the souls that love his name.

When they move at duty's call,
He is with them by the way;
He is ever with them all,
Those who go, and those who stay.

From his holy mercy-seat
Nothing can their souls confine;
Still in spirit they may meet,
And in sweet communion join.

For a season call'd to part,
Let us then ourselves commend
To the gracious eye and heart,
Of our ever-present Friend.

JESUS, hear our humble pray'r!
Tender Shepherd of thy sheep!
Let thy mercy and thy care
All our souls in safety keep.

In thy strength may we be strong,
Sweeten ev'ry cross and pain;
Give us, if we live, ere long
Here to meet in peace again.

Then, if thou thy help afford,
Ebenezers shall be rear'd;
And our souls shall praise the LORD
Who our poor petitions heard.

ON THE DEATH OF A BELIEVER.

IN vain my fancy strives to paint
    The moment after death;
The glories that surround the saint,
    When yielding up its breath.

One gentle sigh their fetters breaks,
    We scarce can say, "They're gone!"
Before the willing spirit takes
    Her mansion near the throne.

Faith strives, but all its efforts fail,
    To trace her in her flight:
No eye can pierce within the vail
    Which hides that world of light.

Thus much (and this is all) we know,
    They are completely blest;
Have done with sin, and care, and woe,
    And with their Saviour rest.

On harps of gold they praise his name,
    His face they always view;
Then let us follow'rs be of them,
    That we may praise him too.

Their faith and patience, love and zeal,
    Should make their mem'ry dear;
And, LORD, do thou the pray'rs fulfil,
    They offer'd for us here!

While they have gain'd, we losers are,
    We miss them day by day;
But thou canst ev'ry breach repair,
    And wipe our tears away.

We pray, as in Elisha's case,
    When great Elijah went,
May double portions of thy grace,
    To us who stay, be sent.

THE TOLLING BELL.

OFT as the bell, with solemn toll,
Speaks the departure of a soul;
Let each one ask himself; "Am I
Prepar'd, should I be call'd to die?"

Only this frail and fleeting breath
Preserves me from the jaws of death;
Soon as it fails, at once I'm gone,
And plung'd into a world unknown.

Then, leaving all I lov'd below,
To GOD's tribunal I must go;
Must hear the Judge pronounce my fate,
And fix my everlasting state.

But could I bear to hear him say,
"Depart, accursed, far away!
With Satan, in the lowest hell,
Thou art for ever doom'd to dwell."

LORD JESUS! help me now to flee,
And seek my hope alone in thee;
Apply thy blood, thy Spirit give,
Subdue my sin, and in me live.

Then, when the solemn bell I hear,
If sav'd from guilt, I need not fear;
Nor would the thought distressing be,
Perhaps it next may toll for me.

Rather, my spirit would rejoice,
And long, and wish, to hear thy voice;
Glad when it bids me earth resign,
Secure of heav'n, if thou art mine.

HOPE BEYOND THE GRAVE.

MY soul, this curious house of clay,
    Thy present frail abode;
Must quickly fall to worms a prey,
    And thou return to GOD.

Canst thou, by faith, survey with joy
    The change, before it come?
And say, "Let death this house destroy,
    I have a heav'nly home!"

The Saviour, whom I then shall see
    With new admiring eyes,
Already has prepar'd for me,
    A mansion in the skies.[1]

I feel this mud-wall'd cottage shake,
    And long to see it fall;
That I my willing flight may take
    To him who is my all.

Burden'd and groning, then no more,
    My rescu'd soul shall sing,
As up the shining path I soar,
    "Death, thou hast lost thy sting."

Dear Saviour, help us now to seek,
    And know thy grace's power;
That we may all this language speak,
    Before the dying hour.

---

1 2 Corinthians 5:1—For we know that if our earthly house of this tabernacle were dissolved, we have a building of God, an house not made with hands, eternal in the heavens.

THERE THE WEARY ARE AT REST.

COURAGE, my soul! behold the prize
   The Saviour's love provides;
Eternal life beyond the skies,
   For all whom here he guides.

The wicked cease from troubling there,
   The weary are at rest;[1]
Sorrow and sin, and pain and care,
   No more approach the blest.

A wicked world and wicked heart,
   With Satan now are join'd;
Each acts a too successful part
   In harassing my mind.

In conflict with this threefold troop,
   How weary, LORD, am I?
Did not thy promise bear me up,
   My soul must faint and die.

But fighting in my Saviour's strength,
   Tho' mighty are my foes,
I shall a conqu'ror be at length,
   O'er all that can oppose.

Then why, my soul, complain or fear?
   The crown of glory see!
The more I toil and suffer here,
   The sweeter rest will be.

THE DAY OF JUDGMENT.

DAY of judgment, day of wonders!
Hark! the trumpet's awful sound,
Louder than a thousand thunders,
Shakes the vast creation round!
   How the summons will the sinner's heart
     confound!

See the Judge our nature wearing,
Clothed in majesty divine!
You who long for his appearing,
Then shall say, "This GOD is mine!"
   Gracious Saviour, own me in that day for
     thine!

At his call the dead awaken,
Rise to life from earth and sea;
All the pow'rs of nature shaken
By his look, prepares to flee:
   Careless sinner, what will then become of
     thee!

Horrors, past imagination,
Will surprize your trembling heart,
When you hear your condemnation,
"Hence, accursed wretch, depart!
   Thou, with Satan and his angels, have thy
     part!"

Satan, who now tries to please you,
Lest you timely warning take,
When that word is past, will seize you,
Plunge you in the burning lake:
   Think, poor sinner, thy eternal all's at
     stake.

But to those who have confessed,
Lov'd and serv'd the LORD below;
He will say, "Come near ye blessed,
See the kingdom I bestow:
   You for ever shall my love and glory
     know."

Under sorrows and reproaches,
May this thought your courage raise!
Swiftly GOD's great day approaches,
Sighs shall then be chang'd to praise:
   We shall triumph when the world is in a
     blaze.

---

1 Job 3:17—There the wicked cease from troubling; and
  there the weary be at rest.

THE DAY OF THE LORD.[1]

GOD, with one piercing glance, looks thro'
Creation's wide extended frame;
The past and future in his view,
And days and ages are the same.[2]

Sinners, who dare provoke his face,
Who on his patience long presume,
And trifle out his day of grace,
Will find he has a day of doom.

As pangs the lab'ring woman feels,
Or as the thief, in midnight sleep;
So comes that day, for which the wheels
Of time, their ceaseless motion keep!

Hark! from the sky, the trump proclaims
JESUS, the Judge approaching nigh!
See, the creation wrapt in flames,
First kindled by his vengeful eye!

When thus the mountains melt like wax,
When earth, and air, and sea, shall burn;
When all the frame of nature breaks,
Poor sinner, whither wilt thou turn?

The puny works which feeble men
Now boast, or covet, or admire;
Their pomp, and arts, and treasures, then
Shall perish in one common fire.

LORD, fix our hearts and hopes above!
Since all below to ruin tends;
Here may we trust, obey, and love,
And there be found amongst thy friends.

THE GREAT TRIBUNAL.[3]

JOHN in vision saw the day
When the Judge will hasten down;
Heav'n and earth shall flee away
From the terror of his frown:
Dead and living, small and great,
Raised from the earth and sea;
At his bar shall hear their fate,
What will then become of me?

Can I bear his awful looks?
Shall I stand in judgment then,
When I see the open'd books,
Written by th' Almighty's pen?
If he to remembrance bring,
And expose to public view,
Ev'ry work and secret thing,
Ah, my soul, what canst thou do?

When the list shall be produc'd
Of the talents I enjoy'd;
Means and mercies, how abus'd!
Time and strength, how misemploy'd!
Conscience then, compell'd to read,
Must allow the charge is true;
Say, my soul, what canst thou plead
In that hour, what wilt thou do?

But the book of life I see,
May my name be written there!
Then from guilt and danger free,
Glad I'll meet him in the air:
That's the book I hope to plead,
'Tis the gospel open'd wide;
LORD, I am a wretch indeed!
I have sinn'd, but thou hast dy'd.[4]

(Continued on the next page.)

---

1 Book III. Hymn 4.
2 2 Peter 3:8–10—But, beloved, be not ignorant of this one thing, that one day is with the Lord as a thousand years, and a thousand years as one day. The Lord is not slack concerning his promise, as some men count slackness; but is longsuffering to us-ward, not willing that any should perish, but that all should come to repentance. But the day of the Lord will come as a thief in the night; in the which the heavens shall pass away with a great noise, and the elements shall melt with fervent heat, the earth also and the works that are therein shall be burned up.

---

3 Revelation 20:11–12—And I saw a great white throne, and him that sat on it, from whose face the earth and the heaven fled away; and there was found no place for them. And I saw the dead, small and great, stand before God; and the books were opened: and another book was opened, which is the book of life: and the dead were judged out of those things which were written in the books, according to their works.
4 Romans 8:34—Who is he that condemneth? It is Christ that died, yea rather, that is risen again, who is even at the right hand of God, who also maketh intercession for us.

Now my soul knows what to do;
Thus I shall with boldness stand,
Number'd with the faithful few,
Own'd and sav'd, at thy right hand:
If thou help a foolish worm
To believe thy promise now;
Justice will at last confirm
What thy mercy wrought below.

THE OLD AND NEW CREATION.

THAT was a wonder-working word
Which could the vast creation raise!
Angels, attendant on their LORD,[1]
Admir'd the plan, and sung his praise.

From what a dark and shapeless mass,
All nature sprang at his command!
Let there be light, and light there was,
And sun and stars, and sea and land.

With equal speed the earth and seas,
Their mighty Maker's voice obey'd;
He spake, and strait the plants and trees,
And birds, and beasts, and man were made.

But man, the lord and crown of all,
By sin his honor soon defac'd;
His heart (how alter'd since the fall!)
Is dark, deform'd, and void, and waste.

The new creation of the soul
Does now no less his pow'r display;[2]
Than when he form'd the mighty whole,
And kindled darkness into day.

Tho' self-destroy'd, O LORD, we are,
Yet let us feel what thou canst do;
Thy word the ruin can repair,
And all our hearts create anew.

---

1 Job 38:7—When the morning stars sang together, and all the sons of God shouted for joy?
2 2 Corinthians 4:6—For God, who commanded the light to shine out of darkness, hath shined in our hearts, to give the light of the knowledge of the glory of God in the face of Jesus Christ.

THE BOOK OF CREATION.

THE book of nature open lies,
  With much instruction stor'd;
But till the LORD anoints our eyes
  We cannot read a word.

Philosophers have por'd in vain,
  And guess'd, from age to age;
For reason's eye could ne'er attain
  To understand a page.

Tho' to each star they give a name,
  Its size and motions teach;
The truths which all the stars proclaim,
  Their wisdom cannot reach.

With skill to measure earth and sea;
  And weigh the subtle air;
They cannot, LORD, discover thee
  Tho' present ev'ry where.

The knowledge of the saints excels
  The wisdom of the schools;
To them his secrets GOD reveals,
  Tho' men account them fools.

To them the sun and stars on high,
  The flow'rs that paint the field,[1]
And all the artless birds that fly,
  Divine instruction yield.

The creatures on their senses press,
  As witnesses to prove
Their Saviour's pow'r, and faithfulness,
  His providence and love.

Thus may we study nature's book
  To make us wise indeed!
And pity those who only look
  At what they cannot read.[2]

---

1 Matthew 6:26–28—Behold the fowls of the air: for they sow not, neither do they reap, nor gather into barns; yet your heavenly Father feedeth them. Are ye not much better than they? Which of you by taking thought can add one cubit unto his stature? And why take ye thought for raiment? Consider the lilies of the field, how they grow; they toil not, neither do they spin.

2 Romans 1:20—For the invisible things of him from the creation of the world are clearly seen, being understood by the things that are made, even his eternal power and Godhead; so that they are without excuse.

THE RAINBOW.

WHEN the sun, with cheerful beams,
Smiles upon a low'ring sky;
Soon its aspect soft'ned seems,
And a rainbow meets the eye:
  While the sky remains serene,
  This bright arch is never seen.

Thus the LORD's supporting pow'r
Brightest to his saints appears,
When affliction's threat'ning hour
Fills their sky with clouds and fears:
  He can wonders then perform,
  Paint a rainbow on the storm.[3]

All their graces doubly shine
When their troubles press them sore;
And the promises divine
Give them joys unknown before:
  As the colours of the bow,
  To the cloud their brightness owe.

Favor'd John a rainbow saw[4]
Circling round the throne above;
Hence the saints a pledge may draw
Of unchanging cov'nant love:
  Clouds awhile may intervene,
  But the bow will still be seen.

---

3 Genesis 9:14—And it shall come to pass, when I bring a cloud over the earth, that the bow shall be seen in the cloud.

4 Revelation 4:3—And he that sat was to look upon like a jasper and a sardine stone: and there was a rainbow round about the throne, in sight like unto an emerald.

THUNDER.

When a black overspreading cloud
  Has darkned all the air;
And peals of thunder roaring loud
  Proclaim the tempest near.

Then guilt and fear, the fruits of sin,
  The sinner oft pursue;
A louder storm is heard within,
  And conscience thunders too.

The law a fiery language speaks,
  His danger he perceives;
Like Satan, who his ruin seeks,
  He trembles and believes.

But when the sky serene appears,
  And thunders roll no more;
He soon forgets his vows and fears,
  Just as he did before.

But whither shall the sinner flee,
  When nature's mighty frame,
The pond'rous earth, and air, and sea,[1]
  Shall all dissolve in flame?

Amazing day! it comes apace!
  The Judge is hasting down!
Will sinners bear to see his face,
  Or stand before his frown.

Lord, let thy mercy find a way
  To touch each stubborn heart;
That they may never hear thee say,
  "Ye cursed ones depart."

Believers, you may well rejoice!
  The thunders loudest strains
Should be to you a welcome voice,
  That tells you, "Jesus reigns!"

LIGHTNING IN THE NIGHT.

A glance from heav'n, with sweet effect,
Sometimes my pensive spirit cheers;
But, ere I can my thoughts collect,
As suddenly it disappears.

So light'ning in the gloom of night,
Affords a momentary day;
Disclosing objects full in sight,
Which soon as seen, are snatch'd away.

Ah! what avail these pleasing scenes!
They do but aggravate my pain;
While darkness quickly intervenes,
And swallows up my joys again.

But shall I murmur at relief?
Tho' short, it was a precious view;
Sent to controll my unbelief,
And prove that what I read is true.

The light'nings flash did not create
The op'ning prospect it reveal'd;
But only shew'd the real state
Of what the darkness had conceal'd.

Just so, we by a glimpse discern
The glorious things within the vail;
That when in darkness, we may learn
To live by faith, till light prevail.

The Lord's great day will soon advance,
Dispersing all the shades of night;
Then we no more shall need a glance,
But see by an eternal Light.

---

1 2 Peter 3:10—But the day of the Lord will come as a thief in the night; in the which the heavens shall pass away with a great noise, and the elements shall melt with fervent heat, the earth also and the works that are therein shall be burned up.

ON THE ECLIPSE OF THE MOON.

July 30, 1776.

THE moon in silver glory shone,
   And not a cloud in sight;
When suddenly a shade begun
   To intercept her light.

How fast across her orb it spread,
   How fast her light withdrew!
A circle, ting'd with languid red,
   Was all appear'd in view.

While many with unmeaning eye
   Gaze on thy works in vain;
Assist me, LORD, that I may try
   Instruction to obtain.

Fain would my thankful heart and lips
   Unite in praise to thee;
And meditate on thy eclipse,
   In sad Gethsemane.

Thy peoples guilt, a heavy load!
   (When standing in their room)
Depriv'd thee of the light of GOD,
   And fill'd thy soul with gloom.

How punctually eclipses move,
   Obedient to thy will!
Thus shall thy faithfulness and love,
   Thy promises fulfill.

Dark, like the moon without the sun
   I mourn thine absence, LORD!
For light or comfort I have none,
   But what thy beams afford.

But lo! the hour draws near apace,
   When changes shall be o'er;
Then I shall see thee face to face,
   And be eclips'd no more.

MOON-LIGHT.

THE moon has but a borrow'd light,
   A faint and feeble ray;
She owes her beauty to the night,
   And hides herself by day.

No cheering warmth her beam conveys,
   Tho' pleasing to behold;
We might upon her brightness gaze
   Till we were starv'd with cold.

Just such is all the light to man
   Which reason can impart;
It cannot shew one object plain,
   Nor warm the frozen heart.

Thus moon-light views of truths divine
   To many fatal prove;
For what avail in gifts to shine,[1]
   Without a spark of love?

The gospel, like the sun at noon,
   Affords a glorious light;
Then fallen reason's boasted moon
   Appears no longer bright.

And grace, not light alone, bestows,
   But adds a quickning pow'r;
The desart blossoms like the rose,[2]
   And sin prevails no more.

---

1 1 Corinthians 13:1—Though I speak with the tongues of men and of angels, and have not charity, I am become as sounding brass, or a tinkling cymbal.

2 Isaiah 35:1—The wilderness and the solitary place shall be glad for them; and the desert shall rejoice, and blossom as the rose.

THE SEA.[1]

IF for a time the air be calm,
Serene and smooth the sea appears;
And shews no danger to alarm
The unexperienc'd landsman's fears.

But if the tempest once arise,
The faithless water swells and raves;
Its billows, foaming to the skies,
Disclose a thousand threat'ning graves.

My untry'd heart thus seem'd to me,
(So little of myself I knew)
Smooth as the calm unruffled sea,
But ah! it prov'd as treach'rous too!

The peace, of which I had a taste,
When JESUS first his love reveal'd;
I fondly hop'd would always last,
Because my foes were then conceal'd.

But when I felt the tempter's pow'r
Rouse my corruptions from their sleep;
I trembled at the stormy hour,
And saw the horrors of the deep.

Now, on presumption's billows borne,
My spirit seem'd the LORD to dare;
Now, quick as thought, a sudden turn
Plung'd me in gulphs of black despair.

LORD, save me, or I sink, I pray'd,
He heard, and bid the tempest cease;
The angry waves his word obey'd,
And all my fears were hush'd to peace.

The peace is his, and not my own,
My heart (no better than before)
Is still to dreadful changes prone,
Then let me never trust it more.

THE FLOOD.

THO' small the drops of falling rain,
    If one be singly view'd;
Collected, they o'erspread the plain,
    And form a mighty flood.

The house it meets with in its course,
    Should not be built on clay;
Lest, with a wild resistless force,
    It sweep the whole away.

Tho' for awhile it seem'd secure,
    It will not bear the shock;
Unless it has foundations sure,
    And stands upon a rock.

Thus sinners think their evil deeds,
    Like drops of rain, are small;
But it the pow'r of thought exceeds,
    To count the sum of all.

One sin can raise, tho' small it seems,
    A flood to drown the soul;
What then, when countless million streams
    Shall join, to swell the whole.

Yet, while they think the weather fair,
    If warn'd, they smile or frown;
But they will tremble and despair,
    When the fierce flood comes down!

Oh! then on JESUS ground your hope,
    That stone in Zion laid;[2]
Lest your poor building quickly drop,
    With ruin, on your head.

---

2 Matthew 7:24—Therefore whosoever heareth these sayings of mine, and doeth them, I will liken him unto a wise man, which built his house upon a rock.

1 Peter 2:6—Wherefore also it is contained in the scripture, Behold, I lay in Sion a chief corner stone, elect, precious: and he that believeth on him shall not be confounded.

---

1 Book I. Hymn 115.

THE THAW.

THE ice and snow we lately saw,
    Which cover'd all the ground;
Are melted soon before the thaw,
    And can no more be found.

Could all the art of man suffice
    To move away the snow,
To clear the rivers from the ice,
    Or make the waters flow?

No, 'tis the work of GOD alone;
    An emblem of the pow'r
By which he melts the heart of stone,
    In his appointed hour.

All outward means, till he appears,
    Will ineffectual prove;
Tho' much the sinner sees and hears,
    He cannot learn to love.

But let the stoutest sinner feel
    The soft'ning warmth of grace;
Tho' hard as ice, or rocks, or steel,
    His heart dissolves apace.

Seeing the blood which JESUS spilt,
    To save his soul from woe,
His hatred, unbelief, and guilt,
    All melt away like snow.

JESUS, we in thy name intreat,
    Reveal thy gracious arm;
And grant thy Spirit's kindly heat,
    Our frozen hearts to warm.

THE LOADSTONE.

As needles point towards the pole,
    When touch'd by the magnetic stone;
So faith in JESUS, gives the soul
    A tendency before unknown.

Till then, by blinded passions led,
    In search of fancy'd good we range;
The paths of disappointment tread,
    To nothing fix'd, but love of change.

But when the Holy Ghost imparts
    A knowledge of the Saviour's love;
Our wand'ring, weary, restless hearts,
    Are fix'd at once, no more to move.

Now a new principle takes place,
    Which guides and animates the will;
This love, another name for grace,
    Constrains to good, and bars from ill.

By love's sure light we soon perceive
    Our noblest bliss, and proper end;
And gladly ev'ry idol leave,
    To love and serve our LORD and Friend.

Thus borne along by faith and hope,
    We feel the Saviour's words are true;
"And I, if I be lifted up,[1]
Will draw the sinner upward too."

---

1 John 12:32—And I, if I be lifted up from the earth, will draw all men unto me.

THE SPIDER AND BEE.

ON the same flow'r we often see
The lothsome spider and the bee;
But what they get by working there,
Is diff'rent as their natures are.

The bee a sweet reward obtains,
And honey well repays his pains;
Home to the hive he bears the store,
And then returns in quest of more.

But no sweet flow'rs that grace the field,
Can honey to the spider yield;
A cobweb all that he can spin,
And poison all he stores within.

Thus in that sacred field the word,
With flow'rs of GOD's own planting stor'd,
Like bees his children feed and thrive,
And bring home honey to the hive.

There, spider-like, the wicked come,
And seem to taste the same perfume;
But the vile venom of their hearts,
To poison all their food converts.

From the same truths believers prize,
They weave vain refuges of lies;
And from the promise licence draw,
To trifle with the holy law!

LORD, shall thy word of life and love,
The means of death to numbers prove!
Unless thy grace our hearts renew,[1]
We sink to hell, with heav'n in view.

THE BEE SAVED FROM THE SPIDER.

THE subtle spider often weaves
    His unsuspected snares,
Among the balmy flow'rs and leaves,
    To which the bee repairs.

When in his web he sees one hang,
    With a malicious joy,
He darts upon it with his fang,
    To poison and destroy.

How welcome then, some pitying friend,
    To save the threat'ned bee!
The spider's treach'rous web to rend,
    And set the captive free!

My soul has been in such a case,
    When first I knew the LORD,
I hasted to the means of grace,
    Where sweets I knew were stor'd.

Little I thought of danger near,
    That soon my joys would ebb;
But ah! I met a spider there,
    Who caught me in his web.

Then Satan rais'd his pois'nous sting,
    And aim'd his blows at me;
While I, poor helpless trembling thing,
    Could neither fight nor flee.

But oh! the Saviour's pitying eye
    Reliev'd me from despair;
He saw me at the point to die
    And broke the fatal snare.

My case his heedless saints should warn,
    Or cheer them if afraid;
May you from me your danger learn,
    And where to look for aid.

---

1 Book III. Hymn 71.

THE TAMED LION.

A LION, tho' by nature wild,
   The art of man can tame;
He stands before his keeper, mild,
   And gentle as a lamb.

He watches, with submissive eye,
   The hand that gives him food;
As if he meant to testify
   A sense of gratitude.

But man himself, who thus subdues
   The fiercest beasts of prey;
A nature, more unfeeling shews,
   And far more fierce than they.

Tho' by the LORD preserv'd and fed,
   He proves rebellious still;
And while he eats his Maker's bread,
   Resists his holy will.

Alike in vain, of grace that saves,
   Or threat'ning law he hears;
The savage scorns, blasphemes, and raves,
   But neither loves nor fears.

O Saviour! how thy wond'rous pow'r
   By angels is proclaim'd!
When in thine own appointed hour,
   They see this lion tam'd.

The love thy bleeding cross displays,
   The hardest heart subdues;
Here furious lions while they gaze,
   Their rage and fierceness lose.[1]

Yet are we but renew'd in part,
   The lion still remains;
LORD, drive him wholly from my heart,
   Or keep him fast in chains.

SHEEP.

THE Saviour calls his people sheep,
   And bids them on his love rely;
For he alone their souls can keep,
   And he alone their wants supply.

The bull can fight, the hare can flee,
   The ant, in summer, food prepare;
But helpless sheep, and such are we,
   Depend upon the Shepherd's care.

JEHOVAH is our Shepherd's name,[2]
   Then what have we, tho' weak, to fear?
Our sin and folly we proclaim,
   If we despond while he is near.

When Satan threatens to devour,
   When troubles press on ev'ry side;
Think of our Shepherd's care and pow'r,
   He can defend, he will provide.

See the rich pastures of his grace,
   Where, in full streams, salvation flows!
There he appoints our resting place,
   And we may feed, secure from foes.

There, 'midst the flock the Shepherd dwells,
   The sheep around in safety lie;
The wolf, in vain, with malice swells,
   For he protects them with his eye.[3]

Dear LORD, if I am one of thine,
   From anxious thoughts I would be free;
To trust, and love, and praise, is mine,
   The care of all belongs to thee.

---

1 Isaiah 11:6—The wolf also shall dwell with the lamb, and the leopard shall lie down with the kid; and the calf and the young lion and the fatling together; and a little child shall lead them.

2 Psalm 23:1—The LORD is my shepherd; I shall not want.

3 Micah 5:4—And he shall stand and feed in the strength of the LORD, in the majesty of the name of the LORD his God; and they shall abide: for now shall he be great unto the ends of the earth.

THE GARDEN.

A GARDEN contemplation suits,
    And may instruction yield,
Sweeter than all the flow'rs and fruits
    With which the spot is fill'd.

Eden was Adam's dwelling place,
    While blest with innocence;
But sin o'erwhelm'd him with disgrace,
    And drove the rebel thence.

Oft as the garden-walk we tread,
    We should bemoan his fall;
The trespass of our legal head
    In ruin plung'd us all.

The garden of Gethsemane,
    The second Adam saw,
Oppress'd with woe, to set us free
    From the avenging law.

How stupid we, who can forget,
    With gardens in our sight,
His agonies and bloody sweat,
    In that tremendous night!

His church as a fair garden stands,
    Which walls of love enclose;
Each tree is planted by his hand,[1]
    And by his blessing grows.

Believing hearts are gardens too,
    For grace has sown its seeds;
Where once, by nature, nothing grew
    But thorns and worthless weeds.

Such themes to those who JESUS love,
    May constant joys afford;
And make a barren desert prove
    The garden of the LORD.

FOR A GARDEN-SEAT, OR SUMMER-HOUSE.

A SHELTER from the rain or wind,[2]
    A shade from scorching heat;
A resting place you here may find,
    To ease your weary feet.

Enter but with a serious thought,
    Consider who is near!
This is a consecrated spot,
    The LORD is present here!

A question of the utmost weight,
    While reading, meets your eye;
May conscience witness to your state,
    And give a true reply!

Is JESUS to your heart reveal'd,
    As full of truth and grace?
And is his name your hope and shield,
    Your rest and hiding place?

If so, for all events prepar'd,
    Whatever storms may rise,
He, whom you love, will safely guard,
    And guide you to the skies.

No burning sun, or storm, or rain,
    Will there your peace annoy;
No sin, temptation, grief, or pain,
    Intrude to damp your joy.

But if his name you have not known,
    Oh, seek him while you may!
Lest you should meet his awful frown,
    In that approaching day.

When the avenging Judge you see,
    With terrors on his brow;
Where can you hide, or whither flee,
    If you reject him now?

---

1 Isaiah 61:3—To appoint unto them that mourn in Zion, to give unto them beauty for ashes, the oil of joy for mourning, the garment of praise for the spirit of heaviness; that they might be called trees of righteousness, the planting of the LORD, that he might be glorified.

---

2 Isaiah 32:2—And a man shall be as an hiding place from the wind, and a covert from the tempest; as rivers of water in a dry place, as the shadow of a great rock in a weary land.

THE CREATURES IN THE LORD'S HANDS.

THE water stood like walls of brass,
To let the sons of Israel pass;[1]
And from the rock in rivers burst,[2]
At Moses' prayer to quench their thirst.

The fire restrain'd by GOD's commands,
Could only burn his people's bands;[3]
Too faint, when he was with them there,
To singe their garments or their hair.

At Daniel's feet the lions lay[4]
Like harmless lambs, nor touch'd their prey;
And ravens, which on carrion fed,
Procur'd Elijah flesh and bread.

Thus creatures only can fulfill
Their great Creator's holy will;
And when his servants need their aid,
His purposes must be obey'd.

So if his blessing he refuse,
Their pow'r to help they quickly lose,
Sure as on creatures we depend,
Our hopes in disappointment end.

Then let us trust the LORD alone,
And creature-confidence disown;
Nor if they threaten need we fear,
They cannot hurt if he be near.

If instruments of pain they prove,
Still they are guided by his love;
As lancets by the surgeon's skill,
Which wound to cure, and not to kill.

1 Exodus 14:22—And the children of Israel went into the midst of the sea upon the dry ground: and the waters were a wall unto them on their right hand, and on their left.
2 Numbers 20:11—And Moses lifted up his hand, and with his rod he smote the rock twice: and the water came out abundantly, and the congregation drank, and their beasts also.
3 Daniel 3:27—And the princes, governors, and captains, and the king's counsellors, being gathered together, saw these men, upon whose bodies the fire had no power, nor was an hair of their head singed, neither were their coats changed, nor the smell of fire had passed on them.
4 Daniel 6:23—Then was the king exceedingly glad for him, and commanded that they should take Daniel up out of the den. So Daniel was taken up out of the den, and no manner of hurt was found upon him, because he believed in his God.

ON DREAMING.

WHEN slumber seals our weary eyes,
The busy fancy wakeful keeps;
The scenes which then before us rise,
Prove, something in us never sleeps.

As in another world we seem,
A new creation of our own;
All appears real, tho' a dream,
And all familiar, tho' unknown.

Sometimes the mind beholds again
The past days bus'ness in review;
Resumes the pleasure or the pain,
And sometimes all we meet is new.

What schemes we form, what pains we take!
We fight, we run, we fly, we fall;
But all is ended when we wake,
We scarcely then a trace recall.

But tho' our dreams are often wild,
Like clouds before the driving storm;
Yet some important may be stil'd,
Sent to admonish or inform.

What mighty agents have access,
What friends from heav'n, or foes from hell,
Our minds to comfort or distress,
When we are sleeping, who can tell?

One thing, at least, and 'tis enough,
We learn from this surprising fact;
Our dreams afford sufficient proof,
The soul, without the flesh, can act.

This life, which mortals so esteem,
That many choose it for their all,
They will confess, was but a dream,[5]
When 'waken'd by death's awful call.

5 Isaiah 29:8—It shall even be as when an hungry man dreameth, and, behold, he eateth; but he awaketh, and his soul is empty: or as when a thirsty man dreameth, and, behold, he drinketh; but he awaketh, and, behold, he is faint, and his soul hath appetite: so shall the multitude of all the nations be, that fight against mount Zion.

THE WORLD.

SEE, the world for youth prepares,
Harlot like, her gaudy snares!
Pleasures round her seem to wait,
But 'tis all a painted cheat.

Rash and unsuspecting youth
Thinks to find thee always smooth,
Always kind, till better taught,
By experience dearly bought.

So the calm, but faithless sea,
(Lively emblem, world, of thee)
Tempts the shepherd from the shore,
Foreign regions to explore.

While no wrinkled wave is seen,
While the sky remains serene;
Fill'd with hopes, and golden schemes,
Of a storm he little dreams.

But ere long the tempest raves,
Then he trembles at the waves;
Wishes then he had been wise,
But too late—he sinks and dies.

Hapless thus, are they, vain world,
Soon on rocks of ruin hurl'd;
Who admiring thee, untry'd,
Court thy pleasure, wealth, or pride.

Such a shipwreck had been mine,
Had not JESUS (Name Divine!)
Sav'd me with a mighty hand,
And restor'd my soul to land.

Now, with gratitude I raise
Ebenezers to his praise;
Now my rash pursuits are o'er,
I can trust thee, world, no more.

THE INCHANTMENT DISSOLVED.

BLINDED in youth by Satan's arts,
The world to our unpractis'd hearts,
　A flatt'ring prospect shows;
Our fancy forms a thousand schemes,
Of gay delights, and golden dreams,
　And undisturb'd repose.

So in the desarts dreary waste,
By magic pow'r produc'd in haste,
　(As ancient fables say)
Castles, and groves, and music sweet,
The senses of the trav'ller meet,
　And stop him in his way.

But while he listens with surprize,
The charm dissolves, the vision dies,
　'Twas but inchanted ground;
Thus if the LORD our spirits touch,
The world, which promis'd us so much,
　A wilderness is found.

At first we start, and feel distress'd,
Convinc'd we never can have rest,
　In such a wretched place;
But he whose mercy breaks the charm,
Reveals his own almighty arm,
　And bids us seek his face.

Then we begin to live indeed,
When from our sin and bondage freed,
　By this beloved Friend;
We follow him from day to day,
Assur'd of grace thro' all the way,
　And glory at the end.

EXPOSTULATION.

No words can declare,
No fancy can paint,
What rage and despair,
What hopeless complaint,
Fill Satan's dark dwelling,
The prison beneath;
What weeping and yelling,
And gnashing of teeth!

Yet sinners will choose
This dreadful abode,
Each madly persues
The dangerous road;
Tho' GOD give them warning
They onward will go,
They answer with scorning,
And onward do go.

How sad to behold
The rich and the poor,
The young and the old,
All blindly secure!
All posting to ruin,
Refusing to stop;
Ah! think what you're doing,
While yet there is hope!

How weak is your hand
To fight with the LORD!
How can you withstand
The edge of his sword?
What hope of escaping
For those who oppose,
When hell is wide gaping
To swallow his foes?

How oft have you dar'd
The LORD to his face!
Yet still you are spar'd
To hear of his grace;
Oh pray for repentance
And life-giving faith,
Before the just sentence
Consign you to death.

(Continued in the next column.)

It is not too late
To JESUS to flee,
His mercy is great,
His pardon is free;
His blood has such virtue
For all that believe,
That nothing can hurt you,
If him you receive.

ALARM.

STOP, poor sinner! stop and think
    Before you farther go!
Will you sport upon the brink
    Of everlasting woe?
Once again I charge you, stop!
For, unless you warning take,
Ere you are aware, you drop
    Into the burning lake!

Say, have you an arm like GOD,
    That you his will oppose?
Fear you not that iron rod
    With which he breaks his foes?
Can you stand in that dread day,
When he judgment shall proclaim,
And the earth shall melt away
    Like wax before the flame?

Palefac'd death will quickly come
    To drag you to his bar;
Then to hear your awful doom
    Will fill you with despair:
All your sins will round you croud,
Sins of a blood-crimson dye;
Each for vengeance crying loud,
    And what can you reply?

Tho' your heart be made of steel,
    Your forehead lin'd with brass,
GOD at length will make you feel,
    He will not let you pass:
Sinners then in vain will call,
(Tho' they now despise his grace)
Rocks and mountains on us fall,[1]
    And hide us from his face.

But as yet there is a hope
    You may his mercy know;
Tho' his arm is lifted up,
    He still forbears the blow:
'Twas for sinners JESUS dy'd,
Sinners he invites to come;
None who come shall be deny'd,
He says, "There still is room."[2]

WE WERE ONCE AS YOU ARE.

SHALL men pretend to pleasure
    Who never knew the LORD?
Can all the worldling's treasure
    True peace of mind afford?
They shall obtain this jewel
    In what their hearts desire,
When they by adding fuel
    Can quench the flame of fire.

Till you can bid the ocean,
    When furious tempests roar,[3]
Forget its wonted motion,
    And rage, and swell, no more:
In vain your expectation
    To find content in sin;
Or freedom from vexation,
    While passions reign within.

Come, turn your thoughts to JESUS,
    If you would good possess;
'Tis he alone that frees us
    From guilt, and from distress:
When he, by faith, is present,
    The sinner's troubles cease;
His ways are truly pleasant,[4]
    And all his paths are peace.

Our time in sin we wasted,
    And fed upon the wind;
Until his love we tasted,
    No comfort could we find:
But now we stand to witness
    His pow'r and grace to you;
May you perceive its fitness,
    And call upon him too!

Our pleasure and our duty,
    Tho' opposite before;
Since we have seen his beauty,
    Are join'd to part no more:
It is our highest pleasure,
    No less than duty's call;
To love him beyond measure,
    And serve him with our all.

---

1 Revelation 6:16—And said to the mountains and rocks,
  Fall on us, and hide us from the face of him that sitteth
  on the throne, and from the wrath of the Lamb.
2 Luke 14:22—And the servant said, Lord, it is done as
  thou hast commanded, and yet there is room.

3 Isaiah 57:20–21—But the wicked are like the troubled
  sea, when it cannot rest, whose waters cast up mire and
  dirt. There is no peace, saith my God, to the wicked.
4 Proverbs 3:17—Her ways are ways of pleasantness,
  and all her paths are peace.

PREPARE TO MEET GOD.

SINNER, art thou still secure?
Wilt thou still refuse to pray?
Can thy heart or hands endure
In the LORD's avenging day?
See, his mighty arm is bar'd!
Awful terrors clothe his brow!
For his judgment stand prepar'd,
Thou must either break or bow.

At his presence nature shakes,
Earth affrighted hastes to flee;
Solid mountains melt like wax,
What will then become of thee?
Who his advent may abide?
You that glory in your shame,
Will you find a place to hide
When the world is wrapt in flame?

Then the rich, the great, the wise,
Trembling, guilty, self-condemn'd;
Must behold the wrathful eyes
Of the Judge they once blasphem'd:
Where are now their haughty looks?
Oh their horror and despair!
When they see the open'd books
And their dreadful sentence hear!

LORD prepare us by thy grace!
Soon we must resign our breath;
And our souls be call'd, to pass
Thro' the iron gate of death:
Let us now our day improve,
Listen to the gospel voice;
Seek the things that are above,
Scorn the world's pretended joys.

Oh! when flesh and heart shall fail,
Let thy love our spirits cheer;
Strengthen'd thus, we shall prevail
Over Satan, sin, and fear:
Trusting in thy precious name,
May we thus our journey end;
Then our foes shall lose their aim,
And the Judge will be our Friend.

INVITATION.

SINNER, hear the Saviour's call,
  He now is passing by;
He has seen thy grievous thrall,
  And heard thy mournful cry.
He has pardons to impart,
Grace to save thee from thy fears,
See the love that fills his heart,
  And wipe away thy tears.

Why art thou afraid to come
  And tell him all thy case?
He will not pronounce thy doom,
  Nor frown thee from his face:
Wilt thou fear EMMANUEL?
Wilt thou dread the Lamb of GOD,
Who, to save thy soul from hell,
  Has shed his precious blood?

Think, how on the cross he hung
  Pierc'd with a thousand wounds!
Hark, from each as with a tongue
  The voice of pardon sounds!
See, from all his bursting veins,
Blood, of wond'rous virtue, flow!
Shed to wash away thy stains,
  And ransom thee from woe.

Tho' his majesty be great,
  His mercy is no less;
Tho' he thy transgressions hate,
  He feels for thy distress:
By himself the LORD has sworn,
He delights not in thy death;[1]
But invites thee to return,
  That thou mayst live by faith.

Raise thy downcast eyes, and see
  What throngs his throne surround!
These, tho' sinners once like thee,
  Have full salvation found:
Yield not then to unbelief!
While he says, "There yet is room;"
Tho' of sinners thou art chief,
  Since JESUS calls thee, come.

---

1 Ezekiel 33:11—Say unto them, As I live, saith the Lord GOD, I have no pleasure in the death of the wicked; but that the wicked turn from his way and live: turn ye, turn ye from your evil ways; for why will ye die, O house of Israel?

THE BURDENED SINNER.

AH, what can I do,
Or where be secure!
If justice pursue
What heart can endure!
When GOD speaks in thunder,
And makes himself known,
The heart breaks asunder,
Tho' hard as a stone.

With terror I read
My sins heavy score,
The numbers exceed
The sands on the shore;
Guilt makes me unable
To stand or to flee,
So Cain murder'd Abel,
And trembled like me.

Each sin, like his blood,
With a terrible cry,
Calls loudly on GOD
To strike from on high:
Nor can my repentance
Extorted by fear,
Reverse the just sentence,
'Tis just tho' severe.

The case is too plain,
I have my own choice;
Again, and again,
I slighted his voice;
His warnings neglected,
His patience abus'd,
His gospel rejected,
His mercy refus'd.

And must I then go,
Forever to dwell
In torments and woe
With devils in hell?
Oh where is the Saviour
I scorn'd in times past?
His word in my favour
Would save me at last.

(Continued in the next column.)

LORD JESUS, on thee
I venture to call,
Oh look upon me
The vilest of all!
For whom didst thou languish,
And bleed on the tree?
Oh pity my anguish,
And say, "'Twas for thee."

A case such as mine
Will honor thy pow'r;
All hell will repine,
All heav'n will adore;
If in condemnation
Strict justice takes place,
It shines in salvation
More glorious thro' grace.

BEHOLD I AM VILE!

O Lord, how vile am I,
Unholy, and unclean!
How can I dare to venture nigh
With such a load of sin?

Is this polluted heart
A dwelling fit for thee?
Swarming, alass! in ev'ry part,
What evils do I see!

If I attempt to pray,
And lisp thy holy name;
My thoughts are hurry'd soon away,
I know not where I am.

If in thy word I look,
Such darkness fills my mind,
I only read a sealed book,
But no relief can find.

Thy gospel oft I hear,
But hear it still in vain;
Without desire, or love, or fear,
I like a stone remain.

Myself can hardly bear
This wretched heart of mine;
How hateful then must it appear
To those pure eyes of thine?

And must I then indeed
Sink in despair and die?
Fain would I hope that thou didst bleed
For such a wretch as I.

That blood which thou hast spilt,
That grace which is thine own;
Can cleanse the vilest sinner's guilt,
And soften hearts of stone.

Low at thy feet I bow,
Oh pity and forgive;
Here will I lie and wait, till thou
Shalt bid me rise and live.

ENCOURAGEMENT.

My soul is beset
With grief and dismay,
I owe a vast debt
And nothing can pay:
I must go to prison,
Unless that dear Lord,
Who dy'd and is risen,
His pity afford.

The death that he dy'd,
The blood that he spilt,
To sinners apply'd,
Discharge from all guilt:
This great Intercessor
Can give, if he please,
The vilest transgressor
Immediate release.

When nail'd to the tree,
He answer'd the pray'r
Of one, who like me,
Was nigh to despair;[1]
He did not upbraid him
With all he had done,
But instantly made him,
A saint and a son.

The jailor, I read,
A pardon receiv'd;[2]
And how was he freed?
He only believ'd:
His case mine resembled,
Like me he was foul,
Like me too he trembled,
But faith made him whole.

Tho' Saul in his youth,
To madness enrag'd,
Against the Lord's truth,
And people, engag'd;

(Continued on the next page.)

---

1 Luke 23:43—And Jesus said unto him, Verily I say unto thee, Today shalt thou be with me in paradise.
2 Acts 16:31—And they said, Believe on the Lord Jesus Christ, and thou shalt be saved, and thy house.

Yet JESUS, the Saviour,
Whom long he revil'd,[1]
Receiv'd him to favor
And made him a child.

A foe to all good,
In wickedness skill'd,
Manasseh, with blood,
Jerusalem fill'd;[2]
In evil long harden'd,
The LORD he defy'd,
Yet he too was pardon'd,
When mercy he cry'd.

Of sinners the chief,
And viler than all,
The jailor or thief,
Manasseh or Saul:
Since they were forgiven
Why should I despair,
While CHRIST is in heaven,
And still answers pray'r?

THE EFFORT.

CHEER up, my soul, there is a mercy-seat
Sprinkled with blood, where JESUS answers
    pray'r;
There humbly cast thyself, beneath his feet,
For never needy sinner perish'd there.

LORD, I am come! thy promise is my plea,
Without thy word I durst not venture nigh;
But thou hast call'd the burden'd soul to thee,
A weary burden'd soul, O LORD, am I!

Bow'd down beneath a heavy load of sin,
By Satan's fierce temptations sorely prest,
Beset without, and full of fears within,
Trembling and faint I come to thee for rest.

Be thou my refuge, LORD, my hiding-place,
I know no force can tear me from thy side;
Unmov'd I then may all accusers face,
And answer ev'ry charge, with, "JESUS dy'd."

Yes, thou didst weep, and bleed, and groan,
    and die,
Well hast thou known what fierce temptations
    mean;
Such was thy love, and now, enthron'd on
    high,
The same compassions in thy bosom reign.

LORD give me faith—he hears—what grace is
    this!
Dry up thy tears, my soul, and cease to grieve:
He shews me what he did, and who he is,
I must, I will, I can, I do believe.

---

1 1 Timothy 1:16—Howbeit for this cause I obtained
mercy, that in me first Jesus Christ might shew forth
all longsuffering, for a pattern to them which should
hereafter believe on him to life everlasting.

2 2 Chronicles 33:12–13—And when he was in afflic-
tion, he besought the LORD his God, and humbled him-
self greatly before the God of his fathers, And prayed
unto him: and he was intreated of him, and heard his
supplication, and brought him again to Jerusalem
into his kingdom. Then Manasseh knew that the LORD
he was God.

THE EFFORT—IN ANOTHER MEASURE.

APPROACH, my soul, the mercy-seat
  Where JESUS answers pray'r;
There humbly fall before his feet,
  For none can perish there.

Thy promise is my only plea,
  With this I venture nigh;
Thou callest burden'd souls to thee,
  And such, O LORD, am I.

Bow'd down beneath a load of sin,
  By Satan sorely prest;
By war without, and fears within,
  I come to thee for rest.

Be thou my shield and hiding-place!
  That, shelter'd near thy side,
I may my fierce accuser face,
  And tell him, "Thou hast dy'd."

Oh wond'rous love! to bleed and die,
  To bear the cross and shame;
That guilty sinners, such as I,
  Might plead thy gracious name.

"Poor tempest-tossed soul, be still,
  My promis'd grace receive;"
'Tis JESUS speaks—I must, I will,
  I can, I do believe.

REST FOR WEARY SOULS.

DOES the gospel-word proclaim
Rest, for those who weary be?[1]
Then, my soul, put in thy claim,
Sure that promise speaks to thee:
Marks of grace I cannot shew,
All polluted is my best;
Yet I weary am I know,
And the weary long for rest.

Burden'd with a load of sin,
Harass'd with tormenting doubt,
Hourly conflicts from within,
Hourly crosses from without:
All my little strength is gone,
Sink I must without supply;
Sure upon the earth is none
Can more weary be than I.

In the ark, the weary dove[2]
Found a welcome resting-place;
Thus my spirit longs to prove
Rest in CHRIST, the ark of grace:
Tempest-toss'd I long have been,
And the flood increases fast;
Open, LORD, and take me in,
Till the storm be overpast.

Safely lodg'd within thy breast,
What a wond'rous change I find!
Now I know thy promis'd rest
Can compose a troubled mind:
You that weary are like me,
Hearken to the gospel call;
To the ark for refuge flee,
JESUS will receive you all!

---

1 Matthew 11:28—Come unto me, all ye that labour
  and are heavy laden, and I will give you rest.
2 Genesis 8:9—But the dove found no rest for the sole
  of her foot, and she returned unto him into the ark, for
  the waters were on the face of the whole earth: then
  he put forth his hand, and took her, and pulled her in
  unto him into the ark.

THE STORM HUSHED.

'TIS past—the dreadful stormy night
  Is gone, with all its fears!
And now I see returning light,
  The LORD, my Sun, appears.

The tempter, who but lately said,
  I soon shall be his prey;
Has heard my Saviour's voice and fled
  With shame and grief away.

Ah! LORD, since thou didst hide thy face,
  What has my soul endur'd?
But now 'tis past, I feel thy grace,
  And all my wounds are cur'd!

Oh wond'rous change! but just before
  Despair beset me round;
I heard the lion's horrid roar,
  And trembled at the sound.

Before corruption, guilt and fear,
  My comforts blasted fell;
And unbelief discover'd near
  The dreadful depths of hell.

But JESUS pity'd my distress,
  He heard my feeble cry;
Reveal'd his blood and righteousness,
  And brought salvation nigh.

Beneath the banner of his love,
  I now secure remain;
The tempter frets, but dares not move
  To break my peace again.

LORD, since thou thus hast broke my bands,
  And set the captive free;
I would devote my tongue, my hands,
  My heart, my all to thee.

HELP IN TIME OF NEED.

UNLESS the LORD had been my stay
(With trembling joy my soul may say)
  My cruel foe had gain'd his end:
But he appear'd for my relief,
And Satan sees, with shame and grief,
  That I have an almighty Friend.

Oh, 'twas a dark and trying hour,
When harass'd by the tempter's pow'r,
  I felt my strongest hopes decline!
You only who have known his arts,
You only who have felt his darts,
  Can pity such a case as mine.

Loud in my ears a charge he read,
(My conscience witness'd all he said)
  My long black list of outward sin;
Then bringing forth my heart to view,
Too well what's hidden there he knew,
  He shew'd me ten-times worse within.

'Tis all too true, my soul reply'd,
But I remember JESUS dy'd,
  And now he fills a throne of grace;
I'll go, as I have done before,
His mercy I may still implore,
  I have his promise, "Seek my face."

But, as when sudden fogs arise,
The trees and hills, the sun and skies,
  Are all at once conceal'd from view;
So clouds of horror, black as night,
By Satan rais'd, hid from my sight,
  The throne of grace and promise too.

Then, while beset with guilt and fear,
He try'd to urge me to despair,
  He try'd, and he almost prevail'd;
But JESUS, by a heav'nly ray,
Drove clouds, and guilt, and fear away,
  And all the tempter's malice fail'd.

REJOICE THE SOUL OF
THY SERVANT.

WHEN my pray'rs are a burden and task,
No wonder I little receive;
O LORD, make me willing to ask,
Since thou art so ready to give:
Altho' I am bought with thy blood,
And all thy salvation is mine;
At a distance from thee my chief good,
I wander, and languish, and pine.

Of thy goodness of old when I read,
To those who were sinners like me,
Why may I not wrestle and plead,
With them a partaker to be?
Thine arm is not shortned since then,
And those who believe in thy name,
Ever find thou art Yea, and Amen,
Thro' all generations the same.

While my spirit within me is prest
With sorrow, temptation, and fear;
Like JOHN I would flee to thy breast,[1]
And pour my complaints in thine ear:
How happy and favor'd was he,
Who could on thy bosom repose!
Might this favor be granted to me,
I'd smile at the rage of my foes.

I have heard of thy wonderful name,
How great and exalted thou art;
But ah! I confess to my shame,
It faintly impresses my heart:
The beams of thy glory display,
As PETER once saw thee appear;
That transported like him I may say,
"It is good for my soul to be here."[2]

What a sorrow and weight didst thou feel,
When nail'd, for my sake, to the tree!
My heart sure is harder than steel,
To feel no more sorrow for thee:

(Continued in the next column.)

Oh let me with THOMAS descry
The wounds in thy hands and thy side;
And have feelings like his, when I cry,
"My GOD and my Saviour has dy'd!"[3]

But if thou hast appointed me still
To wrestle, and suffer, and fight;
Oh make me resign'd to thy will,
For all thine appointments are right:
This mercy, at least, I intreat,
That knowing how vile I have been,
I with MARY may wait at thy feet,[4]
And weep o'er the pardon of sin.

---

1 John 13:25—He then lying on Jesus' breast saith
  unto him, Lord, who is it?
2 Matthew 17:4—Then answered Peter, and said unto
  Jesus, Lord, it is good for us to be here: if thou wilt, let
  us make here three tabernacles; one for thee, and one
  for Moses, and one for Elias.

3 John 20:28—And Thomas answered and said unto
  him, My LORD and my God.
4 Luke 7:38—And stood at his feet behind him weep-
  ing, and began to wash his feet with tears, and did
  wipe them with the hairs of her head, and kissed his
  feet, and anointed them with the ointment.

BITTER AND SWEET.

KINDLE, Saviour, in my heart
   A flame of love divine;
  Hear, for mine I trust thou art,
   And sure I would be thine:
If my soul has felt thy grace,
If to me thy name is known;
Why should trifles fill the place,
   Due to thyself alone.

'Tis a strange mysterious life
   I live from day to day;
  Light and darkness, peace and strife,
   Bear an alternate sway:
When I think the battle won
I have to fight it o'er again;
When I say I'm overthrown,
   Relief I soon obtain.

Often at the mercy-seat
   While calling on thy name;
  Swarms of evil thoughts I meet,
   Which fill my soul with shame.
Agitated in my mind,
Like a feather in the air;
Can I thus a blessing find?
   My soul, can this be pray'r?

But when CHRIST, my LORD and Friend,
   Is pleas'd to shew his pow'r;
  All at once my troubles end,
   And I've a golden hour:
Then I see his smiling face,
Feel the pledge of joys to come;
Often, LORD, repeat this grace
   Till thou shalt call me home.

WHY SHOULD I COMPLAIN?

WHEN my Saviour, my Shepherd is near,
How quickly my sorrows depart!
New beauties around me appear,
New spirits enliven my heart:
His presence gives peace to my soul,
And Satan assaults me in vain;
While my Shepherd his pow'r controls,
I think I no more shall complain.

But alass! what a change do I find,
When my Shepherd withdraws from my sight?
My fears all return to my mind,
My day is soon chang'd into night:
Then Satan his efforts renews
To vex and ensnare me again;
All my pleasing enjoyments I lose,
And can only lament and complain.

By these changes I often pass thro',
I am taught my own weakness to know;
I am taught what my Shepherd can do,
And how much to his mercy I owe:
It is he who supports me thro' all,
When I faint he revives me again;
He attends to my pray'r when I call,
And bids me no longer complain.

Wherefore then should I murmur and grieve?
Since my Shepherd is always the same,
And has promis'd he never will leave[1]
The soul that confides in his name:
To relieve me from all that I fear,
He was buffeted, tempted, and slain;
And at length he will surely appear,
Tho' he leaves me awhile to complain.

While I dwell in an enemy's land,
Can I hope to be always in peace?
'Tis enough that my Shepherd's at hand,
And that shortly this warfare will cease;
For ere long he will bid me remove[2]
From this region of sorrow and pain,
To abide in his presence above,
And then I no more shall complain.

---

1 Jeremiah 1:19—And they shall fight against thee;
  but they shall not prevail against thee; for I am with

(Footnote continued on the next page.)

RETURN, O LORD, HOW LONG.

RETURN to bless my waiting eyes,
And cheer my mourning heart, O LORD!
Without thee, all beneath the skies
No real pleasure can afford.

When thy lov'd presence meets my sight,
It softens care, and sweetens toil;
The sun shines forth with double light,
The whole creation wears a smile.

Upon thine arm of love I rest,
Thy gracious voice forbids my fear;
No storms disturb my peaceful breast,
No foes assault when thou art near.

But ah! since thou hast been away,
Nothing but trouble have I known;
And Satan marks me for his prey
Because he sees me left alone.

My sun is hid, my comforts lost,
My graces droop, my sins revive;
Distress'd, dismay'd, and tempest-toss'd,
My soul is only just alive!

LORD, hear my cry and come again!
Put all mine enemies to shame,
And let them see, 'tis not in vain
That I have trusted in thy name.

CAST DOWN, BUT NOT DESTROYED.

THO' sore beset with guilt and fear,
I cannot, dare not, quite despair;
If I must perish, would the LORD
Have taught my heart to love his word?
Would he have giv'n me eyes to see[1]
My danger, and my remedy,
Reveal'd his name, and bid me pray,
Had he resolv'd to say me nay?

No—tho' cast down I am not slain;
I fall, but I shall rise again;[2]
The present Satan is thy hour,
But JESUS shall control thy pow'r:
His love will plead for my relief,
He hears my grones, he sees my grief;
Nor will he suffer thee to boast,
A soul, that sought his help, was lost.

'Tis true, I have unfaithful been,
And griev'd his Spirit by my sin;
Yet still his mercy he'll reveal,
And all my wounds and follies heal:
Abounding sin, I must confess,[3]
But more abounding is his grace;
He once vouchsaf'd for me to bleed,
And now he lives my cause to plead.

I'll cast myself before his feet,
I see him on his mercy-seat,
('Tis sprinkled with atoning blood)
There sinners find access to GOD:
Ye burden'd souls approach with me,
And make the Saviour's name your plea;
JESUS will pardon all who come,
And strike our fierce accuser dumb.

---

1 Judges 13:23—But his wife said unto him, If the LORD were pleased to kill us, he would not have received a burnt offering and a meat offering at our hands, neither would he have shewed us all these things, nor would as at this time have told us such things as these.

2 Micah 7:8—Rejoice not against me, O mine enemy: when I fall, I shall arise; when I sit in darkness, the LORD shall be a light unto me.

3 Romans 5:20—Moreover the law entered, that the offence might abound. But where sin abounded, grace did much more abound.

(Footnote continued from the previous page.)

thee, saith the LORD, to deliver thee.

2 Revelation 2:10—Fear none of those things which thou shalt suffer: behold, the devil shall cast some of you into prison, that ye may be tried; and ye shall have tribulation ten days: be thou faithful unto death, and I will give thee a crown of life.

THE BENIGHTED TRAVELLER.

FOREST beasts, that live by prey,
Seldom shew themselves by day;
But when day-light is withdrawn,[1]
Then they rove and roar till dawn.

Who can tell the traveller's fears,
When their horrid yells he hears?
Terror almost stops his breath,
While each step he looks for death.

Thus when JESUS is in view,
Cheerful I my way pursue;
Walking by my Saviour's light,
Nothing can my soul affright.

But when he forbears to shine,
Soon the travell'rs case is mine;
Lost, benighted, struck with dread,
What a painful path I tread!

Then, my soul with terror hears
Worse than lions, wolves, or bears,
Roaring loud in ev'ry part,
Thro' the forest of my heart.

Wrath, impatience, envy, pride,
Satan and his host beside,
Press around me to devour;
How can I escape their pow'r?

Gracious LORD afford me light,
Put these beasts of prey to flight;
Let thy pow'r and love be shewn,[2]
Save me, for I am *thine* own.

THE PRISONER.

WHEN the poor pris'ner thro' a grate
    Sees others walk at large;
How does he mourn his lonely state,
    And long for a discharge?

Thus I, confin'd in unbelief,
    My loss of freedom mourn;
And spend my hours in fruitless grief,
    Until my LORD return.

The beam of day, which pierces thro'
    The gloom in which I dwell;
Only discloses to my view,
    The horrors of my cell.

Ah! how my pensive spirit faints,
    To think of former days!
When I could triumph with the saints,
    And join their songs of praise!

But now my joys are all cut off,
    In prison I am cast;
And Satan, with a cruel scoff,[3]
    Says, "Where's your GOD at last?"

Dear Saviour, for thy mercies sake,
    My strong, my only plea,
These gates and bars in pieces break,[4]
    And set the pris'ner free!

Surely my soul shall sing to thee,
    For liberty restor'd;
And all thy saints admire to see
    The mercies of the LORD.

---

1 Psalm 104:20—Thou makest darkness, and it is night:
  wherein all the beasts of the forest do creep forth.
2 Psalm 119:94—I am thine, save me: for I have sought
  thy precepts.

3 Psalm 115:2—Wherefore should the heathen say,
  Where is now their God?
4 Psalm 142:7—Bring my soul out of prison, that I
  may praise thy name: the righteous shall compass me
  about; for thou shalt deal bountifully with me.

PERPLEXITY RELIEVED.

UNCERTAIN how the way to find
  Which to salvation led;
I list'ned long, with anxious mind,
  To hear what others said.

When some of joys and comforts told
  I fear'd that I was wrong;
For I was stupid, dead, and cold,
  Had neither joy nor song.

The LORD my lab'ring heart reliev'd,
  And made my burden light;
Then for a moment I believ'd,
  Supposing all was right.

Of fierce temptations others talk'd,
  Of anguish and dismay;
Thro' what distresses they had walk'd,
  Before they found the way.

Ah! then I thought my hopes were vain,
  For I had liv'd at ease;
I wish'd for all my fears again,
  To make me more like these.

I had my wish, the LORD disclos'd
  The evils of my heart;
And left my naked soul, expos'd
  To Satan's fiery dart.

Alass! "I now must give it up,"
  I cry'd in deep despair;
How could I dream of drawing hope
  From what I cannot bear!

Again my Saviour brought me aid,
  And when he set me free;
"Trust simply on my word, he said,
  And leave the rest to me."

PRAYER ANSWERED BY CROSSES.

I ASK'D the LORD that I might grow
In faith, and love, and ev'ry grace;
Might more of his salvation know,
And seek, more earnestly, his face.

'Twas he who taught me thus to pray,
And he, I trust, has answer'd pray'r;
But it has been in such a way,
As almost drove me to despair.

I hop'd that in some favor'd hour,
At once he'd answer my request;
And by his love's constraining pow'r,
Subdue my sins, and give me rest.

Instead of this, he made me feel
The hidden evils of my heart;
And let the angry pow'rs of hell
Assault my soul in ev'ry part.

Yea more, with his own hand he seem'd
Intent to aggravate my woe;
Cross'd all the fair designs I schem'd,
Blasted my gourds, and laid me low.

LORD, why is this, I trembling cry'd,
Wilt thou pursue thy worm to death?
"'Tis in this way, the LORD reply'd,
I answer pray'r for grace and faith.

These inward trials I employ,
From self, and pride, to set thee free;
And break thy schemes of earthly joy,
That thou may'st find thy all in me."

I WILL TRUST AND NOT
BE AFRAID.

BEGONE unbelief,
My Saviour is near,
And for my relief
Will surely appear:
By pray'r let me wrestle,
And he will perform,
With CHRIST in the vessel,
I smile at the storm.

Tho' dark be my way,
Since he is my guide,
'Tis mine to obey,
'Tis his to provide;
Tho' cisterns be broken,
And creatures all fail,
The word he has spoken
Shall surely prevail.

His love in time past
Forbids me to think
He'll leave me at last
In trouble to sink;
Each sweet Ebenezer
I have in review,
Confirms his good pleasure
To help me quite thro'.

Determin'd to save,
He watch'd o'er my path,
When Satan's blind slave,
I sported with death;
And can he have taught me
To trust in his name,
And thus far have brought me,
To put me to shame?

Why should I complain
Of want or distress,
Temptation or pain?
He told me no less:
The heirs of salvation,
I know from his word,
Thro' much tribulation
Must follow their LORD.[1]

(Continued in the next column.)

How bitter that cup,
No heart can conceive,
Which he drank quite up,
That sinners might live!
His way was much rougher,
And darker than mine;
Did JESUS thus suffer,
And shall I repine?

Since all that I meet
Shall work for my good,
The bitter is sweet,
The med'cine is food;
Tho' painful at present,
Will cease before long,
And then, oh! how pleasant,
The conqueror's song![2]

---

1 Acts 14:22—Confirming the souls of the disciples, and
exhorting them to continue in the faith, and that we must
through much tribulation enter into the kingdom of God.
2 Romans 8:37—Nay, in all these things we are more than
conquerors through him that loved us.

QUESTIONS TO UNBELIEF.

IF to JESUS for relief
    My soul has fled by pray'r;
Why should I give way to grief,
    Or heart-consuming care?
Are not all things in his hand?
Has he not his promise past?
Will he then regardless stand
    And let me sink at last?

While I know his providence
    Disposes each event;
Shall I judge by feeble sense,
    And yield to discontent?
If he worms and sparrows feed,
Clothe the grass in rich array;[1]
Can he see a child in need,
    And turn his eye away?

When his name was quite unknown,
    And sin my life employ'd;
Then he watch'd me as his own,
    Or I had been destroy'd:
Now his mercy-seat I know,
Now by grace am reconcil'd;
Would he spare me while a foe,[2]
    To leave me when a child?

If he all my wants supply'd
    When I disdain'd to pray;
Now his Spirit is my guide,
    How can he say me nay?
If he would not give me up,
When my soul against him fought;
Will he disappoint the hope,
    Which he himself has wrought?

(Continued in the next column.)

If he shed his precious blood
    To bring me to his fold;
Can I think that meaner good[3]
    He ever will withhold?
Satan, vain is thy device!
Here my hope rests well-assur'd,
In that great redemption-price,
    I see the whole secur'd.

---

1 Matthew 6:26–30—Behold the fowls of the air: for they sow not, neither do they reap, nor gather into barns; yet your heavenly Father feedeth them. Are ye not much better than they? Which of you by taking thought can add one cubit unto his stature? And why take ye thought for raiment? Consider the lilies of the field, how they grow; they toil not, neither do they spin: And yet I say unto you, That even Solomon in all his glory was not arrayed like one of these. Wherefore, if God so clothe the grass of the field, which to day is, and to morrow is cast into the oven, shall he not much more clothe you, O ye of little faith?

2 Romans 5:10—For if, when we were enemies, we were reconciled to God by the death of his Son, much more, being reconciled, we shall be saved by his life.

3 Romans 8:32—He that spared not his own Son, but delivered him up for us all, how shall he not with him also freely give us all things?

GREAT EFFECTS BY WEAK MEANS.

UNBELIEF the soul dismays,
What objections will it raise!
But true faith securely leans
On the promise, in the means.

If to faith it once be known,
GOD has said, "It shall be done,
And in this appointed way;"
Faith has then no more to say.

Moses' rod, by faith uprear'd,[1]
Thro' the sea a path prepar'd;
Jericho's devoted wall,[2]
At the trumpet's sound must fall.

With a pitcher and a lamp,[3]
Gideon overthrew a camp;
And a stone, well aim'd by faith,[4]
Prov'd the arm'd Philistine's death.

Thus the LORD is pleas'd to try
Those who on his help rely;
By the means he makes it known,
That the pow'r is all his own.

Yet the means are not in vain,
If the end we would obtain;
Tho' the breath of pray'r be weak,
None shall find, but they who seek.

GOD alone the heart can reach,
Yet the ministers must preach;
'Tis their part the seed to sow,
And 'tis his to make it grow.

---

1 Exodus 14:21—And Moses stretched out his hand over
the sea; and the LORD caused the sea to go back by a
strong east wind all that night, and made the sea dry
land, and the waters were divided.

2 Joshua 6:20—So the people shouted when the priests
blew with the trumpets: and it came to pass, when the
people heard the sound of the trumpet, and the people
shouted with a great shout, that the wall fell down flat, so
that the people went up into the city, every man straight
before him, and they took the city.

3 Judges 7:22—And the three hundred blew the trumpets,
and the LORD set every man's sword against his fellow,
even throughout all the host: and the host fled to Beth-
shittah in Zererath, and to the border of Abelmeholah,
unto Tabbath.

4 1 Samuel 17:49—And David put his hand in his bag,
and took thence a stone, and slang it, and smote the
Philistine in his forehead, that the stone sunk into his
forehead; and he fell upon his face to the earth.

WHY ART THOU CAST DOWN?

BE still my heart! these anxious cares
To thee are burdens, thorns, and snares,
They cast dishonor on thy LORD,
And contradict his gracious word!

Brought safely by his hand thus far,
Why wilt thou now give place to fear?
How canst thou want if he provide,
Or lose thy way with such a guide?

When first before his mercy-seat,
Thou didst to him thy all commit;
He gave thee warrant, from that hour,
To trust his wisdom, love, and pow'r.

Did ever trouble yet befall,
And he refuse to hear thy call?
And has he not his promise past,
That thou shalt overcome at last?

Like David, thou may'st comfort draw,
Sav'd from the bear's and lion's paw,
Goliath's rage I may defy,
For GOD, my Saviour, still is nigh.

He who has help'd me hitherto,
Will help me all my journey thro';
And give me daily cause to raise
New Ebenezers to his praise.

Tho' rough and thorny be the road,
It leads thee home, apace, to GOD;
Then count thy present trials small,
For heav'n will make amends for all.

THE WAY OF ACCESS.

ONE glance of thine, eternal LORD,
  Pierces all nature thro';
Nor heav'n, nor earth, nor hell, afford
  A shelter from thy view!

The mighty whole, each smaller part,
  At once before thee lies;
And ev'ry thought, of ev'ry heart,
  Is open to thine eyes.

Tho' greatly from myself conceal'd,
  Thou see'st my inward frame;
To thee I always stand reveal'd,
  Exactly as I am.

Since therefore I can hardly bear
  What in myself I see;
How vile and black must I appear,
  Most holy GOD, to thee.

But since my Saviour stands between,
  In garments dy'd in blood;
'Tis he, instead of me, is seen,
  When I approach to GOD.

Thus, tho' a sinner, I am safe;
  He pleads before the throne,
His life and death, in my behalf,
  And calls my sins his own.

What wond'rous love, what mysteries,
  In this appointment shine!
My breaches of the Law are his,[1]
  And his obedience mine.

THE PILGRIM'S SONG.

FROM Egypt lately freed
  By the Redeemer's grace;
A rough and thorny path we tread,
  In hopes to see his face.

The flesh dislikes the way,
  But faith approves it well;
This only leads to endless day,
  All others lead to hell.

The promis'd land of peace
  Faith keeps in constant view;
How diff'rent from the wilderness
  We now are passing thro'!

Here often from our eyes
  Clouds hide the light divine;
There we shall have unclouded skies,
  Our Sun will always shine.

Here griefs, and cares, and pains,
  And fears, distress us sore;
But there eternal pleasure reigns,
  And we shall weep no more.

LORD pardon our complaints,
  We follow at thy call;
The joy, prepar'd for suff'ring saints,
  Will make amends for all.

---

1 2 Corinthians 5:21—For he hath made him to be sin
  for us, who knew no sin; that we might be made the
  righteousness of God in him.

FAITH A NEW AND COMPREHENSIVE SENSE.

SIGHT, hearing, feeling, taste and smell,
　Are gifts we highly prize;
But faith does singly each excel,
　And all the five comprize.

More piercing than the eagle's sight
　It views the world unknown;
Surveys the glorious realms of light,
　And JESUS on the throne.

It hears the mighty voice of GOD,
　And ponders what he saith;
His word and works, his gifts and rod,
　Have each a voice to faith.

It feels the touch of heavenly pow'r,[1]
　And from that boundless source,
Derives fresh vigor ev'ry hour,
　To run its daily course.

The truth and goodness of the LORD,
　Are suited to its taste;[2]
Mean is the worldling's pamper'd board,
　To faith's perpetual feast.

It smells the dear Redeemer's name
　Like ointment poured forth;[3]
Faith only knows or can proclaim,
　Its savor or its worth.

Till saving faith possess the mind,
　In vain of sense we boast;
We are but senseless, tasteless, blind,
　And deaf, and dead, and lost.

JESUS MY ALL.

WHY should I fear the darkest hour,
Or tremble at the tempter's pow'r?
JESUS vouchsafes to be my tow'r.

Tho' hot the fight; why quit the field?
Why must I either flee or yield,
Since JESUS is my mighty shield?

When creature comforts fade and die,
Worldlings may weep; but why should I?
JESUS still lives, and still is nigh.

Tho' all the flocks and herds were dead,
My soul a famine need not dread,
For JESUS is my living bread.

I know not what may soon betide,
Or how my wants shall be supply'd;
But JESUS knows, and will provide.

Tho' sin would fill me with distress,
The throne of grace I dare address;
For JESUS is my righteousness.

Tho' faint my pray'rs, and cold my love,
My stedfast hope shall not remove,
While JESUS intercedes above.

Against me earth and hell combine;
But on my side is pow'r divine;
JESUS is all, and he is mine.

---

1 Luke 8:46—And Jesus said, Somebody hath touched
　me: for I perceive that virtue is gone out of me.
2 Psalm 119:103—How sweet are thy words unto my
　taste! yea, sweeter than honey to my mouth!
3 Song of Solomon 1:3—Because of the savour of thy
　good ointments thy name is as ointment poured forth,
　therefore do the virgins love thee.

CONFIDENCE.

YES! since GOD himself has said it,
On the promise I rely;
His good word demands my credit,
What can unbelief reply?
    He is strong and *can* fulfill,
    He is truth and therefore *will.*

As to all the doubts and questions,
Which my spirit often grieve,
These are Satan's sly suggestions,
And I need no answer give;
    He would fain destroy my hope,
    But the promise bears it up.

Sure the LORD thus far has brought me
By his watchful tender care;
Sure 'tis he himself has taught me
How to seek his face by pray'r:
    After so much mercy past,
    Will he give me up at last?

True, I've been a foolish creature,
And have sinn'd against his grace;
But forgiveness is his nature,
Tho' he justly hides his face:
    Ere he call'd me well he knew,[1]
    What a heart like mine would do.

In my Saviour's intercession
Therefore I will still confide;
LORD accept my free confession,
I have sinn'd, but thou hast dy'd:[2]
    This is all I have to plead,
    This is all the plea I need.

PEACE RESTORED.

OH, speak that gracious word again,
    And cheer my drooping heart!
No voice but thine can sooth my pain,
    Or bid my fears depart.

And canst thou still vouchsafe to own
    A wretch so vile as I?
And may I still approach thy throne,
    And Abba, Father, cry?

Oh then let saints and angels join,
    And help me to proclaim,
The grace that heal'd a breach like mine,
    And put my foes to shame!

How oft did Satan's cruel boast
    My troubled soul affright!
He told me I was surely lost,
    And GOD had left me quite.[3]

Guilt made me fear, lest all were true
    The lying tempter said!
But now the LORD appears in view,
    My enemy is fled.

My Saviour, by his pow'rful word,
    Has turn'd my night to day;
And his salvation's joys restor'd,
    Which I had sinn'd away.

Dear LORD I wonder and adore,
    Thy grace is all divine;
Oh keep me, that I sin no more
    Against such love as thine!

---

1 Isaiah 48:8—Yea, thou heardest not; yea, thou knewest not; yea, from that time that thine ear was not opened: for I knew that thou wouldest deal very treacherously, and wast called a transgressor from the womb.

2 Romans 8:34—Who is he that condemneth? It is Christ that died, yea rather, that is risen again, who is even at the right hand of God, who also maketh intercession for us.

---

3 Psalm 71:11—Saying, God hath forsaken him: persecute and take him; for there is none to deliver him.

HEAR WHAT HE HAS DONE
FOR MY SOUL!

SAV'D by blood I live to tell,
What the love of CHRIST hath done;
He redeem'd my soul from hell,
Of a rebel made a son:
Oh I tremble still, to think
How secure I liv'd in sin;
Sporting on destruction's brink,
Yet preserv'd from falling in.

In his own appointed hour,
To my heart the Saviour spoke;
Touch'd me by his Spirit's pow'r,
And my dang'rous slumber broke.
Then I saw and own'd my guilt,
Soon my gracious LORD reply'd;
"Fear not, I my blood have spilt,
'Twas for such as thee I dy'd."

Shame and wonder, joy and love,
All at once possess'd my heart;
Can I hope thy grace to prove,
After acting such a part?
"Thou hast greatly sinn'd, he said,
But I freely all forgive;
I myself thy debt have paid,
Now I bid thee rise and live."

Come, my fellow-sinners, try,
JESUS' heart is full of love;
Oh that you, as well as I,
May his wond'rous mercy prove!
He has sent me to declare,
All is ready, all is free;
Why should any soul despair,
When he sav'd a wretch like me?

FREEDOM FROM CARE.

WHILE I liv'd without the LORD,
(If I might be said to live)
Nothing could relief afford,
Nothing satisfaction give.

Empty hopes and groundless fear,
Mov'd by turns my anxious mind;
Like a feather in the air,
Made the sport of ev'ry wind.

Now, I see, whate'er betide,
All is well if CHRIST be mine;
He has promis'd to provide,
I have only to resign.

When a sense of sin and thrall,
Forc'd me to the sinner's Friend;
He engag'd to manage all,
By the way, and to the end.

"Cast, he said, on me thy care,[1]
'Tis enough that I am nigh;
I will all thy burdens bear,
I will all thy wants supply.

Simply follow as I lead,
Do not reason but believe;
Call on me in time of need,
Thou shalt surely help receive."

LORD I would, I do, submit,
Gladly yield my all to thee;
What thy wisdom sees most fit,
Must be, surely, best for me.

Only when the way is rough,
And the coward flesh would start,
Let thy promise and thy love,
Cheer and animate my heart.

---

1 Psalm 55:22—Cast thy burden upon the LORD, and he
  shall sustain thee: he shall never suffer the righteous
  to be moved.
  1 Peter 5:7—Casting all your care upon him; for he
  careth for you.

HUMILIATION AND PRAISE.

(Imitated from the German.)

WHEN the wounded spirit hears
　The voice of JESUS' blood;
How the message stops the tears
　Which else in vain had flow'd:
Pardon, grace, and peace proclaim'd,
And the sinner call'd a child;
Then the stubborn heart is tam'd,
　Renew'd, and reconcil'd.

Oh! 'twas grace indeed, to spare,
　And save a wretch like me!
Men or angels could not bear
　What I have offer'd thee:
Were thy bolts at their command,
Hell, ere now, had been my place;
Thou alone couldst silent stand,
　And wait to shew thy grace.

If in one created mind
　The tenderness and love
Of thy saints on earth were join'd,
　With all the hosts above;
Still that love were weak and poor,
If compar'd, my LORD, with thine;
Far too scanty to endure
　A heart so vile as mine.

Wond'rous mercy I have found,
　But ah! how faint my praise!
Must I be a cumber-ground,
　Unfruitful all my days?
Do I in thy garden grow,
Yet produce thee only leaves?
LORD, forbid it should be so!
　The thought my spirit grieves.

Heavy charges Satan brings
　To fill me with distress;
Let me hide beneath thy wings,
　And plead thy righteousness:
LORD, to thee for help I call,
'Tis thy promise bids me come;
Tell him thou hast paid for all,
　And that shall strike him dumb.

HOME IN VIEW.

As when the weary travell'r gains
The height of some o'er-looking hill;
His heart revives, if cross the plains
He eyes his home, tho' distant still.

While he surveys the much-lov'd spot,
He slights the space that lies between;
His past fatigues are now forgot,
Because his journey's end is seen.

Thus, when the christian pilgrim views
By faith, his mansion in the skies;
The sight his fainting strength renews,
And wings his speed to reach the prize.

The thought of home his spirit cheers,
No more he grieves for troubles past;
Nor any future trial fears,[1]
So he may safe arrive at last.

'Tis there, he says, I am to dwell
With JESUS, in the realms of day;
Then I shall bid my cares farewel,
And he will wipe my tears away.

JESUS, on thee our hope depends,
To lead us on to thine abode;
Assur'd our home will make amends
For all our toil while on the road.

---

1 Acts 20:24—But none of these things move me, neither count I my life dear unto myself, so that I might finish my course with joy, and the ministry, which I have received of the Lord Jesus, to testify the gospel of the grace of God.

OLD THINGS ARE PASSED AWAY.

LET worldly minds the world pursue,
    It has no charms for me;
Once I admir'd its trifles too,
    But grace has set me free.

Its pleasures now no longer please,
    No more content afford;
Far from my heart be joys like these,
    Now I have seen the LORD.

As by the light of op'ning day
    The stars are all conceal'd;
So earthly pleasures fade away,
    When JESUS is reveal'd.

Creatures no more divide my choice,
    I bid them all depart;
His name, and love, and gracious voice,
    Have fix'd my roving heart.

Now, LORD, I would be thine alone,
    And wholly live to thee;
But may I hope that thou wilt own
    A worthless worm, like me?

Yes! tho' of sinners I'm the worst,
    I cannot doubt thy will;
For if thou hadst not lov'd me first
    I had refus'd thee still.[1]

THE POWER OF GRACE.

HAPPY the birth where grace presides
    To form the future life!
In wisdom's paths the soul she guides,
    Remote from noise and strife.

Since I have known the Saviour's name
    And what for me he bore;
No more I toil for empty fame,
    I thirst for gold no more.

Plac'd by his hand in this retreat,
    I make his love my theme;
And see that all the world calls great,
    Is but a waking dream.

Since he has rank'd my worthless name
    Amongst his favor'd few;
Let the mad world who scoff at *them*
    Revile and hate *me* too.

O thou whose voice the dead can raise,
    And soften hearts of stone,
And teach the dumb to sing thy praise,
    This work is all thine own!

Thy wond'ring saints rejoice to see
    A wretch, like me, restor'd;
And point, and say, "How chang'd is he,
    Who once defy'd the LORD!"

Grace bid me live, and taught my tongue
    To aim at notes divine;
And grace accepts my feeble song,
    The glory, LORD, be thine!

---

1 Jeremiah 31:3—The LORD hath appeared of old unto
me, saying, Yea, I have loved thee with an everlasting
love: therefore with lovingkindness have I drawn thee.

THE CHILD.[1]

Quiet, Lord, my froward heart,
Make me teachable and mild,
Upright, simple, free from art,
Make me as a weaned child:
    From distrust and envy free,
    Pleas'd with all that pleases thee.

What thou shalt to-day provide,
Let me as a child receive;
What to-morrow may betide,
Calmly to thy wisdom leave:
    'Tis enough that thou wilt care,
    Why should I the burden bear?

As a little child relies
On a care beyond his own;
Knows he's neither strong nor wise,
Fears to stir a step alone:
    Let me thus with thee abide,
    As my Father, Guard, and Guide.

Thus preserv'd from Satan's wiles,
Safe from dangers, free from fears;
May I live upon thy smiles,
Till the promis'd hour appears;
    When the sons of God shall prove
    All their Father's boundless love.

TRUE HAPPINESS.

Fix my heart and eyes on thine!
What are other objects worth?
But to see thy glory shine,
Is a heav'n begun on earth:
Trifles can no longer move,
Oh, I tread on all beside,
When I feel my Saviour's love,
And remember how he dy'd.

Now my search is at an end,
Now my wishes rove no more!
Thus my moments I would spend,
Love, and wonder, and adore:
Jesus, source of excellence!
All thy glorious love reveal!
Kingdoms shall not bribe me hence,
While this happiness I feel.

Take my heart, 'tis all thine own,
To thy will my spirit frame;
Thou shalt reign, and thou alone,
Over all I have, or am:
If a foolish thought shall dare
To rebel against thy word,
Slay it, Lord, and do not spare,
Let it feel thy Spirit's sword.

Making thus the Lord my choice
I have nothing more to choose,
But to listen to thy voice,
And my will in thine to lose:
Thus, whatever may betide,
I shall safe and happy be;
Still content and satisfy'd,
Having all, in having thee.

---

1 Psalm 131:2—Surely I have behaved and quieted myself, as a child that is weaned of his mother: my soul is even as a weaned child.

  Matthew 18:3–4—And said, Verily I say unto you, Except ye be converted, and become as little children, ye shall not enter into the kingdom of heaven. Whosoever therefore shall humble himself as this little child, the same is greatest in the kingdom of heaven.

THE HAPPY DEBTOR.

Ten thousand talents once I ow'd,
    And nothing had to pay;
But Jesus freed me from the load,
    And wash'd my debt away.

Yet since the Lord forgave my sin,
    And blotted out my score;
Much more indebted I have been,
    Than e'er I was before.

My guilt is cancell'd quite, I know,
    And satisfaction made;
But the vast debt of love I owe,
    Can never be repaid.

The love I owe for sin forgiv'n,
    For power to believe,
For present peace, and promis'd heav'n,
    No angel can conceive.

That love of thine! thou sinner's Friend!
    Witness thy bleeding heart!
My little all can ne'er extend
    To pay a thousandth part.

Nay more, the poor returns I make
    I first from thee obtain;[1]
And 'tis of grace, that thou wilt take
    Such poor returns again.

'Tis well—it shall my glory be
    (Let who will boast their store)
In time and to eternity,
    To owe thee more and more.

TRUE AND FALSE ZEAL.

Zeal is that pure and heav'nly flame,
    The fire of love supplies;
While that which often bears the name,
    Is self in a disguise.

True zeal is merciful and mild,
    Can pity and forbear;
The false is headstrong, fierce and wild,
    And breathes revenge and war.

While zeal for truth the christian warms,
    He knows the worth of peace;
But self contends for names and forms,
    Its party to increase.

Zeal has attain'd its highest aim,
    Its end is satisfy'd;
If sinners love the Saviour's name,
    Nor seeks it ought beside.

But self, however well employ'd,
    Has its own ends in view;
And says, as boasting Jehu cry'd,[2]
    "Come, see what I can do."

Self may its poor reward obtain,
    And be applauded here;
But zeal the best applause will gain,
    When Jesus shall appear.

Dear Lord, the idol self dethrone,
    And from our hearts remove;
And let no zeal by us be shewn,
    But that which springs from love.

---

1 1 Chronicles 29:14—But who am I, and what is my people, that we should be able to offer so willingly after this sort? for all things come of thee, and of thine own have we given thee.

2 2 Kings 10:16—And he said, Come with me, and see my zeal for the Lord. So they made him ride in his chariot.

SIN'S DECEIT.

Sin, when view'd by scripture light,
Is a horrid, hateful sight;
But when seen in Satan's glass,
Then it wears a pleasing face.

When the gospel trumpet sounds,
When I think how grace abounds,
When I feel sweet peace within,
Then I'd rather die than sin.

When the cross I view by faith,
Sin is madness, poison, death;
Tempt me not, 'tis all in vain,
Sure I ne'er can yield again.

Satan, for awhile debarr'd,
When he finds me off my guard,
Puts his glass before my eyes,
Quickly other thoughts arise.

What before excited fears,
Rather pleasing now appears;
If a sin, it seems so small,
Or, perhaps, no sin at all.

Often thus, thro' sin's deceit,
Grief, and shame, and loss I meet;
Like a fish, my soul mistook,
Saw the bait, but not the hook.

O my Lord, what shall I say?
How can I presume to pray?
Not a word have I to plead,
Sins, like mine, are black indeed!

Made, by past experience, wise,
Let me learn thy word to prize;
Taught by what I've felt before,
Let me Satan's glass abhor.

ARE THERE FEW THAT SHALL BE SAVED?

Destruction's dangerous road
What multitudes pursue!
While that which leads the soul to God,
Is known or sought by few.

Believers enter in
By Christ, the living gate;
But they who will not leave their sin,
Complain it is too strait.

If self must be deny'd,
And sin forsaken quite;
They rather choose the way that's wide,
And strive to think it right.

Encompass'd by a throng,
On numbers they depend;
So many surely can't be wrong,
And miss a happy end.

But numbers are no mark
That men will right be found;
A few were sav'd in Noah's ark,[1]
For many millions drown'd.

Obey the gospel call,
And enter while you may;
The flock of Christ is always small,[2]
And none are safe but they.

Lord, open sinners eyes
Their awful state to see;
And make them, ere the storm arise,
To thee for safety flee.

---

1 1 Peter 3:20—Which sometime were disobedient, when once the longsuffering of God waited in the days of Noah, while the ark was a preparing, wherein few, that is, eight souls were saved by water.

2 Luke 12:32—Fear not, little flock; for it is your Father's good pleasure to give you the kingdom.

THE SLUGGARD.

THE wishes that the sluggard frames,[1]
    Of course must fruitless prove;
With folded arms he stands and dreams,
    But has no heart to move.

His field from others may be known,
    The fence is broken thro';
The ground with weeds is overgrown,
    And no good crop in view.

No hardship, he, or toil, can bear,
    No difficulty meet;
He wastes his hours at home, for fear
    Of lions in the street.

What wonder then if sloth and sleep,
    Distress and famine bring!
Can he in harvest hope to reap,
    Who will not sow in spring?

'Tis often thus, in soul concerns,
    We gospel-sluggards see;
Who if a wish would serve their turns,
    Might true believers be.

But when the preacher bids them watch,
    And seek, and strive, and pray;[2]
At ev'ry poor excuse they catch,
    A lion's in the way!

To use the means of grace, how loth!
    We call them still in vain;
They yield to their beloved sloth,
    And fold their arms again.

Dear Saviour, let thy pow'r appear,
    The outward call to aid;
These drowsy souls, can only hear
    The voice, that wakes the dead.

---

1 Proverbs 6:10—Yet a little sleep, a little slumber, a little folding of the hands to sleep.
  Proverbs 24:30—I went by the field of the slothful, and by the vineyard of the man void of understanding.
  Proverbs 22:13—The slothful man saith, There is a lion without, I shall be slain in the streets.
  Proverbs 20:4—The sluggard will not plow by reason of the cold; therefore shall he beg in harvest, and have nothing.

2 1 Corinthians 9:24—Know ye not that they which run in a race run all, but one receiveth the prize? So run, that ye may obtain.
  Luke 13:24—Strive to enter in at the strait gate: for many, I say unto you, will seek to enter in, and shall not be able.

NOT IN WORD, BUT IN POWER.

HOW soon the Saviour's gracious call,
Disarm'd the rage of bloody Saul![3]
JESUS, the knowledge of thy name,
Changes the lion to a lamb!

Zaccheus, when he knew the LORD,[4]
What he had gain'd by wrong, restor'd;
And of the wealth he priz'd before,
He gave the half to feed the poor.

The woman who so vile had been,[5]
When brought to weep o'er pardon'd sin,
Was from her evil ways estrang'd,
And shew'd that grace her heart had chang'd.

And can we think the pow'r of grace
Is lost, by change of time and place?
Then it was mighty, all allow,
And is it but a notion now?

Can they whom pride and passion sway,
Who Mammon and the world obey,
In envy or contention live,
Presume that they indeed believe?

True faith unites to CHRIST the root,
By him producing holy fruit;
And they who no such fruit can show,
Still on the stock of nature grow.

LORD, let thy word effectual prove,
To work in us obedient love!
And may each one who hears it dread
A name to live; and yet be dead.[6]

---

3 Acts 9:6—And he trembling and astonished said, Lord, what wilt thou have me to do? And the Lord said unto him, Arise, and go into the city, and it shall be told thee what thou must do.

4 Luke 19:8—And Zacchaeus stood, and said unto the Lord: Behold, Lord, the half of my goods I give to the poor; and if I have taken any thing from any man by false accusation, I restore him fourfold.

5 Luke 7:47—Wherefore I say unto thee, Her sins, which are many, are forgiven; for she loved much: but to whom little is forgiven, the same loveth little.

6 Revelation 3:1—And unto the angel of the church in Sardis write; These things saith he that hath the seven Spirits of God, and the seven stars; I know thy works, that thou hast a name that thou livest, and art dead.

PRAISE FOR REDEEMING LOVE.

LET us *love*, and *sing*, and *wonder*,
Let us *praise* the Saviour's name!
He has hush'd the Law's loud thunder,
He has quench'd mount Sinai's flame:
  He has wash'd us with his blood,
  He has brought us nigh to GOD.

Let us *love* the LORD who bought us,
Pity'd us when enemies;
Call'd us by his grace, and taught us,
Gave us ears, and gave us eyes:
  He has wash'd us with his blood,
  He presents our souls to GOD.

Let us *sing* tho' fierce temptations
Threaten hard to bear us down!
For the LORD, our strong salvation,[1]
Holds in view the conqu'rors crown:
  He who wash'd us with his blood,
  Soon will bring us home to GOD.

Let us *wonder*, grace and justice,
Join and point to mercy's store;
When thro' grace in CHRIST our trust is,
Justice smiles; and asks no more:
  He who wash'd us with his blood,
  Has secur'd our way to GOD.

Let us *praise*, and join the chorus
Of the saints, enthron'd on high;
Here they trusted him before us,
Now their praises fill the sky:[2]
  "Thou hast wash'd us with thy blood,
  Thou art worthy, Lamb of GOD!"

Hark! the name of JESUS, sounded
Loud, from golden harps above!
LORD, we blush, and are confounded,
Faint our praises, cold our love!
  Wash our souls and songs with blood,
  For by thee we come to GOD.

1 Revelation 2:10—Fear none of those things which thou
  shalt suffer: behold, the devil shall cast some of you into
  prison, that ye may be tried; and ye shall have tribulation
  ten days: be thou faithful unto death, and I will give thee
  a crown of life.
2 Revelation 5:9—And they sung a new song, saying, Thou
  art worthy to take the book, and to open the seals thereof:
  for thou wast slain, and hast redeemed us to God by thy
  blood out of every kindred, and tongue, and people, and
  nation.

PERSEVERANCE.

REJOICE, believer, in the LORD
  Who makes your cause his own;
The hope that's built upon his word,
  Can ne'er be overthrown.

Tho' many foes beset your road,
  And feeble is your arm;
Your life is hid with CHRIST in GOD,[3]
  Beyond the reach of harm.

Weak as you are, you shall not faint,
  Or fainting shall not die;
JESUS, the strength of ev'ry saint,[4]
  Will aid you from on high.

Tho' sometimes unperceiv'd by sense,
  Faith sees him always near;
A Guide, a Glory, a Defence,
  Then what have you to fear?

As surely as he overcame,
  And triumph'd once for you;
So surely you, that love his name,
  Shall triumph in him too.

3 Colossians 3:3—For ye are dead, and your life is hid with
  Christ in God.
4 Isaiah 40:29—He giveth power to the faint; and to them
  that have no might he increaseth strength.

SALVATION.

Salvation! what a glorious plan,
    How suited to our need!
The grace that raises fallen man,
    Is wonderful indeed!

'Twas wisdom form'd the vast design,
    To ransom us when lost;
And love's unfathomable mine
    Provided all the cost.

Strict Justice, with approving look,
    The holy cov'nant seal'd;
And Truth, and Power, undertook
    The whole should be fulfill'd.

Truth, Wisdom, Justice, Pow'r and Love,
    In all their glory shone;
When Jesus left the courts above,
    And dy'd to save his own.

Truth, Wisdom, Justice, Pow'r and Love,
    Are equally display'd;
Now Jesus reigns enthron'd above,
    Our Advocate and Head.

Now sin appears deserving death,
    Most hateful and abhorr'd;
And yet the sinner lives by faith,
    And dares approach the Lord.

REIGNING GRACE.

Now may the Lord reveal his face,
    And teach our stamm'ring tongues
To make his sovereign, reigning grace,[1]
    The subject of our songs!
No sweeter subject can invite
    A sinner's heart to sing;
Or more display the glorious right
    Of our exalted King.

This subject fills the starry plains
    With wonder, joy, and love;
And furnishes the noblest strains
    For all the harps above:
While the redeem'd in praise combine
    To grace upon the throne;[2]
Angels in solemn chorus join,
    And make the theme their own.

Grace reigns, to pardon crimson sins,
    To melt the hardest hearts;
And from the work it once begins,[3]
    It never more departs.
The world and Satan strive in vain,
    Against the chosen few;[4]
Secur'd by grace's conqu'ring reign,
    They all shall conquer too.

(Continued on the next page.)

1 Romans 5:21—That as sin hath reigned unto death, even so might grace reign through righteousness unto eternal life by Jesus Christ our Lord.

2 Revelation 5:9—And they sung a new song, saying, Thou art worthy to take the book, and to open the seals thereof: for thou wast slain, and hast redeemed us to God by thy blood out of every kindred, and tongue, and people, and nation.

Revelation 5:12—Saying with a loud voice, Worthy is the Lamb that was slain to receive power, and riches, and wisdom, and strength, and honour, and glory, and blessing.

3 Philippians 1:6—Being confident of this very thing, that he which hath begun a good work in you will perform it until the day of Jesus Christ.

4 Romans 8:35–39—Who shall separate us from the love of Christ? shall tribulation, or distress, or persecution, or famine, or nakedness, or peril, or sword? As it is written, For thy sake we are killed all the day long; we are accounted as sheep for the slaughter. Nay, in all these things we are more than conquerors through him that loved us. For I am persuaded, that neither death, nor life, nor angels, nor principalities, nor powers, nor things present, nor things to come, Nor height, nor depth, nor any other creature, shall be able to separate us from the love of God, which is in Christ Jesus our Lord.

Grace tills the soil, and sows the seeds,
   Provides the sun and rain;
Till from the tender blade proceeds
   The ripen'd harvest grain.
'Twas grace that call'd our souls at first,
   By grace thus far we're come,
And grace will help us thro' the worst,
   And lead us safely home.

LORD, when this changing life is past
   If we may see thy face;
How shall we praise, and love, at last,
   And sing the reign of grace![1]
Yet let us aim while here below
   Thy mercy to display;
And own at least the debt we owe,
   Altho' we cannot pay.

---

1 Psalm 115:1—Not unto us, O LORD, not unto us, but unto thy name give glory, for thy mercy, and for thy truth's sake.

PRAISE TO THE REDEEMER.

PREPARE a thankful song
   To the Redeemer's name!
His praises should employ each tongue
   And ev'ry heart inflame!

He laid his glory by,
   And dreadful pains endur'd;
That rebels, such as you and I,
   From wrath might be secur'd.

Upon the cross he dy'd,
   Our debt of sin to pay;
The blood and water from his side
   Wash guilt and filth away.

And now he pleading stands
   For us, before the throne;
And answers all the Law's demands,
   With what himself hath done.

He sees us, willing slaves
   To sin, and Satan's pow'r;
But, with an outstretch'd arm, he saves,
   In his appointed hour.

The Holy Ghost he sends
   Our stubborn souls to move;
To make his enemies his friends,
   And conquer them by love.

The love of sin departs,
   The life of grace takes place,
Soon as his voice invites our hearts
   To rise and seek his face.

The world and Satan rage,
   But he their pow'r controls;
His wisdom, love, and truth, engage
   Protection for our souls.

Tho' press'd, we will not yield,
   But shall prevail at length,
For JESUS is our sun and shield,
   Our righteousness and strength.

Assur'd that CHRIST our king,
   Will put our foes to flight;
We, on the field of battle, sing
   And triumph, while we fight.

MAN BY NATURE, GRACE AND GLORY.

LORD, what is man! extremes how wide,
In this mysterious nature join!
The flesh, to worms and dust ally'd,
The soul, immortal and divine!

Divine at first, a holy flame
Kindled by the Almighty's breath;
Till, stain'd by sin, it soon became
The seat of darkness, strife, and death,

But JESUS, Oh! amazing grace!
Assum'd our nature as his own,
Obey'd and suffer'd in our place,
Then took it with him to his throne.

Now what is man, when grace reveals
The virtue of a Saviour's blood?
Again a life divine he feels,
Despises earth, and walks with GOD.

And what, in yonder realms above,
Is ransom'd man ordain'd to be?
With honor, holiness, and love,
No seraph more adorn'd than he.

Nearest the throne, and first in song,
Man shall his hallelujahs raise;
While wond'ring angels round him throng,
And swell the chorus of his praise.

HYMN 89.

CONFIRM the hope thy word allows,
Behold us waiting to be fed;
Bless the provisions of thy house,
And satisfy thy poor with bread:
Drawn by thine invitation, LORD,
Athirst and hungry we are come;
Now from the fulness of thy word,
Feast us, and send us thankful home.

HYMN 90.

Now, LORD, inspire the preacher's heart,
   And teach his tongue to speak;
Food to the hungry soul impart,
   And cordials to the weak.

Furnish us all with light and pow'rs
   To walk in Wisdom's ways;
So shall the benefit be ours,
   And thou shalt have the praise.

HYMN 91.

THY promise, LORD, and thy command
  Have brought us here to-day;
And now, we humbly waiting stand
  To hear what thou wilt say.[1]

Meet us, we pray, with words of peace,
  And fill our hearts with love;
That from our follies we may cease,
  And henceforth faithful prove.

HYMN 92.

HUNGRY, and faint, and poor,
  Behold us, LORD, again
Assembled at thy mercies door,
  Thy bounty to obtain.

Thy word invites us nigh
  Or we must starve indeed;
For we no money have to buy,
  No righteousness to plead.

The food our spirits want
  Thy hand alone can give;
Oh, hear the pray'r of faith, and grant
  That we may eat, and live.

HYMN 93.

Remember me, O LORD, with the favour that thou bearest unto thy people: O visit me with thy salvation; That I may see the good of thy chosen, that I may rejoice in the gladness of thy nation, that I may glory with thine inheritance.—PSALM 106:4–5.

REMEMBER us, we pray thee, LORD,
With those who love thy gracious name,
And to our souls that good afford,
Thy promise has prepar'd for them.

To us thy great salvation show,
Give us a taste of love divine;
That we thy peoples joy may know;
And in their holy triumph join.

HYMN 94.

NOT to Sinai's dreadful blaze,[2]
But to Zion's throne of grace,
By a way mark'd out with blood,
Sinners now approach to GOD.

Not to hear the fiery Law,
But with humble joy to draw
Water, by that well supply'd,[3]
JESUS open'd when he dy'd.

LORD, there are no streams but thine,
Can assuage a thirst like mine!
'Tis a thirst thyself didst give,
Let me therefore drink and live.

---

1 Psalm 85:8—I will hear what God the LORD will speak: for he will speak peace unto his people, and to his saints: but let them not turn again to folly.

2 Hebrews 12:18—For ye are not come unto the mount that might be touched, and that burned with fire, nor unto blackness, and darkness, and tempest.
  Hebrews 12:22—But ye are come unto mount Sion, and unto the city of the living God, the heavenly Jerusalem, and to an innumerable company of angels.
3 Isaiah 12:3—Therefore with joy shall ye draw water out of the wells of salvation.

HYMN 95.

Oᶠᵗᴇɴ thy public means of grace,
Thy thirsty peoples wat'ring place,
    The archers have beset;[1]
Attack'd them in thy house of pray'r,
To prison dragg'd, or to the bar,
    When thus together met.

But we from such assaults are freed,
Can pray, and sing, and hear, and read,
    And meet, and part, in peace:
May we our privileges prize,
In their improvement make us wise,
    And bless us with increase.

Unless thy presence thou afford,
Unless thy blessing clothe the word,
    In vain our liberty!
What would it profit to maintain
A name for life, should we remain
    Formal and dead to thee?

HYMN 96.

There is none like unto the God of Jeshurun, who rideth upon the heaven in thy help, and in his excellency on the sky. The eternal God is thy refuge, and underneath are the everlasting arms: and he shall thrust out the enemy from before thee; and shall say, Destroy them. Israel then shall dwell in safety alone: the fountain of Jacob shall be upon a land of corn and wine; also his heavens shall drop down dew. Happy art thou, O Israel: who is like unto thee, O people saved by the Lᴏʀᴅ, the shield of thy help, and who is the sword of thy excellency! and thine enemies shall be found liars unto thee; and thou shalt tread upon their high places.
                    —Dᴇᴜᴛᴇʀᴏɴᴏᴍʏ 33:26–29.

Wɪᴛʜ Israel's Gᴏᴅ who can compare?
Or who, like Israel, happy are?
O people saved by the Lᴏʀᴅ,
He is thy shield and great reward!

Upheld by everlasting arms,
Thou art secur'd from foes and harms!
In vain their plots, and false their boasts,
Our refuge is the Lᴏʀᴅ of Hosts.

HYMN 97.

Although the fig tree shall not blossom, neither shall fruit be in the vines; the labour of the olive shall fail, and the fields shall yield no meat; the flock shall be cut off from the fold, and there shall be no herd in the stalls: Yet I will rejoice in the Lᴏʀᴅ, I will joy in the God of my salvation.
                    —Hᴀʙᴀᴋᴋᴜᴋ 3:17–18.

Jᴇsᴜs is mine! I'm now prepar'd
To meet with what I thought most hard;
Yes, let the winds of trouble blow,
And comforts melt away like snow:
No blasted trees, or failing crops,
Can hinder my eternal hopes;
Tho' creatures change, the Lᴏʀᴅ's the same,
Then let me triumph in his name.

---

1 Judges 5:11—They that are delivered from the noise of archers in the places of drawing water, there shall they rehearse the righteous acts of the Lᴏʀᴅ, even the righteous acts toward the inhabitants of his villages in Israel: then shall the people of the Lᴏʀᴅ go down to the gates.

HYMN 98.

WE seek a rest beyond the skies,
  In everlasting day;
Thro' floods and flames the passage lies,
  But JESUS guards the way:
The swelling flood, and raging flame,
  Hear and obey his word;
Then let us triumph in his name,
  Our Saviour is the LORD.

HYMN 99.

For the LORD's portion is his people; Jacob is the lot of his inheritance. He found him in a desert land, and in the waste howling wilderness; he led him about, he instructed him, he kept him as the apple of his eye.—DEUTERONOMY 32:9–10.

THE saints EMMANUEL'S portion are,
Redeem'd by price, reclaim'd by pow'r;
His special choice, and tender care,
Owns them and guards them ev'ry hour.

He finds them in a barren land
Beset with sins, and fears, and woes;
He leads and guides them by his hand,
And bears them safe from all their foes.

HYMN 100.

Now the God of peace, that brought again from the dead our Lord Jesus, that great shepherd of the sheep, through the blood of the everlasting covenant.—HEBREWS 13:20.

Salute all them that have the rule over you, and all the saints. They of Italy salute you.—HEBREWS 13:24.

Now may He who from the dead
Brought the Shepherd of the sheep,
JESUS CHRIST, our King and Head,
All our souls in safety keep!

May he teach us to fulfill
What is pleasing in his sight;
Perfect us in all his will,
And preserve us day and night!

To that dear Redeemer's praise,
Who the cov'nant seal'd with blood,
Let our hearts and voices raise
Loud thanksgivings to our GOD.

HYMN 101.

The grace of the Lord Jesus Christ, and the love of God, and the communion of the Holy Ghost, be with you all. Amen.—2 CORINTHIANS 13:14.

MAY the grace of CHRIST our Saviour
And the FATHER's boundless love,
With the holy SPIRIT's favor,
Rest upon us from above!
Thus may we abide in union
With each other, and the LORD;
And possess, in sweet communion,
Joys which earth cannot afford.

HYMN 102.

THE peace which GOD alone reveals,
And by his word of grace imparts,
Which only the believer feels,[1]
Direct and keep, and cheer your hearts:
And may the holy Three in One,
The FATHER, WORD, and COMFORTER,
Pour an abundant blessing down
On ev'ry soul assembled here!

HYMN 103.

To thee our wants are known,
From thee are all our pow'rs;
Accept what is thine own,
And pardon what is ours:
Our praises, LORD, and pray'rs receive,
And to thy word a blessing give.

Oh, grant that each of us
Now met before thee here,
May meet together thus,
When thou and thine appear!
And follow thee to heav'n our home,
E'en so, amen, LORD JESUS, come![2]

HYMN 104.

THE FATHER we adore,
And everlasting SON;
The SPIRIT of his love and pow'r,
The glorious Three in One.

At the creation's birth
This song was sung on high,
Shall sound, thro' ev'ry age, on earth,
And thro' eternity.

HYMN 105.

FATHER of angels and of men,
SAVIOUR, who hast us bought,
SPIRIT by whom we're born again,
And sanctify'd and taught!

Thy glory, holy Three in One,
Thy peoples song shall be,
Long as the wheels of time shall run,
And to eternity.

HYMN 106.

GLORY to GOD, the FATHER's name,
To JESUS, who for sinners dy'd;
The holy SPIRIT claims the same,
By whom our souls are sanctify'd.

Thy praise was sung when time began
By angels, thro' the starry spheres;
And shall, as now, be sung by man
Thro' vast eternity's long years.

HYMN 107.

YE saints on earth ascribe with heav'ns high
    host,
Glory and honour to the One in three;
To GOD the FATHER, SON, and HOLY GHOST,
As was, and is, and evermore shall be.

---

1 Philippians 4:7—And the peace of God, which passeth
  all understanding, shall keep your hearts and minds
  through Christ Jesus.
2 Revelation 22:20—He which testifieth these things
  saith, Surely I come quickly. Amen. Even so, come,
  Lord Jesus.

APPENDIX.

APPENDIX

GLOSSARY.

Alass — Alas
Altho' — Although
Athirst — Thirsty
Betide — To come to pass
Blithe — Merry or joyous
Candlestic — Candlestick
Canst — Can (second person singular present tense)
Carr — Chariot
Chear — Cheer
Cloyed — Choked up or satiated
Comprize — Comprise
Couldst — Can (second person singular simple past)
Crost — Crossed
Croud — Crowd
Cruise — Cruse, a small bottle
Cumber-ground — an unprofitable person.
Dearth — A shortage
Desart — Desert
Distrest — Distressed
Dost — Do (second person singular present tense)
Drest — Dressed
Durst — Dare
Dy'd — Died
E'en — Even
E'er — Ever
Ebenezer — Symbol of divine assistance
Encumber — To impede with burden
Ere — Before
Ev'ry — Every
Fain — Gladly
Farewel — Farewell, goodbye
Farther — Further
Feint — A mock attack
Forebore — forebear (simple past tense)
Froward — Disobedient
Gainsay — To contradict or oppose
Gay — Delightful
Goaler — Keeper of the prison
Gron'd — Groaned
Grone — Groan
Gulph — Gulf
Hast — Have (second person singular present tense)
Hasted — Hurried
Hence — From this time or place
Henceforth — From this time forward
Hitherto — Up to this time or place
Hoary — Gray hair, old age

Imprest — Impressed
Inchantment — Enchantment
Kine — Cows
Loth — Loath, reluctant
Meat — Meal
Methinks — It seems to me
Methought — It seemed to me
Ne'er — Never
Nigh — Near
O'er — Over
Oft — Often
Opprest — Oppressed
Overborne — Overbear (past participle)
Overcloud — To cast gloom
Overpast — Passed by
Passest — passed
Pelf — Money
Ply'd — Plied, used diligently
Possest — Possessed
Pray'r — Prayer
Prest — Pressed
Rue — Lament
Shew — Show
Shewn — Shown
Sooth — Soothe
Stil'd — Styled, characterized or designated
Stile — Style, characterize or designate
Succour — Succor, relief
Surprize — Surprise
T' — To
Th' — The
Thee — Thou (objective case solemn style)
Thence — From that time or place
Thine — Your (solemn style)
Tho' — Though
Thou — Second personal pronoun (solemn style)
Thrall — Enslave
Thro' — Through
Thy — Of thee (solemn style)
'Tis — It is
'Twere — It were
Vail — Veil, covering
Vouchsafe — Condescend to grant or bestow
Whence — From what time, place or circumstance
Wilt — Will (second person singular)
Worldling — A person engrossed in temporal things

SIMILAR HYMNS FOR BOOK III.

SOLEMN ADDRESSES TO SINNERS.
BOOK I. HYMN 75, 91.
BOOK II. HYMN 1, 2, 3, 4, 6, 35, 77, 78, 83.

SEEKING, PLEADING, HOPING.
BOOK I. HYMN 45, 69, 82, 83, 84, 96.
BOOK II. HYMN 29.

CONFLICT.
BOOK I. HYMN 10, 13, 21, 22, 24, 27, 40, 43, 44, 51, 56, 63, 76, 88, 107, 115, 126, 130, 131, 136, 142.
BOOK II. HYMN 30, 31, 84, 87, 92.

COMFORT.
BOOK I. HYMN 4, 7, 9, 11, 25, 35, 36, 39, 41, 46, 47, 48, 70, 95, 128, 132.
BOOK II. HYMN 45, 46, 47.

DEDICATION AND SURRENDER.
BOOK I. HYMN 27, 50, 70, 93, 122.
BOOK II. HYMN 23, 90.

CAUTIONS.
BOOK I. HYMN 8, 20, 85, 87, 91, 104, 125, 139, 141.
BOOK II. HYMN 34, 49, 86, 91, 99.

PRAISE.
BOOK I. HYMN 57, 58, 59, 79, 80.
BOOK II. HYMN 37, 38, 39, 41, 42.

ALPHABETICAL FIRST LINE INDEX.

Made in the USA
Monee, IL
30 May 2024

59136370R00103